'I hope Robert Holden's beautiful books, like this one, Higher Purpose, keep reaching more and more people and aid their heart to unfurl. And in case you wanted to know: The moon, asked about her luminosity, said, "I am perched on a limb in the sky; I found my Higher Purpose. And you can join me there and give light to others too, 'cause dear Robert can help."'

— **Daniel Ladinsky**, author of *The Gift* and *The Subject Tonight Is Love*

'Higher Purpose *offers much-needed inspiration and nourishment for everyone who has ever pondered how to take the next step, questioned their faith walk, or doubted that their life has meaning and purpose. Every word is a blessing for all who choose to accept this gift.*'

— **Deborah Egerton PhD**, author of *Know Justice Know Peace: A Transformative Journey of Social Justice, Anti-Racism, and Healing through the Power of the Enneagram*

'At a time when so many people are hungry, even starving for meaning, purpose, passion, and aliveness, Higher Purpose *shines a clear and steady beam illuminating the path ahead. If you are ready to claim your right to live a more soulful life, this rare book, loaded with wisdom and heart, will surely take you there.'*

— **Alan Cohen**, bestselling author of *A Course in Miracles Made Easy* and *Soul and Destiny: Why You Are Here and What You Came to Do*

'If you've ever wondered why you're here and what your purpose is, Robert Holden's wonderful new book not only helps you answer the question, it does it by entertaining your mind, warming your heart, and calling out to your soul that it's time to come home.'

— **Michael Neill**, bestselling author of *The Inside-Out Revolution* and *Creating the Impossible*

Praise for

HIGHER PURPOSE

'The best book on purpose I've ever read! Masterfully presented.
Robert is a consummate storyteller and impassioned teacher, meticulously
sequencing both for maximum effect. Accept this invitation to awaken to
the very reason you're here on Earth and to your sacred role in life.'

— **Mike Dooley**, *New York Times* bestselling author of
Infinite Possibilities and *Life on Earth*

'Higher Purpose *is a masterpiece! This wonderful book is a luminous
and original presentation that offers some of the finest thoughts ever
conjured on our life's purpose – and I expect it will serve our
human journey for many generations to come.'*

— **Jean Houston PhD**, author of *A Mythic Life: Learning
to Live Our Greater Story* and *The Possible Human*

'Life is only the journey of seeking your higher purpose. Everything we
experience is in service to that, for we only begin to feel the gift and
power of our life when we have animated our deeper purpose. But like
all the deep treasures of the soul, we require guidance to recognize what
purpose really means and then how to sense its force awakening within
us. Robert Holden has provided us with that precious guidebook.'

— **Caroline Myss**, *New York Times* bestselling author of *Sacred Contracts:
Awakening Your Divine Potential* and *Intimate Conversations with the Divine*

'In our demanding times, it is a blessing to hear a voice of such
clarity, breadth, and depth coming our way in this spiritual memoir
from Robert Holden. His life of hunting-gathering after spiritual wisdom,
his wounds turned to grace, and his articulate and generous telling of
his journey has birthed a book where Spirit breathes copiously!'

— **Matthew Fox**, *New York Times* bestselling author of
Original Blessing and *The Reinvention of Work*

'Higher Purpose *is a wise, profound, and deliciously openhearted
book written by one of our most skillful and luminous spiritual guides.
Inside this book you will find all the inspiration, encouragement, and
guidance you need to fulfill your most empowered destiny.'*

— **Andrew Harvey**, author of *The Hope* and
Engoldenment: A Year with Kabir

'If you long to know your purpose or be renewed in answering the Call of Soul's Purpose, prepare to have your heart ignited. Robert's depth of understanding, practical wisdom, and rich life experience weave an illuminating tapestry revealing the golden thread of purpose available for anyone to discover and activate! We can't wait to share it with our students. It is a masterpiece!'

— **Mary and Ron Hulnick**, co-directors of University of Santa Monica and co-authors of *Loyalty to Your Soul*

'This is a life-changing book. Each page I turned captured my attention more and more. It answered some of my deepest questions about life and helped to point my inner rudder where I needed to go. I quite simply couldn't put it down.'

— **David Hamilton PhD**, author of *Choice Point* and *Destiny vs Free Will*

'Higher Purpose *is a magical book, full of stories that go straight to the heart and speak to the connectedness of us all. As I read its pages of inquiry, insights, and gentle humor, I felt I was on a long walk in a beautiful place with a wise and trusted friend, and I didn't want it to end. This book will stay with me and beside me for a very long time.'*

— **Liz Trubridge**, producer of the *Downton Abbey* series and films

'I love this book! Higher Purpose *weaves a golden thread that connects you to your higher purpose, reminds you of what is important, and guides you in practical ways to live your most joyful, blissful life.'*

— **Rebecca Campbell**, author of *Rise Sister Rise* and *Light Is the New Black*

'Robert Holden's life and work is the epitome of living with purpose – any time I am in his company I am inspired to dive deeper into living more purposefully. His new book, Higher Purpose, *is a truly heart-inspiring offering that will help you to live with a greater meaning, alignment, and service in your life.'*

— **Kyle Gray**, bestselling author of *Light Warrior* and *Raise Your Vibration*

HIGHER PURPOSE

ALSO BY ROBERT HOLDEN

Finding Love Everywhere

Life Loves You (with Louise Hay)

Holy Shift!

Loveability

Shift Happens!

Authentic Success

Be Happy

Happiness NOW!

All of the above are available at your local bookstore,
or may be ordered by visiting:

Hay House UK: www.hayhouse.co.uk
Hay House USA: www.hayhouse.com®
Hay House Australia: www.hayhouse.com.au
Hay House India: www.hayhouse.co.in

***

HIGHER PURPOSE

HOW TO FIND MORE INSPIRATION, MEANING AND PURPOSE IN YOUR LIFE

ROBERT HOLDEN

HAY HOUSE

Carlsbad, California • New York City
London • Sydney • New Delhi

Published in the United Kingdom by:
Hay House UK Ltd, The Sixth Floor, Watson House,
54 Baker Street, London W1U 7BU
Tel: +44 (0)20 3927 7290; Fax: +44 (0)20 3927 7291; www.hayhouse.co.uk

Published in the United States of America by:
Hay House Inc., PO Box 5100, Carlsbad, CA 92018-5100
Tel: (1) 760 431 7695 or (800) 654 5126
Fax: (1) 760 431 6948 or (800) 650 5115; www.hayhouse.com

Published in Australia by:
Hay House Australia Ltd, 18/36 Ralph St, Alexandria NSW 2015
Tel: (61) 2 9669 4299; Fax: (61) 2 9669 4144; www.hayhouse.com.au

Published in India by:
Hay House Publishers India, Muskaan Complex, Plot No.3, B-2,
Vasant Kunj, New Delhi 110 070
Tel: (91) 11 4176 1620; Fax: (91) 11 4176 1630; www.hayhouse.co.in

Text © Robert Holden, 2022

Cover design: Jemima Giffard-Taylor • *Interior design*: Karim J. Garcia
Interior illustrations: Jemima Giffard-Taylor

The moral rights of the author have been asserted.

A catalogue record for this book is available from the British Library.

Tradepaper ISBN: 978-1-78817-751-1
Hardback ISBN: 978-1-4019-6547-1
E-book ISBN: 978-1-4019-6548-8
Audiobook ISBN: 978-1-4019-6905-9

*This book is a thank-you
to everyone who has helped me
to recognize and follow the
Golden Thread that ties me to
my Higher Purpose.*

*May this book be a help to you
in following the pull and
unmistakable tug of
your Golden Thread.*

Use me, God.
Show me how to take who I am,
who I want to be, and what I can do,
and use it for a purpose greater
than myself.

— a prayer by Martin Luther King Jr.

CONTENTS

FOREWORD

For over a decade I've had the privilege of sharing many stages with my dear friend, Robert Holden. Watching him speak, I've witnessed many moments where he bravely answers an audience member's common question, *What is my life's purpose?*

What am I born to do? people want to know. They've searched high and low, and come up empty. They've sought others' opinions, gone on far-flung retreats . . . or hit the tarot cards hard! But rarely do they achieve the kind of clarity that Robert can bring them in mere minutes.

Robert has been given a profound gift in this life. He has an extraordinary ability to crack people open to the power and the purpose that's already within them. And now, he's bringing his message out into the world through his powerful new book.

As *Higher Purpose* illustrates, your soul's true calling is already in you—and in everything around you. Your purpose is woven through your life like a golden thread, guiding you to service and inspiration.

In the pages that follow, Robert will guide you toward your soul's highest calling with heart, spirit, and a whole lot of experience.

Higher Purpose will take you on a joyful journey toward tapping into your passion, doing more of what inspires you and busting through any blocks that stand between you and a sense of meaning in your life.

You are here to make a difference and have fun while doing it! And now you have a roadmap to do just that.

— Gabrielle Bernstein, *New York Times* best-selling author of
Super Attractor and *Happy Days*

INTRODUCTION

For 10 years, I hosted a talk-radio show called *Shift Happens!* for Hay House Radio.[1] Each week, I focused on a specific theme. The most popular shows had the word *purpose* in the title. And the most common question I was asked by my callers—in over 500 shows—was far and away this one: *How do I find my purpose?*

Everybody is looking for their purpose, and most of us struggle with how to find it. The purpose of this book is to help you recognize your purpose and live a purpose-centered life.

Yes, you do have a purpose. Everyone does. You are here in this world for a reason, even if that reason isn't always clear. Your life is not a mistake. You are not an accident. Creation doesn't make administrative errors. You are meant to be here, and no one has the authority to tell you otherwise. A big purpose has birthed you. We are each born with *a pre-birth intention*, as Rudolf Steiner described it. Throughout this book, I will draw on the insights of Steiner and other magnificent, visionary philosophers that will help you to realize and live your purpose.

Since I was a young boy, I've felt that a golden thread was tied to me and that it connected me to my purpose. This golden thread has pulled me toward people I needed to meet, books I needed to read, and places I needed to go. You have a golden thread too, and it ties you to your purpose. *It's a ribbon in the sky*, to quote Stevie Wonder. It's invisible to the naked eye, yet it's always with you.

And it's vital that you learn to recognize and follow the unmistakable tug of your golden thread if you are to show up for your life and live your purpose.

I promise you this: *Your purpose goes with you wherever you go.* You can never be apart from your purpose. Your purpose is with you even when you feel lost and are struggling to find direction and meaning in your life. Stop looking for your purpose on the horizon or over the rainbow. You don't need to take a pilgrimage to some far-off place to find it; you simply need to be more present to where you are. Adjust your sights, your purpose is closer than you realize.

> *"You don't create your mission in life—you detect it."*
>
> — Viktor Frankl

On my first pilgrimage to India, I remember squeezing into a two-seat rickshaw with my friend and heading into Delhi city center. We were stopped at a red light at a busy intersection surrounded by huge trucks, buses, cars, and motorbikes when suddenly an elephant appeared from nowhere and stuck its head inside our tiny carriage.

"Oh my God! An elephant!" I shouted.

"Where?" said my friend.

"What do you mean, *where*?!" I shouted back. Its long grey trunk was sniffing at our shoes!

"I can't see it!" he said.

"Right here!" I shouted.

"Oh my God! An elephant!" he shouted in turn.

"How could you not see it?" I asked

"It was so close, I *couldn't* see it!"

Your purpose is bigger than you can see sometimes. It is bigger than your ego, bigger than who you take yourself to be. Your purpose doesn't belong only to you. It is part of a bigger picture. You must adjust your sights to see your purpose in its true glory.

In *Higher Purpose*, I will show you that what most of us call "my purpose" is really part of a much larger story. Look closely and you will see that your purpose has three golden threads or levels that are woven into one. The first is your *individual purpose* that is unique to you; the second is your *shared purpose* that you have in common with others; and the third is your *universal purpose* that fastens you to one cosmic, unified purpose for all of life.

Every living being has this threefold purpose. In this book, I will show you how whales and dolphins have a threefold purpose, and bees too. Trees also have a threefold purpose. William Wordsworth, who makes several appearances in this book, wrote a wonderful poem, "Yew-Trees," about a thousand-year-old yew tree that still stands in the village of Lorton, in the Lake District.[2] It "stands single," with its own unique purpose, and it has generously offered itself as a shelter, a temple, and an altar to countless people across the centuries. As with all flora and fauna, its existence is also woven into an even greater tapestry of an ecosystem, Mother Nature, and the universe.

> *"I live my life in widening circles, that reach out across the world."*
>
> — Rainer Maria Rilke

Why do we have a purpose? On an individual level, living your purpose helps you to grow, to cultivate skills and talents, and to become the person you most want to be. On a shared level, your purpose enables you to overcome your sense of separateness, to be an instrument for a greater good, and to be of service to others. On a universal level, your purpose aligns you with a much bigger plan, a higher power, and a COSMIC-SIZED love, as Caroline Myss calls it, that works through you so that your presence is a blessing to others.

In *Higher Purpose*, I share with you my own journey of finding my purpose—the highs and the lows. You will read stories and sketches from my life. You will meet some of my friends who have helped me to live my purpose. They include Winny and Kees, who swim in the wild with whales and dolphins; John Willoner, who looks after the bees in Findhorn; Viva, who drives a red London bus; and Sue Boyd, who started up a project to plant hanging flower baskets in her village. The purpose of each story I tell is to help you pay attention to *your* life and recognize who and what is helping you to live *your* purpose.

I also share a lifetime of conversations with remarkable people who have taught me important lessons about purpose. As you turn the pages of this book, you will meet my first spiritual mentor, Avanti Kumar, who gave me a copy of the *Bhagavad Gita*; and Jean Houston, the philosopher and mystic, who teaches about the Godseed that we each carry in our heart; and Freddie Frankl, nephew of Victor Frankl, the author of *Man's Search for Meaning*; and Bob Thurman, the Buddhist professor, who lost an eye and found his dharma; and Maya Angelou, the civil rights activist, whom I interviewed three times. In one of our meetings, she told me, "My mission in life is not merely to survive, but to thrive; and to do so with some passion, some compassion, some humor, and some style."

In *Higher Purpose*, I take you on an epic journey from looking for your purpose to living it.

This journey has four parts to it.

In Part I, *The Call*, we explore "the calling" that wants you to live a more meaningful and purpose-centered life. This calling is the pull of your golden thread. Deep down, we all know that there is more to life than finding a steady job, paying the bills, buying a bigger TV, attracting a soul mate, getting more "likes" and "followers" on social media, and fitting into our jeans. Your purpose is to escape the chains of your narrow self and express your true self—what Wordsworth calls your soul's immensity—with courage, imagination, and love. Here in Part I, we also meet Carl Jung, the Swiss psychologist and mystic, and I share with you how his work helped me to recognize my calling.

In Part II, *The Path*, I help you to recognize when you are most "on purpose" in your life. I share with you some powerful self-inquiry exercises that I devised for myself and that I share with students who take my courses and with people whom I mentor. These exercises will help you to pay attention and to notice when you feel most alive, when you are following your joy, when you feel truly inspired, and when you are doing what you love. Here in Part II, I introduce you to Joseph Campbell's work on the hero journey, which I teach on my retreats and Mastermind programs. Learning to navigate the three stages of your hero journey is immensely helpful for staying on track with your purpose.

> *"The privilege of a lifetime is being who you are."*
>
> — Joseph Campbell

In Part III, *The Ordeal*, I address the most common inner blocks we each must overcome if we are to live our purpose. We start with a pilgrimage to Assisi, where we walk in the footsteps of St. Francis and St. Clare. St. Francis is my Patron Saint of Purpose, and St. Clare is my Patron Saint of Vision. These two young spiritual rebels offer us a perfect blueprint for working with our threefold purpose. They were nonconformists who gave up a "normal" life for a purpose-centered life. They identified their chief point of inspiration. They made themselves into instruments for a higher purpose.

Here in Part III, I guide you on the *road of trials*—a term Joseph Campbell coined—in which you experience the death of normal, you become lost in a dark wood, you encounter the dark night of the soul, and you survive the death of your ego. I also reflect on the COVID-19 pandemic and how this terrible collective ordeal has been a catalyst for so many of us to be more purpose-centered in our life.

In Part IV, *The Victory*, I tell you that it is never too late to say YES to your purpose. I start with some key messages from a commencement speech I gave to graduates at the University of Santa Monica. One message is *you don't need to be entirely ready to start living your purpose; you only need to be ready enough.* Another message is *your purpose is too big for you to do on your own.* To live your purpose, you must give up what I call *dysfunctional independence.* You must be open to guidance, to support, and to *supernatural aid*—another Joseph Campbell term—that will come to you in delightful and surprising ways when you say YES to your purpose.

Here in Part IV, I spotlight some specific challenges that may seriously tempt you to give up on your purpose. Many of these happen just before the Victory. I examine the uses of failure, how to handle criticism, the fear of rejection, not selling yourself short, coming out of your cage, and the gift of forgiveness. We also pay a visit to Findhorn and its resident bees, and take inspiration from them on how to live our threefold purpose.

I encourage you to keep a journal while you read this book. I have carefully inserted spiritual practices and inquiries through-out for you to work with. Please feel free to use a marker pen to scribble in the margins and to underline the good bits as you go. Hopefully, you will find some! And please do get into some good conversations about your purpose while you read this book. We evolve and grow through the conversations we are often too busy and afraid to have. If by the end of this book, you are still not sure how to find your purpose, I will make it very simple for you. Your purpose is to love the world. You are here to be a presence of love. Your work is to be the most loving person you can be.

Robert Holden
London
April 2022

PART I

THE CALL

A BIGGER ME

My three-year-old son, Christopher, and I are playing Test match cricket on the beach at Encinitas, California. It's 9 A.M. The beach is quiet. The sky is clear and blue. We haven't seen a cloud for days. The morning breeze is cool. It will be super-hot by midday. Too hot to play cricket by then. My wife, Hollie, and our daughter, Bo, who is seven years old, are enjoying a lie-in. They will join us later.

It's great fun playing cricket with little Christopher. Each game is full of imagination and surprises. "I'll be Ian Botham and you can be Stevie Wonder," shouts Christopher as he goes in to bat. I'm happy with that. We both love Stevie Wonder. And Ian Botham was one of my cricketing heroes when I was a young boy.

Halfway through Ian Botham's innings, Christopher decides that we should take a break. Christopher is playing well. He's hit the ball into the sea six times already. We sit down on the sand, put raspberries on our fingers, and eat them one by one while we watch two surfers ride the waves.

"Would you like to be a surfer when you grow up, Dad?" he asks me.

"Gosh, that would be fun!" I say.

"Uh-huh," he says, popping another raspberry in his mouth.

"When I was a little boy, I wanted to play cricket for England," I tell him.

"Can I have some water, Dad?"

"Here you are," I say, passing him his water bottle.

Christopher gulps down his water. Some of it goes in his mouth, and the rest spills over his chin and around his lips, which are covered in raspberry stains.

"I know what I want to be when I grow up," he continues.

"That's good, Christopher," I say as we both look out to sea.

"Yeah," he says, eating another raspberry.

"What do you want to be when you grow up?"

"A bigger me," he says.

Christopher has been keen to grow up since he arrived in the world. He has a big appetite for life. As soon as he could talk, he asked "big" questions like "When will I be big?" and "What is it like being big?" He's always been curious to know about the biggest dinosaur, the biggest whale, and the biggest star in the sky. He once asked me, "Daddy, what's bigger than the world?" And to this day, when I wave good-bye to him at the school gates, he shouts, "I love you bigger than space."

My mum told me I was much the same as Christopher. I liked being young. I was full of adventure, in contact with my imagination, and deeply infused with my surroundings. I loved to climb trees, the bigger the better. I enjoyed the view from up above. My best friend was a blackbird who always appeared the moment I went out to the garden. I enjoyed not ever knowing what time it was. And yet, I also felt an urge—some call it a *calling*—to get going with my life. "You were born with fast genes," Mum told me.

In my book *Authentic Success*, I tell the story of when my mum and dad asked me what I wanted for my sixth birthday.[1] I wanted toys, of course. I especially wanted a cricket bat. My first bat was too small for me by then. I also wanted a sword and a shield. I already had an imaginary horse, so I didn't need another one of those. But top of my list was a briefcase.

"Why do you want a briefcase?" asked Mum.

"Grandpa's got one, and Daddy has one too," I explained.

I liked Grandpa's best. It was a handmade brown leather attaché case. The leather was scuffed up and fading, and it had his initials, A.E.L.H., printed on the front.[2]

"Why not wait a while for your briefcase?" suggested Mum.

"Mum, I really need it now!" I pleaded, close to tears.

"Why now?" she asked.

"Because I'm going to do something very important with my life," I told her.

Every child likes to imagine their future. While busy playing, we are rehearsing for our great adventure. In childhood, we direct, produce, and star in our own stories the whole time. We need props—like a cricket bat, a sword, and a briefcase—to act out our adventures. We role-play heroes. We dress up as doctors. We invent stuff. We rescue unicorns. We save the world. We know that life is a big event and that we're here for a big purpose.

> *"If you're going to have a story, have a big story, or none at all."*
>
> — Joseph Campbell

SOME BIG QUESTIONS

I was born in Kenya in East Africa. It's the place where the story of humanity is said to have begun. I wasn't there for very long. Mum went to Kenya at her parents' request. Mum wanted to marry Dad. Her parents didn't like the idea. They didn't think that Dad, a working-class man, was suitable for their high-society debutante daughter. If you've ever seen the TV series *Downton Abbey*, Mum was a lot like Lady Sybil Crawley, the youngest of the Grantham daughters, a rebel who falls in love and marries Tom Branson, the family chauffeur.

Mum's parents told her to go to Kenya for six months, and that if she still wanted to marry "that man" after that time, they would give their consent. Six months passed, and Mum still wanted to marry Dad. It seems you really can't choose whom you fall in love with. Love has its own plan for us. I've still got my parents' love letters in my possession. It's safe to say they were head over heels in love. They both believed that destiny had brought them together.

We left Kenya shortly after my first birthday. "We loved living in Kenya, but something was calling us home to England," Mum told me. It was a call they could not deny. Apparently, we got chased by a rhinoceros with a huge horn on the way to the airport. "This was Africa's way of telling us our time was up!" said Dad, who saw it as another sign. Places have a purpose, just like people do, and they play a vital role in our biography and in helping us live our purpose.

Eventually, we moved to a village called Littleton. This is where my brother, David, and I were raised for most of our childhood. We lived in a bungalow with a small garden patch that had a pond. Littleton was a little village—as you may have guessed—situated somewhere in the south of England. On our Ordnance Survey map, Littleton was halfway down the crease between two pages, so you couldn't find it. We were in the world, but not on the map.

As a young boy, I remember being fascinated by one of my parents' possessions, an antique world globe, 12 inches in diameter, with a mahogany wood stand. The globe piqued my curiosity about life. I'd ask Mum and Dad big questions like these: "Who made the world?" "What is the world for?" "What are we *really* doing here?" I loved to spin the globe around and around. It was one of my favorite toys. "It's not a toy!" Dad kept telling me. It certainly looked like a toy to me.

Dad told me lots of stories about the world. He'd point to places on the globe that he'd visited while serving in the navy. The navy sounded like a lot of fun. Dad didn't say anything about a war. "This is where you were born," he'd say, pointing at Africa. "This is where you live now," he'd say, pointing at Great Britain. I could never find Great Britain by myself. It was too small. Littleton wasn't on this map either. The closest city was London, some

60 miles away. London was far, far away. I never imagined I would visit London, or that I would live there one day.

Life in Littleton was simple and idyllic at first. It had one main road, one bus stop, one post office, one pub, one church, and—praise the Lord—a cricket pitch! Me and my brother, David, who was four years younger, were inseparable. We played together most days until dusk. I also played a lot of cricket for the village team. My first cricket coach was Jeff Levick, whom I am still friends with. Forty years later, we still go to Lord's, the home of cricket, to watch a game, to catch up, and to reminisce about times gone by.

I also experienced my early traumas and dramas in Littleton. The bungalow we lived in was called "Shadows." I ask you, dear reader, who on earth would move into a family home called Shadows? I remember objecting strongly to the name. "Mum, it sounds so scary!" I cried. "I rather like it," was her response.

It was while we were living in Shadows that my mum's experience of depression hospitalized her many times. Later, my father's drinking began to worsen. When I was 15 years old, he moved out. There aren't enough words in the world to tell you how painful this was.

Looking back now, though, I can see that Littleton was the perfect patch of soil for me to grow up in. Everything that happened there served to advance my quest for a greater meaning and wisdom in life. At 18 years old, I left Littleton to go to university in Birmingham, in Middle England. As I packed my bags, I knew that I would not live in Littleton again. I was leaving the Shire for good. I was on my path, and I was following my purpose.

YOUR SOUL'S IMMENSITY

While I was writing this chapter, I spent a morning sorting through some photos of myself as a young boy from birth to about seven years old. I needed them for a course I was taking on biography counseling—a work inspired by Rudolf Steiner, the Austrian philosopher and mystic—that helps you chart your life purpose according to significant stages, cycles, and dates.[3] I look a lot like my son, Christopher, in the photos. As I peer into my own eyes as an infant, I can see a "bigger me" looking back at me.

One of my favorite poems about childhood is "Ode: Intimations of Immortality from Recollections of Early Childhood," by William Wordsworth.[4] In it, he paints a picture of your soul arriving here on earth. You appear from your mother's womb as a little boy or girl, but this is not all that you are. Wordsworth writes,

> *Thou, whose exterior semblance doth belie*
> *Thy soul's immensity;*
> *Thou best Philosopher, who yet dost keep*
> *Thy heritage, thou Eye among the blind,*
> *That, deaf and silent, read'st the eternal deep,*
> *Haunted for ever by the eternal Mind,—*
> *Mighty Prophet! Seer blest!*

"Thy soul's immensity," as Wordsworth describes it, is your true substance; the body is just a shadow or an image of who you are. The essence of you is "Apparelled in celestial light," writes Wordsworth. This light is your true guide and your life's Star. You are Nature's Priest, and as with all of us, you have a divine purpose to fulfill here on earth. Wordsworth goes on:

> *Our birth is but a sleep and a forgetting:*
> *The Soul that rises with us, our life's Star,*
> *Hath had elsewhere its setting,*
> *And cometh from afar:*
> *Not in entire forgetfulness,*
> *And not in utter nakedness,*
> *But trailing clouds of glory do we come*
> *From God, who is our home.*

We come trailing clouds of glory, and Wordsworth tells us how a child at six years old, while enjoying his mother's kisses and his father's admiring gaze, begins to plot out his or her life—with a wedding, a festival, and a funeral. But all this comes with a warning. As we grow up in an increasingly material and cynical world, we will forget about the real glory we came for. "Shades of the prison-house begin to close / Upon the growing Boy," writes Wordsworth.

Our work is to remember the trailing clouds of glory. We must learn (or, rather, relearn) everything we can about the nature of this glory. It is for this glory that we came here. Wordsworth reassures us that this glory accompanies us on our journey until the end, and that it is mirrored to us by birds who "sing a joyous song," by "young Lambs abound," and by the "glory in the flower." No wonder so many of us recover a sense of meaning and purpose when we take a walk in nature.

YOUR GODSEED

Every child who arrives on earth has answered the call. When we are born, we enter the theater of this world. We are here to play our part in the big play of creation. We must plant our feet on the earth and look up to the heavens. We must pitch ourselves inside the tent of our small, physical body, but not forget about our soul's immensity and our life's Star, which will guide us on our way. We must learn how to "play big," so to speak, if we are to stay true to the trailing clouds of glory that sent us. How do we do this?

To start with, let's look more closely at what "playing big" means. Let's examine two distinct types of "playing big": one is a small type of "big" that focuses mostly on self-interest, individual goals, and personal fulfillment; and the other is a much bigger "BIG" that connects everyone, without exception, to a universal story that is far greater than any of us can fully imagine or achieve on our own.

The small type of "big" is an ego-bound approach to life. What is the ego? Your ego is your sense of a separate self. It is the "me," "myself," and "I" that identifies with the physical body and that tends to differentiate itself from the greater "we." The mistake most of us make with our ego-self is that we try to play big by searching for a separate purpose that is independent of others. *You don't have a purpose separate from others; you have a shared purpose with all of creation.* Your task is to give yourself fully to this shared purpose, which is far bigger than your ego. By surrendering to it, you can express this greater purpose *through you* in your own unique and personal way.

Rudolf Steiner describes the ego as the "narrow self." I came across a verse by Steiner about the narrow self a few years ago now. The verse makes a distinction between our narrow self (the ego) and our true being (our soul's immensity). When I first read it, I heard echoes of Wordsworth's "Ode: Intimations of Immortality." The verse is lyrical and cryptic like much of Steiner's writings. It's really a meditation. I recommend that you read this verse a few times to get the hang of it.

> *The I, ever becoming,*
> *Forgetful of itself and yet*
> *Aware of its true origin,*
> *Speaks to the cosmic All:*
> *"As I become more free*
> *From chains of narrow self, in You*
> *I fathom my true being."*[5]

If we are to fathom the depths of our true being and experience a greater sense of purpose, we must undo the *chains of narrow self.* These chains grow heavier, and weigh us down more, when we believe that our ego is the sum of all our parts and insist on giving it a purpose that is separate from others. Conversely, the chains loosen and fall away when we see our ego not as our sole identity but as a vessel for our soul's immensity and an instrument to be used in service of the greater glory of creation.

I'd like to introduce you here to a metaphor that I've found very helpful when thinking about the journey from an ego-bound life to a much bigger life—a journey we must make if we are to experience a greater sense of meaning and a higher purpose. The metaphor is the Godseed. I learned about it from Jean Houston, the philosopher and scholar, and author of the book called *Godseed: The Journey of Christ.*[6]

When I first talked to Jean Houston about her Godseed metaphor, she referred to William Wordsworth and spoke of our soul's immensity. She told me, "I like to remind people that you are not an encapsulated bag of skin dragging around a dreary little ego. You are an evolutionary wonder, a trillion cells singing together in a vast chorale, a marvelous symbiosis of cell and soul. And when cell and soul cooperate with each other, we hear our calling and do great things with our life."

Jean explained that Jesus was a Godseed who became the Christ, and that Siddhartha was a Godseed who became the Buddha, or "the awakened one." She told me, "Every child is a Godseed. Your son, Christopher, and your daughter, Bo, are Godseeds. Everyone who is called to be here on earth is a Godseed. And everyone who reads your book is a Godseed too."

"So what is a Godseed, Jean?" I asked.

"It's a creation of God that is still in potential," she replied.

"What does that mean?"

"It means we are an expression of God, but we haven't realized it yet."

"How do we realize it?"

"We have to see the ego as an embryo that is willing to break through its seed coat, sending its roots down into the earth and its green shoots up toward the sun."

"Why do we want to do this?"

"Because we are here to participate in the flowering of humanity and in the creation of God's Garden here on earth."

As Jean told me about the Godseed, my mind turned to the many seed parables of Jesus Christ and especially to the parable of the grain of wheat, in the Gospel of John, which begins with these words:

> *Very truly, I tell you,*
> *unless a grain of wheat falls into*
> *the earth and dies, it remains just*
> *a single grain; but if it dies, it*
> *bears much fruit.*[7]

The grain of wheat parable is an allegory about playing big and embracing a higher purpose. We are destined to be more than just a single grain of wheat, which is a metaphor for our ego or narrow self. To fulfill our destiny, we must be willing to outgrow our ego. How do we do this? We grow by dying. In this instance, dying means letting go of your narrow self—including your self-image, your psychology, your stories, your theology—and being born again into a greater awareness of who you truly are and why you are here.

Jesus issues a warning immediately after sharing the grain of wheat parable. He advises us not to resist dying to our narrow, separate self. To let go of your small ideas about who you are is a necessary stage in your growth and evolution. It is vital that you embrace a bigger Self (with a capital S) that is connected to all of life and is willing to play its part in the shared purpose and greater story of creation.

> *"Journey from the self to the Self, and find the mine of gold."*
>
> — Rumi

Jesus says in the Gospel of Luke 17:33, "Whoever seeks to save his life will lose it, and whoever loses his life will preserve it." He says something similar in the gospels of Matthew and John.[8] In plain English, what these words mean to me is *If you seek a purpose that belongs exclusively to your ego* (your narrow self) *your life will lose all meaning; but by letting this go, you will discover a purpose that you share with all of humanity and all creation—and this shared purpose will preserve you and greatly fulfill you.*

Resistance to dying to your small self is called *vainglory* (from Medieval Latin), or vanity. Vainglory focuses solely on "my life," "my success," and "my purpose." It tries to replace the bigger picture with a giant selfie. We aim to play big by inflating our ego. We pump ourselves up. We take self-esteem classes. We do our own PR, and we constantly try to make ourselves superior to and more significant than others. All of this is in vain, however, because our sense of separateness makes our victories feel hollow, our successes meaningless, and our life sadly lacking.

Vainglory is "playing small," so to speak, because you are trying to manufacture your own self-made glory. Playing big, on the other hand, is being fully connected to the clouds of glory that sent you. Jesus Christ said in so many ways, "I am not seeking glory for myself."[9] He said, "If I glorify myself, my glory means nothing."[10] Everything he did was not only for his personal purpose, but also for a much greater purpose. This is the secret to true success. *Be who you are, and do what you do, for the greater good of the whole.*

> "Start living and working for the whole, and see how your entire outlook and attitude will change."
>
> — Eileen Caddy

When we follow our true purpose, we are answering a call that takes us on a journey—a big adventure—that Joseph Campbell, the mythologist, called the *hero journey*.[11] I mention his work here because I will refer to it throughout this book. Learning about the hero journey from Joseph Campbell and his close colleagues, like Jean Houston, has helped me to follow the golden thread that ties me to my higher purpose. I have taught classes, retreats, and Masterminds on the hero journey for many years, and I feel very on purpose when I do.

What is a hero? "A hero is someone who has given his or her life to something bigger than oneself," said Joseph Campbell. As the hero, you start out on the journey with your narrow self, but to complete the journey, you must experience a transformation—a death of the narrow, single-grain-of-wheat self and a birth of a greater, fruit-bearing self—which activates a new consciousness and a new way of being in the world.

You return from your hero journey as a "bigger me," as Christopher calls it, and the boon you bring home with you is your gift to everyone. You no longer experience yourself as a separate entity in the world, but rather as an expression of the greater glory of creation. You feel a kinship with the cosmos. You exist in a theater of interrelations. Your purpose is bigger than you. And you are grateful and genuinely delighted to be playing a part—no matter how small—in the larger, emerging, and ongoing story of creation.

QUESTIONS TO LIVE BY

Bo was born at 10:41 on a Sunday morning. Hollie had gone into labor on Friday evening. Now, after 40 hours of laboring and birthing, our daughter was finally here, to consecrate the hour. Knowing her as I do now, some 15 years on, I imagine she must have been busy with some last-minute packing, stuffing essential items into her spiritual backpack in preparation for her journey here on earth. For not in utter nakedness or entire forgetfulness do we come.

Bo arrived with her eyes wide open. "She doesn't want to close her eyes," said Hollie, as she handed our daughter to me. Bo kept her steady gaze fixed on me while I held her tiny body in the palms of my hands. We touched foreheads and noses, as if we were bowing to each other. We continued to look deeply into each other's eyes, for how long I do not know. It was a timeless moment in which I saw Bo as a perfect Godseed. She was full of intent and purpose. She was ready for her life.

Seeing Bo in her physical form for the first time, I sensed in my bones that I had always been destined to be her father. A few days into Bo's life, I wrote an entry in my personal journal about this sense of destiny. I wrote:

> It feels so right that you [Bo] are here. I feel you were destined to be my daughter, that Hollie was destined to be your mother, and I was destined to be your father. What is

destiny? It is the playing out of choices made in another place and at another time . . . We are here, in this great mystery we call life, to play a part in fulfilling each other's destiny and purpose.

After Bo was born, my life was no longer my own. I couldn't keep my heart to myself anymore. My heart was running around inside Bo's body. I loved watching how Bo encountered her life. She was full of wonder. She loved everyone she met, and she loved the world. She loved flowers and animals, snails and stones, yellow leaves on the ground, and inanimate objects like a spoon or a key. Hanging out with Bo, I learned to see through the eye of my heart— the *nous*, some mystics call it—and I saw my life in a new light.

Bo was born with a question mark over her head. She was full of questions—searching questions—that fuelled her never-ending curiosity. Questions came tumbling out of her mouth as soon as she could speak. The early "What's that?" questions were easy to answer, like when she'd point at a rainbow or a butterfly. The next lot of questions were more challenging, like when she asked, *What is that butterfly saying?* and *What is a rainbow for?*

Every first-time parent will tell you that they were in no way prepared for the onslaught of questions that comes at about three years old, which is when children first refer to themselves as "I." Young children, between the ages of three and nine years old, ask their parents up to 300 questions a day, according to research.[1] Bo liked to ask several questions in quick succession, allowing me no time to Google a satisfactory answer to anything.

Fortunately for Bo, and Christopher too, Hollie and I were guided beautifully by their kindergarten teachers on how to meet their inquiring minds. Bo and Christopher both went to Steiner kindergartens. Bo's teacher, Régine, and Christopher's teachers, Leigha and Maria, helped us appreciate the deeper purpose behind a child's love of questions. They taught us the importance of offering age-appropriate answers, leaving questions open, and meeting some questions—like *What is a rainbow for?*—with a reply like "I wonder" or simply "Hmmm . . ."

Hollie and I have taken several classes with Leigha, Christopher's first teacher, in which we've explored the deeper purpose of children asking questions. In a recent conversation, Leigha shared a poem with me by Rainer Maria Rilke called "I Am Much Too Alone in This World, Yet Not Alone." The poem begins,

I am much too alone in this world, yet not alone
enough
to truly consecrate the hour.
I am much too small in this world, yet not small
enough
to be to you just object and thing,
dark and smart.[2]

Young children are not just on a fact-finding mission when they ask questions. They don't want you to be an encyclopedia; they want your attention and a feeling of togetherness: a sense of "I will wonder with you" rather than "I will stand over here and give you my answers!" "Questions help a child overcome their sense of aloneness," Leigha told me. Questions help to orient a young child to their surroundings. They help the growing child move beyond the chains of narrow self and take their place in the larger community of life.

"When a child is asking questions, they are learning to recognize their own voice," said Leigha. "Not just their physical voice, but the voice of their true Self. In a very real sense, children are sharpening their intuition and developing their capacity to recognize truth and wisdom by asking questions." Leigha's insights on this topic could fill a book. "Questions are also how a child learns to engage in a conversation with you about life and how to live it," said Leigha.

Hollie and I learned from Leigha and her fellow teachers that the purpose of education is to teach children a love of learning so they will want to keep on learning for their whole life. Learning shouldn't finish at 16 or at 21. A love of questions is integral to lifelong learning and growth. And for cultivating a greater sense of meaning and purpose along the way. Therefore, our shared purpose as teachers and parents is not so much to answer our children's questions as to keep their questioning alive.

Teachers like Leigha are concerned that too much social media too early on in life can draw a young child away from their questions. Too much screen time, and hearing too many voices from the outside world, can cause infants and adolescents to lose touch with their original voice, the voice they are listening for when they ask questions like *What is a rainbow for?* Their dialogue with truth and beauty is constantly being interrupted by a TV show and by 900 channels bombarding them 24/7 with entertainment and advertising.

In adulthood, our quest is to reconnect ourselves with our original voice. We must keep our eyes wide open, stay awake, and practice inner listening if we are to recognize our true purpose in life. One way to do this is to revisit the big questions you used to ask when you were young. Can you recall the first question that really excited your imagination? What piqued your curiosity? What inspired in you a sense of awe and wonder? What activated the hero archetype in you? Do you remember how you used to answer the question *What do you want to be when you grow up?*

A TEACHER OF INQUIRY

"Were you alive in the olden days, Dad?" Christopher asked, looking up from the Lego set he was working on.

"Where did that question come from?" I asked him.

"I don't know," he said, with a cheeky grin.

"No, I was not!" I told him, but then I realized his olden days and my olden days are not the same. So I amended my answer. "Yes, I was alive in the olden days," I said.

"I thought you must have been," he said as he looked about for another piece of Lego.

When I reflect on the olden days, and on how my work in psychology and philosophy has evolved over the last 30 years, I recognize that I took a path that was mostly self-directed and not very orthodox. I stepped away from academia. I gave up a secure teaching position. I followed my intuition, and I took the road less traveled. I blended psychology with spirituality. I studied mysticism and physics. I practiced yoga philosophy and wrote poetry. Along the way I became a teacher of inquiry, and the purpose of my work was helping people to cultivate an inquiry-based life.

> *"The important thing is not to stop questioning. . . . Never lose a holy curiosity."*
>
> — Albert Einstein

Inquiry is an open-minded approach to life that uses questions as an essential tool for listening to your original voice, recognizing your calling, and finding your direction in life. An essential aim of inquiry work is identifying the big questions—the exciting and scary ones—that serve to bring you alive, ignite your creativity, challenge you to grow, and live a purpose-centered life.

My first major project was my Stress Busters Clinic, which I opened on the National Health Service in England in 1989. It was the first clinic of its kind, and initially my work was educating doctors and health professionals in stress awareness. Most people who came to the clinic were referred through the health service, although some were self-referred. I gave lectures on key questions like "What is stress?" and "What are the causes of stress?" and "What are the most effective solutions for stress?" And, most of all, on "What is the purpose of stress?"

My inquiry into stress taught me that *stress isn't just an illness that requires a medication; it's also an invitation to heal and grow.*[3] I discovered that we are more prone to stress when we don't listen to our inner voice, when we make inauthentic choices, and when we are not living our purpose. I encouraged my clients to get curious about stress and to imagine that their stress was like an angel—a helpful emissary—that has a message for them. I'd ask them questions such as *What is the message of your migraine?*

What is your high blood pressure trying to tell you? What is your stomach ulcer warning you about? And *What is your exhaustion teaching you?*

In 1994 I set up The Happiness Project to conduct an inquiry into life's number one goal. When people around the world, in every country and on every continent, are asked what they most want in life, the top answer is happiness. And yet, in my psychology studies at university, we had only one lecture on happiness in three years. Why was this? One reason is that we didn't appreciate the purpose of happiness. Happiness was dismissed as "a pleasurable emotion with no evolutionary value." We didn't understand, back then in the olden days, that happiness plays a key role in helping you to flourish and live your purpose.[4]

As director of The Happiness Project, I created an eight-week happiness program. The purpose of the program was to test if it was possible to teach people how to be happier. After three years I was approached by True Vision, an award-winning TV production company, to participate in a BBC science documentary on happiness.[5] They assembled two sets of independent scientists— one from Oxford University and the other from the University of Wisconsin–Madison—who measured the progress of three volunteers in my program.

The documentary was called *How to Be Happy*; it was broadcast on BBC 1 at 9:25 P.M. on August 1996; and it has since been watched by millions of TV viewers worldwide. The research findings were positive and enlightening. Professor Richard Davidson, from the University of Wisconsin-Madison, concluded in his report, "This happiness training not only changes the way you feel; it actually changes the way your brain functions." Professor Michael Argyle, from Oxford University, described the happiness program as "a genuine fast track to happiness."[6]

Why was my happiness program so successful? One reason is that the aim of my work was to help people stop searching for happiness and start following their joy. Recognizing the "call to joy" within you, and having the courage to follow your joy, are vital qualities you must cultivate if you are to break free from the chains of narrow self and live your higher purpose. We will explore the theme of joy later in Part II of this book, *The Path*.

After running The Happiness Project full time for seven years, I set up Success Intelligence Ltd., a bespoke consultancy that offered coaching journeys and leadership programs. I've since traveled the world as director of Success Intelligence Ltd., working with leaders of companies and global brands like the Dove Campaign for Real Beauty, IBM, Unilever, Virgin, and Google. I've also worked with schools and universities, public health agencies, government bodies, environmental organizations, and many charities.[7]

My work with Success Intelligence is based on one big question, which is *What is success?* I teach my clients that *the first discipline of success intelligence is to make time to stop and think about what success is.* Why is this so important? It's because your definition of success influences every significant decision in your life. Also, the more attention you give to the question *What is success?*, the clearer you get about who you are, what is real, and what your life is really for.

The purpose of my work with Success Intelligence is to help you create a definition of success that is good for you and good for the planet. Too many of us are living with definitions of success that are too narrow. Our definitions of success are ego-centered and self-serving, and they keep us chained to our narrow self. In the name of success, we play small, we betray ourselves, we get ulcers, we lack imagination, and we miss out on the joy of participating in the larger liturgy and greater glory of life.

To create a truly beautiful definition of success, you must engage your soul's immensity, as Wordsworth named it. In other words, you must bring your whole Self—body, heart, mind, and soul—to the conversation. I also encourage everyone in my Success Intelligence programs to create their vision for success from this starting point: *My success is my gift to the world.* If you do this, I believe the universe will gladly assist you in following your joy and living your true purpose.

One good inquiry always leads to another. The more I researched happiness, and the more I questioned what success was, the more deeply I thought about love. In fact, I found that I couldn't stop thinking about love. Happiness made no sense without love, and neither did success. In my book *Authentic Success*, I wrote, "*If your definition of success has little or no mention of love, get another definition.*"[8]

> *"There is only one question: how to love this world."*
>
> — Mary Oliver

Love came up so often in my inquiries that I decided to start a new project called Loveability. I set up Loveability seven years after I started Success Intelligence. It was the beginning of a new cycle and chapter in my life. I have since written three books on love and lectured all over the world on love as a spiritual path, on love and leadership, and on love and purpose. I'll share more about my work with Loveability later in Part II of this book: *The Path.*

A SELF-INQUIRY PRACTICE

> *Big questions*
> *life questions*
> *have to be answered fully*
> *with your whole life*
> *not just mentally*
> *on the back of an envelope*
>
> — Miller Mair

The purpose of self-inquiry is to help you recognize the golden thread of truth, meaning, and purpose that runs through your life. Self-inquiry cultivates the self-awareness to recognize your inner voice and to make authentic choices that may go against popular opinion. It generates the self-honesty you need to meet the fears and demons that stand before you. Above all, it assists you in your journey of individuation—a term used by Carl Jung—that you take to discover your creative potential, express your talents, and fulfill your destiny.

A good place to begin with self-inquiry is to identify a "life question" that is on your mind at present. This question may be prompted by recent events, or it may have been with you forever. Or both! Your life question is not a trivial matter. It is usually a big question that has big implications for your life. I often work with people who are asking themselves big life questions such as *What is my soul's calling? What is it that inspires me? How can I be a better leader? What is my activism?* and *How can I serve?*

Your life question chooses you as much as you choose it. It hovers over you like an angel, or behind you like a shadow, or by your side like a curious three-year-old. It doesn't leave you alone. It often feels too big for your narrow self to deal with. Don't worry about that, though. Whatever your question is, it comes with an answer. Your willingness to live with the question will greatly assist you in your inquiry.

A lot of people I mentor put undue pressure on themselves to answer a life question like *What is my purpose?* as fast as possible. Many of us have not been schooled in the way of inquiry. We are uncomfortable with uncertainty. We rebuke ourselves for not knowing. We have been educated to answer questions quickly. But being too quick can block courage, imagination, and possibility. A life question needs time and space. It helps to keep a journal, to take your question with you on long walks, to pray on it, and to explore it in conversations with trusted loved ones, a therapist, and a mentor.

One of my favorite books on the practice of inquiry is *Letters to a Young Poet* by Rainer Maria Rilke. The book features a correspondence between Rilke and a poet named Franz Xaver Kappus, who first wrote to him in 1902. In his letters, Rilke encourages the young Kappus to practice a basic openness to help him fathom the depths of his being and connect more fully with the world before him. Questions are very important to Rilke in this matter, and he writes:

> *I want to beg you as much as I can*
> *Be patient toward all that is unsolved in your heart*
> *and try to love the questions themselves,*
> *like locked rooms or like books that are now*
> *written in a very foreign tongue.*
> *Do not now seek the answers,*
> *which cannot be given you because you would*
> *not be able to live them. And the point is,*
> *to live everything.*
> *Live the questions now.*
> *Perhaps you will then gradually,*
> *without noticing it,*
> *live along some distant day into*
> *the answer.*[9]

Rilke's focus never wanders far from destiny and fate. He assures us that we will fulfill our purpose on earth if we live with the questions that want our attention. "Patience is all," he proclaims in one of his letters. Patience, complete trust, and an even temperament are vital. And what makes patience possible is love. "What goes on in your innermost being is worth all your love," he writes in another letter. Love is the heart of inquiry. And learning to love the questions is how we live with them in an open, brave, and appreciative way.

To really love a question, you must train your ears to listen for where the question is coming from. For example, this question—*How do I find my purpose?*—often hides a bunch of fears, such as "I have no purpose" and "I have no significance" and "I have no worth or value." Everyone who has an ego (which is all of us) has encountered these fears. They arise especially when you try to figure out your purpose by yourself, inside your head, and without help from God and other people.

With self-inquiry, it helps sometimes to reword a question so as to free up inspiration. For example, a question like *What is my purpose?* is problematic because the word "my" can narrow your inquiry too soon. Remember, *your purpose is not [only] your purpose.* You might want to read that last sentence again. Your purpose does not exist in isolation; it exists in relationship to the rest of life. What you are calling "my purpose" is really a "shared purpose" that is bigger than you.

To illustrate this idea of a shared purpose, let's look at the physical body for a moment. Do you know what the purpose of your liver organ is? Whatever it is that your liver does, it must be connected to your whole body to do it. While your liver performs its specific purpose, which includes digesting food and eliminating waste, it is also helping your heart and your lungs to fulfill their purpose. Your liver functions simultaneously as a separate organ and as part of a whole. It has an individual purpose and it participates in a shared purpose.

Now let's look at the nature kingdom. Let's examine bees, for example. Each bee is busy with a specific purpose. It buzzes around doing the thing that is "my purpose." Bees that live in hives serve a queen bee and help make honey for the colony. This is their shared purpose. Moreover, the bee community serves Mother Nature by pollinating over 90 percent of the world's flora and crops. They bless the plant kingdom, birds and animals, and humans too, with their presence. This is their universal purpose.

We humans are no different from the whole of life. To better appreciate what our personal purpose is (i.e., "my purpose"), we must consider what is humanity's purpose. *What do you think is the purpose of humanity?* This is a big question, I know, Remember, you are a full member of the human race, and you are qualified, along with everyone else, to make this inquiry. *What is humanity's purpose?* Is it to learn? To explore? To love? To serve? To grow and evolve? To survive? When you say YES to a shared purpose like any of these, you will naturally, organically, express this purpose in your own unique way.

When you live with a big life question, you may find sometimes that the question reveals a basic error in your thinking. For example, the question *How do I find my purpose?* reveals an erroneous belief that you and your purpose are in two separate places. How can your purpose *not* be with you? If you can't find your purpose, the chances are it's because you are not paying attention to your everyday life.

Rainer Maria Rilke frequently encouraged the young poet Kappus to pay close attention to life. In one of his letters, he wrote.

> If your everyday life seems to lack material, do not blame it; blame yourself, tell yourself that you are not poet enough to summon up its riches, for there is no lack for him who creates and no poor, trivial place. And even if you were in a prison whose walls did not let any of the sounds of the world outside reach your senses—would you not have your childhood still, this marvellous, lavish source, this treasure-house of memories?[10]

You won't find your purpose if you're not paying attention to your life. If, however, you are willing to spend some time in the *holy church of noticing,* as my wife, Hollie, calls it in one of her poems, your purpose will reveal itself to you.[11] Your purpose is always right where you are.

When people are struggling to find their purpose, I advise them, *Stop trying to define your purpose, and instead start to recognize when you feel most on purpose.* Trying to define purpose is too heady and academic. Definitions tend to make everything too small anyway. I recommend that you forget about defining your purpose, and try this one simple self-inquiry exercise instead. For the next seven days, keep a daily journal in which you record at least five entries per day by completing this line, *I felt most on purpose today when . . .*

I encourage you to do a version of this self-inquiry practice right now, before you keep reading. Get out a pen and be ready to scribble your answers on this page. Say each line out loud. Listen to your inner voice. And take notes.

I feel on purpose in my life when . . .

I feel on purpose in my life when . . .

I feel on purpose in my life when . . .

I feel on purpose in my life when . . .

I feel on purpose in my life when . . .

A SENSE OF DESTINY

The school run takes about 25 minutes by car. Most mornings we start off late. We aim to leave by 7:50 A.M., but it rarely happens. It's also not unusual to have to turn back to get Bo's ukulele or Christopher's school bag. We take the A316 out of London, over Chiswick Bridge, across the River Thames, down to the Richmond Circus roundabout, and on to the St. Michael Steiner School in Feltham. I often ask the children to say a special prayer to Archangel Metatron, the Angel of Life, for Godspeed on our journey. Amazingly, we arrive on time most days.

The school run normally starts off with an argument between Bo and Christopher over whose turn it is to sit in the front seat. After that, we take turns playing our favorite songs. Stevie Wonder is always on the playlist. We talk about favorite lessons, best friends and annoying friends, and who are the strictest teachers. We play games like guessing the number of red London buses we will see. We also play a game called Questions in which we take turns asking each other a question on absolutely anything that we may or may not want to answer.

When it's the children's turn to ask me a question, they mostly ask about my childhood and my school days. They love hearing about embarrassing moments, funny stories, pranks with friends, and me getting told off by my teachers. Here's what happened the other day.

"Tell us another funny story from when you were young!" said Bo.

"You want another story from the olden days!" I said, not surprised.

"Yeah, the olden days!" they both laughed

"I've run out of funny stories!" I protested.

"No, you haven't!" Bo told me.

"Think, Dad, there *must* be more!" urged Christopher.

At that moment we were approaching the Richmond Circus roundabout. The lights turned red and so we had to stop for a moment. While I searched my mind for a new funny story to tell, I remembered something very mysterious that happened to me at this same roundabout almost 40 years ago.

"I don't have a funny story, but I do have an interesting story to tell you," I said.

"How interesting?" Bo asked, not convinced.

"Is it something *we* would find interesting?" asked Christopher.

"Yes, I think so," I said

"Tell us, Dad," said Christopher.

"Yeah, go on, Dad," said Bo.

Here's what I told them: When I was 17 years old, I took my first road trip from Littleton to London. I went with three friends, Roger, Guy, and Peter. It was a 65-mile journey up the M3 motorway. We were off to celebrate the New Year by getting wet in the fountains at Trafalgar Square in central London. It's what young revelers did in the olden days, I explained, before there was the spectacular annual fireworks display on the River Thames near Big Ben and the London Eye.

The four of us drove up to London in a small Fiat. Our heads were pressed against the ceiling. I was squeezed in the back seat behind Roger, who was our driver. As we were passing Richmond Circus roundabout, I heard a voice say out loud, *"You are going to live here one day."*

I glanced at the car stereo, thinking I must be hearing a voice on the radio. But the radio sounded tinny, and the reception wasn't good. The voice I heard sounded perfectly clear to me. Also,

I somehow knew that the voice was addressing only me, and not my friends. "Did any of you hear that?" I asked.

"Hear what?" asked Roger.

"You are going to live here one day."

Roger and Guy didn't hear it.

"Spooky!" said Peter, who didn't hear it either.

After I heard these words, *"You are going to live here one day,"* I had an intuitive flash of me living and working in the area, being happily married and a father to two children. The voice sounded warm and wise. Its presence filled the car. It was showing me my future, which I could not have predicted. I didn't know that Hollie and her family lived just half a mile from Richmond Circus roundabout. Twenty-one years later, I moved into the area.

"Tell us another interesting story just like that one!" said Bo, who was all ears.

"Yeah, just like that one!" said Christopher.

"I could tell you about the time I nearly died," I said.

"Yes please!" shouted Bo.

"Tell us now, Dad!" urged Christopher.

Here's what I told them: When I was nine years old, my family and I went on holiday for a week to Lyme Regis, in Dorset in the south of England. Each day, we visited a different beach along a beautiful landscape called the Jurassic Coast, which is England's only natural World Heritage Site. My mum had visited Lyme Regis many times as a child. She was also a keen fossil hunter, and there are fossils to be found everywhere on the Jurassic Coast if you have the eyes to see them.

One day we visited Chesil Beach. We spent the morning on the beach, and later in the afternoon we went for a walk along the cliff tops. "Don't leave the path!" warned Dad. "Stay close to us, boys," said Mum firmly. My brother, David, who was five years old, took Mum's hand. I didn't want to hold hands, so I walked behind them. As we wandered along the path, I took a few short steps closer to the cliff edge to look over the side. I told myself I'd be careful. It was an awfully long way down.

As I peered over the edge, I lost my footing. I started to slide on the gravel. I fell to the ground. There was nothing to stop me. I couldn't grip on to anything. I continued to slide. This all happened in slow motion. At one point I was looking down at myself—as if I were a seagull or some other bird—and I saw myself slipping farther down. In desperation, I threw my arms over my head to grasp on to anything that might save me. I closed my eyes. *I'm going to die,* I told myself.

Somehow, I stopped sliding. My right hand was clutching on to something. I opened my eyes and saw that I was holding on to three or four blades of grass. I remember thinking, *This makes no sense.* How on earth was I being supported by a tuft of grass? At that moment, I heard a voice inside me say, "Let's not worry about that now. I am here to help you. Just pull yourself up." I did what the voice said. I scrambled onto higher ground. I dusted myself down. I was shaking. *I nearly died,* I thought.

"*It's not your time yet,*" the voice said.

Somehow, I knew that what the voice said was true. This was not my time to die. The voice spoke with authority. I understood that I still had a life to live. The presence of the voice was loving and wise. It imparted an inner knowing in me that I was alive for a purpose, that I had a divine assignment, and that I would leave only after my work was done. All of this I knew from hearing just those few words.

I looked around for Mum and Dad. No one had come to my rescue. They hadn't seen what had happened to me. *At least I won't get told off!* I thought. But I sorely needed to tell them. I decided it was worth a telling-off! So I raced after them, and, after I got told off, I told them about the blades of grass that made no sense and about the voice that saved my life.

In "Ode: Intimations of Immortality," William Wordsworth tells us about "a Presence [with a capital P] which is not to be put by."[1] Rainer Maria Rilke also recognized this presence in his moments of solitude and when out in nature. In a poem called "Buddha in Glory," he encounters this presence in the "center of all centers" and the "core of cores" of his Self [with a capital S]. He tells us,

> ...a billion stars go spinning through the night,
> glittering high above your head.
> But *in* you is the presence that
> will be when all the stars are dead.[2]

This presence will not allow you "to be misled by the surfaces of things," wrote Rilke in *Letters to a Young Poet*. It offers you inner direction and wise counsel for your life journey. It goes with you wherever you go. It wants to help you fulfill your pre-birth intention. It is never too late to recognize this presence and to listen to its guidance. It will speak to you in ways that you can understand, and it will use every means of communication, not just words, to get through to you.

This presence gets your attention by tapping you on your shoulder. It tugs at your heart. You sense it in your belly. It appears in your dreams. It makes the unconscious conscious. It helps you decipher messages from butterflies, and to notice white feathers and heart-shaped stones that appear at your feet. It recognizes destiny, synchronicity, and fate. It is a future pull. Jean Houston calls it *the lure of your becoming*. And Carl Jung described it as "the good star" that guides you back to your soul and onward to your true vocation.

FOLLOWING YOUR PATH

> *If you travel far enough, one day you will recognize yourself coming down to meet yourself. And you will say—yes.*
>
> — **Marion Woodman**

I was 18 years old, and I had no idea what to do with my life. I had graduated from college. My whole life was before me. I was meant to be excited, but I was overwhelmed by fear and panic. I didn't have a passion. I didn't have a superpower. I wasn't a gifted artist. I wasn't in love. I didn't have a faith. I wasn't particularly academic. There were lots of things I wasn't, and I didn't know who I was or what I wanted. How was I supposed to know what to do next?

As far as I could tell, there were four possible paths ahead for me. But which path was mine? I had no one to talk to. Dad had left home. His alcoholism had worsened. He was living homeless, mostly. One night I found him asleep in the shed in the back garden. My mum's depression had returned. Who knew if this terrible guest that overshadowed my mum would stay for a week, a month, or even longer this time? Her psychiatrist was on standby. David and I had his phone number, just in case.

One possible path was to get a job. Lots of my friends were already working. They didn't like what they did, but the money was good. I was still getting pocket money from my mum. *Maybe I should get a job*, I thought. It didn't feel true, though. The idea of working for money felt like I was betraying myself. I was a conscientious objector who was refusing to do something I didn't believe in. I didn't want a job or a career; I wanted something more meaningful than that.

Another path was to go traveling. One idea I had was to work in a kibbutz in Israel, and then go on to visit Jerusalem and India, two places I'd always felt drawn to. One day my great-uncle Derek Hill, who was an artist, called on the phone to speak to me. "I hear you're thinking of traveling!" he said, in his big, booming voice. The family grapevine was obviously working well. "I think it's an excellent idea!" he told me. "I'm going to give you the name and phone number of a dear friend of mine." He then told me to get a pen and paper, which I duly did.

"Are you ready, Robert?" he asked.

"Yes, Derek," I said, rather nervously.

"Good! My friend is called Teddy Kollek, and he's the mayor of Jerusalem. Shall I help you spell that?"

"No, I'm fine," I said. I was pretty sure I knew how to spell Jerusalem.

"It's 'K,' 'o,' double 'l,' 'e,' 'k,'" he told me.

"Got it! Thank you!" I said, trying to sound like I knew that.

"Don't be shy, Robert. Call him up straightaway!"

Shy was exactly how I felt! The highest-ranking official I'd ever spoken to was the village policeman in Littleton. My great-uncle Derek was a larger-than-life character who traveled the world painting portraits of kings and queens. He was my mother's uncle, and his life was very different from mine. Each year he took HRH Charles, the Prince of Wales, to Mount Athos in the north-east peninsula of Greece to teach the young prince painting and philosophy.[3]

I meant to call Teddy Kollek that day, but something inside me told me to hold off. "Don't look a gift horse in the mouth!" my aunt told me. A few days later, just as I was about to call the mayor of Jerusalem, the conflict between Israel and Palestine erupted again, and the U.K. Foreign Office advised against travel. I was disappointed *and* relieved. Traveling sounded fun, but deep down I felt that I'd be running away from my life. This was not my path for now, but I also knew that I'd visit these places one day when the time was right.

I had two more paths before me. Both were offers for higher education. One was a one-year postgraduate course in journalism at the University of Portsmouth, and the other was a three-year course in communications at the University of Birmingham. Portsmouth was close to home, which was good in case of an emergency with Mum or Dad. I'd skip three years of study, as it was a postgraduate course. Plus I had a guaranteed job in 10 months' time. It seemed like a no-brainer for a young man who was full of ambition and keen to get going with his life.

Birmingham was not close to home. It was a land far, far away, in Middle England, about three hours by car. I didn't know the city, and I'd never thought about going there. The curriculum looked interesting, though. It offered a mix of journalism and psychology, media and sociology, literature and philosophy. Several times I tried to write an acceptance letter to Portsmouth, but my hand could barely hold the pen. It didn't feel true, no matter how hard I tried to convince myself. I was being pulled by an invisible thread to Birmingham.

Choosing Birmingham felt like a big mistake at first. There were only four lectures a week. I wanted more. The travel to and from the campuses took up to an hour. I didn't want to waste my life sitting on buses. I didn't make friends quickly. Everyone was too busy trying to be popular. I told my mum I'd give it until Christmas, and then I'd come home. But everything changed with one fateful meeting with Avanti Kumar, a fellow student who became my best friend and my first spiritual mentor.

Meeting Avanti Kumar set my life on a path I feel I was always destined for. I've written about Avanti in all my major books because he is a central character in the story of my life. So I'll be brief here. Avanti is Indian. He had signed up for the same course as me as a mature student. He was 24 years old when we first met. He had studied Vedanta philosophy since he was nine years old. He was a published writer of fiction. He also had a great love of cricket.

Meeting Avanti felt like a reunion. He was familiar to me, like a brother from another life. It was seven weeks into the first term before I introduced myself to Avanti. He was usually the last person to arrive for class and the first to leave. He lived locally, and he didn't hang out much on campus. One day I decided to catch up with him after class and start up a conversation. I remember it vividly. Here's how it went.

"Hi, my name is Robert," I said.

"Yes, I know," said Avanti.

"So how are you enjoying the course?" I asked.

"Quite so," he replied.

"What made you choose this course?"

"I came to meet you," he said.

"Great," I said.

"Yes," he said.

"Thanks," I said.

Did he mean what he said? Later, Avanti told me that he had felt called to take this course, and that he knew we'd be friends the moment he laid eyes on me. "Why, then, did you take so long to say hello?" I asked him. He told me, "I had a strong sense that you had to approach me first, and that you'd do so when the time was right." After that, we were inseparable. We sat in class together. We talked for hours in our favorite coffee shop. I was adopted into his family. His mother and father treated me like a son.

Everything got better after meeting Avanti. I loved living in Birmingham. I made more friends. I was captain of the university cricket team. My classes were a lot more interesting now because I had Avanti to talk to. I enjoyed the modules on journalism, radio, and television, but what really inspired me were the modules on psychology, sociology, and philosophy. Most of all, I became fascinated with the bridge between Western psychology and Eastern spirituality.

Avanti loaned me lots of his favorite books for further study. The first one he gave me was *The Bhagavad Gita*, a Hindu bible known as "The Song of God." It's a 2,500-year-old spiritual poem full of symbolism, metaphor, and deeper meaning. The heart of it is a dialogue between the young prince Arjuna, who is lost and full of melancholy, and his charioteer, Krishna, who introduces him to three great spiritual paths: *jnana*, the path of wisdom; *karma*, the path of action and service; *and bhakti*, the yoga of love, which Krishna describes as the greatest path because love is our highest purpose.

ADDRESSED BY A VOICE

In the final term of our first year, we had a lecture on Carl Jung and his work. Up until now our classes had been full of "ology" and not much "psyche." We had mostly studied Sigmund Freud's *will to pleasure* theory: that our basic drive is to seek pleasure and avoid pain. Also Alfred Adler's *superiority complex* theory: that our main goal is to overcome feelings of inferiority to feel superior. There were plenty of gaps in the curriculum. My edition of the *Oxford Encyclopedia of Psychology* had no listing in the index for joy, success, love, meaning, or purpose.

During our one and only lecture on Carl Jung's work, the lecturer put up a quote by Jung on his overhead projector that switched a light on in my mind. He took it down before I could write it in my notebook, so I stayed after class and missed taking the bus home with Avanti to make sure I got the full quote and reference. I've shared Carl Jung's quote many times over the years in my work with Stress Busters, The Happiness Project, and Success Intelligence. Here it is:

> About a third of my cases are not suffering from any clearly definable neurosis, but from the senselessness and aimlessness of their lives. I should not object if this were called the general neurosis of our age.[4]

Carl Jung became my new hero, and his work was a "good star" that led me down new paths of inquiry and learning. His work was deep and wide, and it often went over my head. Fortunately for me, I had Avanti as my companion and guide. Jung had freed himself from the narrow chains of Western psychology to take a greater journey beyond the basic will to pleasure and the need for superiority, and into a larger existence and higher purpose in life, which he called *vocation*.

The word *vocation* is described in the *Oxford English Dictionary* as "a person's employment or main occupation." This is a narrow definition of the word and not how Carl Jung used it. Carl Jung was fluent in Latin, and he understood that the Latin root of vocation is *vocare*, which means "to call, invite, or summon." In his collected works, Jung wrote, "The original meaning of 'to have a vocation' is 'to be addressed by a voice.'"[5]

Carl Jung happily embraced words like *fate*, *destiny*, and *synchronicity*. He didn't try to define or rationalize these words because that is impossible, but he didn't delete them either. "From the beginning I had a sense of Destiny," he wrote, "as though my life was assigned to me by fate and had to be fulfilled. This gave me an inner security, and though I could never prove it to myself, it proved itself to me. I did not have this certainty, it had me."[6]

Carl Jung recognized that one's true calling comes not from the ego but from the "bottom of one's own being." Here is where our inner knowing resides. It is the original wisdom that is woven into our spiritual DNA and that seeks a dialogue with us. He wrote, "Somewhere, right at the bottom of one's own being, one generally does know where one should go and what one should do. But there are times when the clown we call 'I' behaves in such a distracting fashion that the inner voice cannot make its presence felt."[7]

The ego's work is to recognize your calling, to honor it, and ultimately to surrender to it. In his book *The Development of Personality*, Jung wrote, "True personality is always a vocation and puts its trust in it as in God, despite its being, as the ordinary man would say, only a personal feeling. But vocation acts like a law of God from which there is no escape. The fact that many a man who goes his own way ends in ruin means nothing to one who has a vocation. He must obey his own law, as if it were a daemon whispering to him of new and wonderful paths."[8]

STAGES ON THE PATH

Carl Jung taught that "man cannot stand a meaningless life." A vocation and a sense of purpose are necessary to help you experience true happiness and fulfillment. Jung used the word *individuation* to describe your most basic need, which is to grow and *to become your whole self*. It's the journey that your ego-self takes to meet your soul's immensity. There's an ancient Greek word that fits with individuation, and it is *anthropos*, which describes a bigger Self that is fully human and fully divine.

In an essay Carl Jung wrote in 1931 entitled "The Stages of Life," he observed four stages of development on the journey to becoming your whole self. These stages generally follow a broad chronological sequence. However, when you are inspired by a vocation, *kairos* (eternal time) can rearrange *chronos* (temporal time) so as to accelerate things. For instance, when building a new business or working on a poem, you might move through all four stages in a matter of weeks or even in a single day.[9]

Stage 1: The Athlete. Early on, we want to make a name for ourselves, create a good impression, and be attractive. We want to feel worthy and to believe that our life means something. We are self-absorbed and full of self-display. We are Narcissus peering at his own reflection in a pool of water. We pursue happiness, we chase success, and we look for love. We are full of ambition, adrenalin, and an excess of anxiety. You might look good, but you don't always feel good. You may exert great willpower, but you haven't yet experienced a higher power than your ego.

Stage 2: The Warrior. Here, we want to conquer the world. Our aim is to be financially independent, to own our own home, and to assert our free will. We want to start our own business, to be king of the hill, and to build our own empire. We are David taking on Goliath. It's very much *me (or a few of us) against the world*. You may think you are playing big, but you are merely a big fish in a small pond—Narcissus's pond—because you have not yet said YES to the great adventure of your life. You are here to love the world, and your circle of love is still narrow, but it is widening.

Stage 3: The Statement. As a warrior you must use both your victories and defeats to go forward to this next stage. You enter this stage often with a sense of disillusionment. "There must be more to life than this!" you cry. The life you have been living feels too small for you now, and you want to play a part—even a very small part—in a bigger story.

"The most important question anyone can ask is, *What myth am I living?*" wrote Carl Jung. A myth is a great story that you want to be part of: a love story, a hero journey, a renaissance, a reformation, a good deed for the world, and a higher purpose that you give yourself fully to.

Jung wrote, "I asked myself, 'What is the myth you are living?' And found that I did not know. . . . So I took it upon myself to get to know 'my' myth, and I regarded this as the task of tasks . . . I simply had to know what unconscious or preconscious myth was forming me."[10]

This is the stage when you work out what truly inspires you and what you want to give your life to. Here is your act of surrender. Now you must submit to the infinite. You must let the single grain of wheat fall to the earth and die so that it will bear new fruit.

Stage 4: Spiritual. Now you are living an inspired life. You are not as rational or small-minded as you once were. Your vocation has freed you from the chains of narrow self. You are emancipated and you enjoy spiritual liberty. You recognize what inspires you. You are following your joy. You are doing what you love. You know you are here for a greater glory. You are happy to affirm, "Thy will be done."

You no longer care about being normal. "To be normal is the ideal aim of the unsuccessful," said Jung. You realize that you are here to be part of the new normal, a better normal, that will help humanity evolve and take its rightful place in the greater story of creation.

YOUR TRUE VOICE

*Anyone with a vocation hears the voice
of the inner man: he is called.*

— Carl Jung

Avanti had arrived at the perfect time to initiate me on my path. I was like Arjuna in *The Bhagavad Gita*, utterly lost and unsure about which direction to take, and Avanti was my Krishna who was offering me guidance and hope. Thanks to Avanti, I immersed myself in spiritual literature from around the world, and I learned about our soul's journey in *The Upanishads*; about dharma, the doctrine of purpose, in the Buddhist text the *Dhammapada*; about spiritual guidance and universal inspiration in the Gospel of John; and about the true way in the *Tao Te Ching*.

Avanti gave me my first spiritual practices. He taught me how to meditate. My first meditation practice was to focus on a candle flame. He told me that the flame represents a light that exists in each of us. It's the same light that Jesus talked about when he said, "I am the light of the world" and when he told his disciples "You are the light of the world."[11] Avanti also gave me a prayer to pray for the world. He said that we come to earth as an answer to each other's prayers.

> *"The sole purpose of human existence is to kindle a light in the darkness of mere being."*
>
> — Carl Jung

Avanti encouraged me to start journaling. "What should I write about?" I asked him. He told me to write about everything that is true. I didn't know how to do that at first. He explained that the purpose of keeping a journal is to learn to be truthful with yourself and to recognize your true voice. He encouraged me to listen for soul guidance, to give voice to my fears, to notice what inspires me, to write down my dreams, and to follow the golden thread, a metaphor Carl Jung used, that connects you to your purpose.

Looking at my journals now, I see that my writing leaned forward, from left to right, pulling me toward my future. My entries were full of imitation. I was busy like a bee collecting inspiration from everywhere. There wasn't much original thought. There was also a lot of angst in my journals. I was terribly in love with one of Avanti's sisters, which was complicated and impossible. Even so, I did manage to write with my true voice every now and then, and it happened more frequently as time went on.

In my journals I made lists of ways I recognized my true voice. I wrote about "a loving presence" that was "infinitely patient," "always affirmative," and "never critical"; and about "wisdom in my bones," "peace of mind," and "joy in my heart." I also made lists of how I block the awareness of my true voice. For example, "worrying about people's opinion," "fear of rejection," "self-comparing unfavorably," "not being emotionally honest with myself," "overworking," "shortening my meditation time," "watching too much TV," and "not doing my journaling."

Making these lists helped me connect more consciously with my inner guidance and true voice. I encourage the people I mentor to make similar lists. For example, I ask them to complete the following sentence 10 times: "One way I experience my true voice is . . ." Another option is, "One way I experience spiritual guidance is . . ." I invite you, dear reader, to try one of these exercises before you finish reading this book.

Rereading my journals, I see that Avanti was always recommending novels and plays to me. He was helping me to find "my myth"—a big story that might ignite in me a sense of destiny and purpose. D. H. Lawrence's *The Rainbow*, George Orwell's *Nineteen Eighty-Four*, J.D. Salinger's *The Catcher in the Rye*, Ernest Hemingway's *The Old Man and the Sea*, and Hermann Hesse's *Siddhartha* all get plenty of mentions in my journals. These books are lifelong companions, and I continue to find new meaning and fresh inspiration in them.

In one journal entry, I tell the story of when Avanti introduced me to a piece of classical music called *The Hymn of Jesus* by Gustav Holst. Avanti's prized possession was his Linn Sondek LP12 turntable, made of rosewood, with an Audiolab amplifier and Wharfedale speakers. We'd sit for hours listening to Beethoven, Mozart, Elgar, Holst, and Radiohead. *The Hymn of Jesus* was Holst's first major work after completing his suite *The Planets*. It is based on the hymn sung at The Last Supper. The lyrics that Holst used come from a Gnostic text, the apocryphal Acts of John.

Avanti encouraged me to use Holst's *Hymn of Jesus* as a spiritual practice for opening myself up to my higher purpose. The *Hymn of Jesus* is 21 minutes long. It opens with a gentle orchestral prelude and then the hymn bursts into life with a full double chorus of "Glory to Thee, Father!" and then "Glory to Thee, Word!" I wrote the lyrics out in full in my journal. They are a call to participate in the greater purpose of creation. One verse begins, "Divine Grace is dancing. Fain would I pipe for you: Dance ye all." This was my first introduction to the Cosmic Christ. The hymn ends with these words:

> *To you who gaze, a lamp am I:*
> *To you that know, a mirror.*
> *To you who knock, a door am I:*
> *To you who fare, the way.*

ANSWERING THE CALL

The grand opening of my Stress Busters Clinic was not as grand as I had hoped for. The first class was scheduled for 11 A.M. one Thursday in April. I'd put posters up everywhere in the local neighborhood. Plenty of people had told me they planned to be there. I blew the budget on posh tea bags and rich biscuits. Eleven A.M. came and went. No one showed up, except for me. Maybe this was a sign I was meant to be doing something different with my life.

At precisely 11:11 A.M., Mary and Jean wandered into the clinic. I welcomed these two angels possibly a bit too enthusiastically. Mary and Jean, two Irish ladies in their 60s, were on a visit from across the other side of the city. I made them both a cup of tea, and we ate digestive biscuits—my mum's favorites—as I told them about my vision for Stress Busters. They listened very politely. I gave them each a copy of the outline for our first class. They told me they could stay for only 30 minutes. "That's absolutely fine by me," I said.

Mary and Jean returned the following week, which is when they confessed that they hadn't meant to come to the first class. My Stress Busters Clinic was based in a health center called the Health Shop. Mary and Jean had wandered into the Health Shop looking for a healthy snack to eat. We didn't sell any food at the Health Shop. Fortunately for me, they settled for Stress Busters instead.

"We both thought what a lovely young man you are," Mary told me as she recounted the tale of last Thursday. "And we realized we were the only ones in your class," said Jean. So while I was busy making them both a cup of tea, Mary and Jean had a little talk and decided to stay. "We didn't have the heart to leave," said Mary, who had kindly brought a packet of digestive biscuits with her this time.

Serendipity had orchestrated my meeting with Mary and Jean, of that I am sure. In our first meeting, I discovered that they had both been born and raised in Letterkenny in County Donegal, which is where my great-uncle Derek, the artist, had a home and an art gallery—called Glebe House and Gallery—that he later bequeathed to Ireland.[1] Mary and Jean knew of Derek Hill. They had grown up with Gracie, Derek's housekeeper, who everyone agreed was the greatest cook and the loveliest person you could ever hope to meet.

I opened my Stress Busters Clinic three years after graduating from the University of Birmingham. In those three years, I had been busy on a quest for greater meaning and purpose. I was living near Avanti and his family. I had organized my own learning curriculum of higher education, which included courses on philosophy, metaphysics, yoga, and a three-year diploma in advanced counseling based on the work of Carl Rogers. I was also busy writing: not just journaling, but essays, articles, and short stories, none of which had been published at that point.

My first paid work was tutoring a stress management course at a local adult education center. It was a series of six classes, and it paid £15 a class. Avanti had worked his magic and recommended me to the head teacher. I relied a lot on Avanti and his sister Anita for help with the design of each class. At the final class, a woman who had attended the whole series introduced herself as the director for public health for the local area. "I've got a good feeling about you, and I want to give you an opportunity," she told me. The opportunity was Stress Busters.

Stress Busters was a pilot scheme. It was the first stress clinic through the National Health Service in the U.K. We were treading new ground. We had started small and took one micro step after another. I was okay with that. We are each born from small beginnings. And most small steps are often not as small as you think. The pay was negligible, but I'd have done it for nothing. The main thing was that I felt truly on purpose. At last, I was doing something meaningful with my studies and I was being of service.

Stress Busters served many purposes. It was a testing apprenticeship for me in lots of ways. The clinic was based in Handsworth, a run-down neighborhood struggling with high unemployment, economic poverty, racial tension, a drug problem, and frequent rioting. Many of my clients lived in the dilapidated high-rise tower blocks, with concrete playgrounds for the kids. The local park was not a safe place to go to after dark. My clients suffered with anxiety, depression, and alcoholism. They weren't only stressed; they were in despair.

My aim was to make my Stress Busters Clinic a safe haven and a sanctuary for the soul. I taught meditation classes. We practiced yoga together. We had a book club, in which I loaned out my favorite books, just as Avanti had done for me. I conducted mind-body research experiments using biofeedback. I offered classes on philosophy. We studied prayer together. I prescribed poems to my clients. I arranged singing lessons to help us find our true voice. And we often ended each class with a dance.

At Stress Busters, I was offering a creative approach to stress that helped my clients relate to stress not merely as an illness but as an invitation to life. In my book *Stress Busters*, I illustrated my approach with a quote from Carl Jung: "Man can meet the demands of outer necessity in an ideal way only if he is adapted to his own inner world, that is if he is in harmony with himself." [2] My aim was to help people find rest in the sanctuary of their soul, learn to recognize their true voice, and follow the golden thread of wisdom, meaning, and purpose in their life.

IN SEARCH OF MEANING

One day I got a call from Gordon Astley, who was the host of a morning talk-radio show for BBC WM at Pebble Mill in Birmingham. He had an invitation for me. "Would you be interested in being a guest presenter on my show for a weekly phone-in on positive mental health?" he asked. We arranged a time to meet up together with his current guest presenter, a much-loved psychiatrist in his 70s who was stepping down after five years on the show. His name was Freddie Frankl.

> *"Synchronicity is an ever-present reality for those who have eyes to see."*
>
> — Carl Jung

Meeting Freddie Frankl was another act of serendipity, or synchronicity as Jung called it. I had recently finished reading *Man's Search for Meaning* by Dr. Viktor Frankl—a book that has sold over 20 million copies and is widely regarded as one of the most inspiring books on meaning and purpose ever written.[3] It had certainly lived up to its billing for me. This book was the new "good star" in my life. I shared passages from it regularly in my Stress Busters classes. Now, here I was talking with Freddie Frankl, who was one of Viktor Frankl's nephews.

Viktor Frankl was a Holocaust survivor who spent three years in Auschwitz and other concentration camps between 1942 and 1945. His first wife, Tilly Grosser, and his mother, father, and brother were all murdered in the camps. In *Man's Search for Meaning*, Frankl shared a "fragment"—as he called it—of his experiences living in that hell. To survive those three terrible years, he found it was "essential to keep practicing the art of living" even in the face of death. He sought inspiration from the Psalms. He repeated daily this line from Psalm 118:

> *I called to the Lord from my narrow prison, and*
> *He answered me in the freedom of space.*[4]

During his time at Auschwitz, Frankl found a "living question" that helped him survive the horrors of the camps and later inspired his life's work. "The question which beset me was, 'Has all this suffering, this dying around us, a meaning?'" he wrote.[5] Frankl deduced that if the answer was no, then that must mean survival had no meaning either. This didn't feel true to Frankl. He recognized that no was the voice of despair, which he described as "suffering without meaning." Frankl said yes to his life, and a deeper meaning and purpose were revealed to him.

Viktor Frankl was the founder of logotherapy, heralded as the *third Viennese school of psychotherapy*, after those of Sigmund Freud and Alfred Adler. "According to logotherapy, this striving to find a meaning in one's life is the primary motivational force in man," wrote Victor Frankl.[6] Logotherapy's main aim is to help you live a meaning-centered life. The *will to meaning*, named by Frankl, is more than just a secondary rationalization to the *will to pleasure* (Freud's theory) and the *will to power* (Adler's theory). The *will to meaning* comes first.

Nine months after Viktor Frankl was liberated from the Nazi concentration camps, he gave a short series of lectures called "Yes to Life in Spite of Everything" at an adult education college in the Ottakring district of Vienna.[7] He taught that your *will to meaning* is a sacred YES that connects you with a higher purpose that is far more meaningful than the pursuit of power and superiority over others. The *will to meaning* also engages a higher power that can help you overcome the wounding and suffering you experience on your path.

I believe that it's your *will to meaning* that helps you grow into a "bigger me," as my son, Christopher, calls it. It activates the God-seed in you and enables you to realize your soul's immensity. Viktor Frankl said it this way: "Logotherapy sees the human patient in all his humanness. I step up to the core of the patient's being. And that is a being in search of meaning, a being that is transcending himself, a being capable of acting in love for others."[8]

Freddie Frankl was an enthusiastic advocate for logotherapy. He spoke about it with passion, and with a twinkle in his eye. He was a rare breed of psychiatrist in that he had a faith, he believed in the soul, and he was happy. In our conversations, Freddie taught me about the three broad levels of meaning and purpose that are outlined in logotherapy.

> **Level 1: Meaning for Self.** Life is full of meaning, but what specifically do you find meaningful? At Level 1, the quest is for personal meaning. Do you know what presses your "This is meaningful" button? Have you worked that out yet? Are you paying attention to your life? At this personal level, Viktor Frankl explained that "the meaning is unique and specific in that it must and can be fulfilled by him [you] alone; only then does it achieve a significance which will satisfy his [your] own will to meaning."[9]

> **Level 2: Shared Meaning.** The *will to meaning* connects you to your true self and to others too. Meaning is intrinsic in every relationship. It is the invisible thread of communication that weaves through your ancestors, your children, and the people you meet. It connects you to butterflies and rainbows, whales and dolphins, and trees and bees. Every relationship has an essential meaning and purpose. The more open you are to this, the more likely you will experience the gift, the lesson, the healing, and the love that each relationship offers.

> **Level 3: A Super Meaning.** Viktor Frankl coined the term *supermeaning* to describe a continuous, universal meaning that unfolds across time and space. This supermeaning belongs to a much larger story than we are aware of at Levels 1 and 2. Frankl said it "necessarily exceeds and surpasses the finite intellectual capacities of man." It takes us beyond the realm of logic and into the mind of universal love.

By doing our inner work on Level 1 and Level 2, we gain glimpses of the supermeaning level. We become increasingly conscious and aware of the part assigned to us in this greater story. Frankl believed that this is true for everyone and that none of us can "completely resist his Zeitgeist, the spirit of his time."

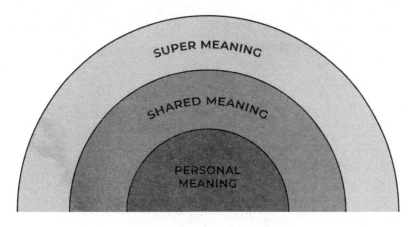

Frankl's Levels of Meaning

One time, while I was having a cup of tea with Freddie Frankl, I asked him for his most helpful advice for experiencing greater meaning and purpose in life. I was preparing to teach a class on life purpose at my Stress Busters Clinic the next day, and I was in need of some good material. "I'll make it nice and simple for you," he said with a twinkle in his eye. "You must learn how to suffer well, to love well, and to work well," he told me.

The meaning of suffering:

Viktor Frankl agreed with the Buddha, with Jesus, and with all the great spiritual teachers who taught that suffering is part of life and that no one can avoid suffering entirely. "When a man finds that it is his destiny to suffer . . . his unique opportunity lies in the way he bears his burden," wrote Frankl. By cultivating an honest and loving approach to our suffering, we can use our suffering for a higher purpose. Also, we do not pass on our suffering to others.

Personally, I knew I still had to address the deeper layers of grief and despair I felt about my mum's depression and my dad's alcoholism. I hadn't been able to save them from their suffering. Mum was hoping to find the right pills, and Dad was looking inside a whisky bottle. Where would I find the answer to my suffering? Freddie told me that a good question to ask myself was *What meaning shall I give to my pain?* In other words, what purpose will I give it? And how can I use it as a catalyst for my growth?

In one of my journals that I kept at this time, I wrote these words:

the meaning that you give to your suffering
is what helps you to overcome your
suffering or not.

The meaning of love:

If you learn to suffer well, you can learn from your suffering, you can grow through it, and ultimately, you are liberated from it. You can use your suffering to experience a greater connection with life, to enjoy deeper and more meaningful relationships, and to continue to step into your soul's immensity. How is this even possible? It is not possible without love.

Viktor Frankl recognized love as a higher power that lives in the "innermost core" of your being. He taught that when you meet suffering with enough love, you can find a meaning for it that helps you to survive and grow. Love has the power to give meaning to your life and it can use your suffering for a higher purpose. Of course, it's impossible to do this on your own. We all need help, and we are here to play a part in each other's healing and liberation. Loving ourselves and each other is our salvation and our shared purpose.

The meaning of work:

Viktor Frankl observed that "ever more people today have the means to live but no meaning to live for." Why do we go to work? What is the real meaning of work? Do we work simply to earn money and acquire wealth, or is there a higher purpose to it? In the Athlete Stage and Warrior Stage of Carl Jung's work, we mainly use work to win medals, climb a ladder, earn a promotion, and rise to the top, but it's never enough. You may end up burying yourself in your work in an effort to avoid your suffering and to compensate for the lack of love in your life.

Freddie Frankl said to me, "The purpose of life is to work out what the *real work* of your life is." Your real work is far greater than learning a trade, having a job, pursuing a career, getting published, being the boss, or owning your business. Yes, it may include some of that, but beyond that, the real work of your life is more about who you are, what you stand for, how you meet your suffering, and how you choose to express your love.

Reading Victor Frankl's works and meeting his nephew Freddie were big turning points in my life. Freddie had picked up the mantle of his uncle's work, and he was handing it on to me. I was asking questions about life, but Freddie was helping me see that *life was also asking questions of me.* It was time for me to trust that I carried the answer to my own questions. And that it was time for me to start living some of those answers.

Ultimately, man should not ask what the meaning of his life is, but rather must recognize that it is he who is asked. In a word, each man is questioned by life; and he can only answer to life by answering for his own life; to life he can only respond by being responsible.

— Victor Frankl

PART II

THE PATH

THE HERO YOU ARE

Around the time I was setting up my Stress Busters Clinic, PBS premiered a documentary called *The Power of Myth*, with mythologist Joseph Campbell and journalist Bill Moyers.[1] It soon became the most viewed documentary in television history, and it introduced the world to Joseph Campbell's work on the hero journey.

The Power of Myth is a series of six conversations filmed at Skywalker Ranch, home of filmmaker George Lucas, and at the American Museum of Natural History in New York. Joseph Campbell is supported masterfully by his great friend Bill Moyers as he takes us on a grand tour of creation mythology, introducing us to the world's first storytellers, the archetype of the hero, the quest for meaning, the ordeal of suffering, and the great victory that happens when you dare to follow your bliss.

Joseph Campbell's map of the hero journey has been a great help to me in my quest for meaning and purpose. I've watched *The Power of Myth* more times than any other documentary, and I am more inspired by it each time I watch it. In a recent interview, I was asked to name my desert island book. That's easy. It's *A Course in Miracles*. I told my interviewer that if I could also take a desert island DVD—with a special solar-powered DVD player—it would be *The Power of Myth* series.

After many years of giving Joseph Campbell special mention in my public events and leadership programs, I gave my first talk on The Hero Journey. It was at a Mind, Body, Spirit Festival in London. Tickets sold out within three days after I announced the talk in my weekly newsletter. I also received many requests from people overseas wanting a longer format. So I followed up with a three-day Hero Journey retreat, and after that a six-month Hero Journey Mastermind program, the first of which included a pilgrimage to Glastonbury in search of the Holy Grail. I always feel very on purpose in my life when I am learning and teaching about Joseph Campbell's work.[2]

In his youth, Joseph Campbell was a great athlete and a gifted musician, but neither of these pursuits felt like his true purpose, and he struggled with his own search for meaning. In one of his early journals, he wrote about the deep need he felt "to justify my existence" and a compelling sense that "I've got to do something for humanity."[3] Young Joe chose higher education over a career. He earned a B.A. in literature, and then an M.A. in Arthurian legends, and after that, during the Great Depression, he embarked upon a program of intensive and rigorous independent study.

Joseph Campbell went in search of the hero myth. He researched the wisdom traditions of every continent, starting with Native Americans. He explored cave paintings in Africa. He visited the pyramids and Stonehenge. He journeyed to Jerusalem. He took a pilgrimage to Bodh Gaya. He read James Joyce's *Ulysses*. Picasso was one of his favorite artists. And with the help of Carl Jung's work on the hero archetype, the human psyche, and the collective unconscious, he eventually presented the hero journey in his seminal work *The Hero with a Thousand Faces*, published in 1949, when he was 45 years old.[4]

THE HERO MYTH

*A hero is someone who has given his or her life
to something bigger than oneself.*

— Joseph Campbell

The hero is an archetype—a big idea—that lives in your psyche and in the collective mind of every culture. It's with you for your whole life, right up until your last breath, and its main aim is to get you to say YES to a hero story—traditionally called a hero myth—that inspires you to fulfill your purpose.

You experience your hero myth on three levels. On a personal level, you are the hero—the main protagonist—in the story of your life. Here, your work is to find a hero storyline you want to pursue in medicine, sport, the arts, media, technology, or ecology, for instance. On a collective level, you are the hero who plays a supporting role—as a friend, a lover, a teacher, a mentor, a healer—helping others become the heroes they are destined to be. On a universal level, the hero archetype works through you in service to humanity, to Gaia, and to the greater story of the universe.

> *"The hero journey is inside of you; tear off the veils and open the mystery of your self."*
>
> — Joseph Campbell

We are all on a hero journey. It is, essentially, the same journey expressed in an infinite variety of ways. That's why Joseph Campbell called his book *The Hero with a Thousand Faces*. We are each participating in a *monomyth*—the great story behind every story—a term that Campbell borrowed from James Joyce's novel *Finnegans Wake*. Your purpose is your unique responsibility, but the copyright doesn't belong solely to you, and the royalties you accrue are for a greater glory.

The hero journey is both an inner and outer journey that you take to become the bigger Self that you truly are. It is a journey you take from self with a small "s" to Self with a big "S." Along the way you may wear an elaborate mask of a research scientist, a rock star, an animal rights campaigner, or a global leader; you also wear an everyday mask of mother, brother, friend, or kind stranger. Beneath the mask is the hero, the fully individuated Self, that you are destined to become and most wish to be.

The hero journey is a path of growth. The hero archetype is packed into the Godseed that arrives with you on earth. The Godseed is full of "aliveness"—one of Campbell's favorite terms—and the hero archetype activates the life force of the Godseed that takes you beyond the chains of narrow self into the realms of your soul's immensity. To do this, you must be willing to die to your old self-image and experience yourself in a new light. You must be born and then born again. In *The Power of Myth*, Joseph Campbell tells Bill Moyers,

> The power of life causes the snake to shed its skin, just as the moon sheds its shadow. The serpent sheds its skin to be born again, as the moon its shadow to be born again.[5]

The hero journey is a transformation drama. The hero who starts the journey is not the same person who completes it. The first Adam dies on the journey, and it is the second Adam who returns. Likewise, the monarch butterfly experiences a complete metamorphosis in four stages: egg, larva (caterpillar), pupa, and adult. The honeybee evolves through a similar cycle. A tree grows through four stages of life, from seedling and primary growth (sapling) to secondary growth and maturity. And the human hero evolves from a small ego that is seeking the meaning of life into a fully fledged life-giving spirit.

THE CALL TO ADVENTURE

The call to adventure signifies that
destiny has summoned the hero.

— Joseph Campbell

The hero journey has three main stages to it. These three stages are similar to the three-act structure of dramatic theory that Aristotle outlined in his work *Poetics*, and that still informs modern writing in novels and on stage and screen. Act One has the setup for the plot. Joseph Campbell called this the Departure Stage. Act Two has the rising action of the story. Campbell called this the Initiation Stage. Act Three holds the climax and resolution. Campbell called this the Return Stage, which is when the hero completes the mythic cycle.

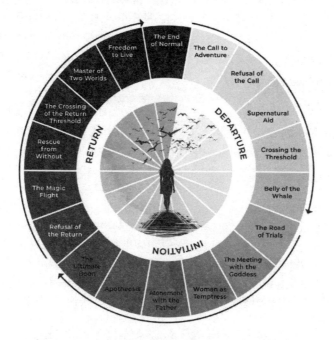

Your hero journey

In dramatic theory, something happens in Act One to stir the main protagonist (i.e., you) into action. This is commonly called the *inciting incident*. Joseph Campbell called it the *call to adventure*. "The hero journey always begins with a call," said Campbell. "One way or another, a guide must come to say 'Look, you're in Sleepy Land. Wake. Come on a trip. There is a whole aspect of your consciousness, your being, that's not been touched. So, you're at home here? Well, there's not enough of you there.' And so, it starts."[6]

Act One, the Departure Stage, can happen at any moment in your life, not just in childhood. "A good life is one hero journey after another," wrote Campbell. "Over and over again, you are called to the realm of adventure, you are called to new horizons."[7] An inciting incident or call to adventure can happen at any age. On my Hero Journey Mastermind program, we draw a biography chart using Rudolf Steiner's life cycles theory, which divides life into septimal cycles of 0–7, 7–14, 14–21, 21–28, 28–35, 35–42, 42–49, 49–56, 56–63, and so on. I find that most people can plot an inciting incident near the start or end of each of these cycles.[8]

> "We must be willing to get rid of the life we've planned, so as to have the life that is waiting for us."
>
> — Joseph Campbell

A call to adventure can take many forms. Broadly speaking, it can be either pleasant or painful. You might be disturbed by some great joy or by a tragedy. Either way, your life is changed. You can't forget what happened. The bones in your body will hold a memory of it for as long as you live. Your heart is touched forever by this event. This inciting incident is a major turning point in your life story. And now you must venture forth from the world of common day—the old normal—into a new life.

Your call to adventure has a question for you. This question is aptly called *the dramatic question* in dramatic theory. It is similar to Rilke's living question in that it urges you to make both an inquiry (an inner journey) and a quest (an outer journey). In *Hamlet*, for example, the first line in the spoken text is "Who's there?" The whole play is about identity. Who will Hamlet be? Will he avenge his father's death and be a murderer, or will he forgive and become his true self? To be or not to be; that is the question life wants us to live.

AN INSPIRING STORY

The Universe is made of stories, not of atoms.

— **Muriel Rukeyser**

When Joseph Campbell was seven years old, his father took him to see Buffalo Bill perform his Wild West show at Madison Square Garden in New York. The evening was a high point—*an inciting incident*—in Campbell's life. While the cowboys were the focus of attention for most in the crowd, young Joseph was captivated by the spirit of the Native Americans. In his journal he later wrote he "became fascinated, seized, obsessed, by the figure of a naked American Indian with his ear to the ground, a bow and arrow in his hand, and a look of special knowledge in his eyes."[9]

For me, one of the joys of being a parent is that I revisit with Bo and Christopher the stories I read in my childhood. Stories like C. S. Lewis's *The Chronicles of Narnia*, Lewis Carroll's *Alice's Adventures in Wonderland*, and L. Frank Baum's *The Wonderful Wizard of Oz* take you on a hero journey. They open with an inciting incident—like stepping through a cupboard door, falling through a rabbit hole, and getting caught up in a cyclone—and then take the reader on an adventure that demands courage, faith, transformation, and love.

Not only in childhood do we encounter inspiring stories. A new story—one that is full of meaning and purpose for you—may appear magically at any time in your life. For example, on my birthday, on April 9, 2018, I took Hollie to see the musical *Hamilton* at London's Victoria Palace Theatre. A friend of ours who has seen the Broadway show over 20 times urged us to get tickets for the London shows as soon as they became available. I had to book 15 months in advance to get our tickets. It was well worth the wait.

Hollie and I were speechless at the end of *Hamilton*. We couldn't move from our seats. "The theater is closing now," said one of the theater ushers to us. She kindly gave us a few moments. "What just happened to us?" Hollie asked me. *Hamilton* had hit us with a full-force gale of storytelling and artistry. It had delivered a shot of inspiration directly into our heart, body, soul, brain, elbows, and toes—the effects of which will hopefully never wear off. Before we went to bed that night, I booked us tickets to see *Hamilton* again.

Hamilton is the Holden family's favorite piece of theater. At last count, Hollie and I have seen it eight times. Bo and Christopher both know the lyrics to all 46 songs on the *Hamilton* soundtrack. On the school run, favorite *Hamilton* songs include "Alexander Hamilton," "My Shot," "The Room Where It Happens," and "History Has Its Eyes on You." It was hard to keep that list to only four songs! When *Hamilton* was streamed on TV by Disney Plus in 2020 (when theaters were closed due to the COVID-19 pandemic), we arranged viewing parties with friends. *Hamilton* lifted our spirits once again.

Hamilton is the story of Alexander Hamilton, one of America's forgotten Founding Fathers. Lin-Manuel Miranda, the creator of *Hamilton*, was inspired to write it after reading Ron Chernow's biography *Alexander Hamilton*. The show has a wide and deep narrative thanks to the well-crafted hip-hop songs that cram more lyrics into songs than any other genre can. In the first song, Miranda introduces us to the protagonist and presents the dramatic question:

> *How does a bastard, orphan, son of a whore*
> *And a Scotsman, dropped in the middle of a forgotten spot*
> *In the Caribbean by providence impoverished*
> *In squalor, grow up to be a hero and a scholar?*

Alexander Hamilton is on a hero journey. He arrives in New York City in 1776. He senses that history has its eyes on him. He recognizes his call to adventure. He says YES to his destiny. "I'm not throwin' away my shot!" he proclaims. He becomes George Washington's right-hand man in the American Revolution, and thereafter the first secretary of the treasury of the United States. He experiences battle, love, betrayal, infidelity (which he commits), the death of his son Philip, forgiveness (by his wife), and redemption before he is killed in a duel with his adversary, "the damn fool" Aaron Burr.

At the end, Lin-Manuel Miranda and the whole cast of *Hamilton* leave us with a dramatic question that we must answer (or pretend we didn't hear). The question is *What will you do with your one shot at life?* Will you say YES to your chance to live? Will you follow the voice that summons you to your vocation? Or will you refuse and throw away your shot?

When you mentor with me or take my Hero Journey retreat, I want to know about the book, movie, play, or TV documentary that is shaking your unconscious and stirring your imagination. What is the story that is emerging in the world right now that you want to be part of? Is it women in leadership, racial equality, better education, reinventing work, the LGBT movement, Earth Justice, ending poverty, re-wilding the planet? Don't throw away your shot—it's all you've got!

WHO IS YOUR HERO?

This morning on the school run, I had a conversation with Bo and Christopher about heroes. I told them that I was writing about heroes today. I was pretty sure they would be up for it.

"Let's have a conversation about heroes," I said.

"Oh yes!" piped Bo, who was sitting in the back seat.

"Yes, yes!" said Christopher, sitting in the front passenger seat.

"Okay, so who is your hero?" I asked.

"Well, Mum is definitely my biggest hero!" said Bo instantly.

"Yes, definitely Mum!" agreed Christopher.

"That's great!" I said.

"Oh, and definitely you too, Dad!" said Bo.

"Oh yeah, you too, Dad!" said Christopher.

"Wow, thanks, guys!"

Hollie is their hero, for sure. I knew that already, so I took it quite well. I was big about it. And I really enjoyed how they tried to reassure me that I had some hero status too.

"Okay, so who else is your hero?" I asked.

"Dolly Parton and Stevie Wonder!" said Bo.

"Why are they your heroes?" I asked.

"They do what they love, and they don't let anything stop them," said Bo.

"Yeah, Stevie Wonder's blind!" exclaimed Christopher.

"And he can see better than any of us," said Bo.

Bo is halfway through her songwriting project for school. She has been busy researching the lives of her favorite singers. She likes how Dolly Parton tells stories in her songs, and how Stevie Wonder gives us songs to help make the world a better place.

"Christopher, who else is your hero?" asked Bo.

"Well, right now it's Spiderman," said Christopher.

"Why Spiderman?" asked Bo.

"Because Peter Parker (aka Spiderman) is more my age than Superman is."

"And why else do you like him?" asked Bo.

"Well, he's trying to do something good in the world. Also, he often makes bad decisions and makes them right again."

"I like that," said Bo.

"Me too," said Christopher.

On the way back from school, I called my brother, David. I asked him who was his favorite hero growing up. It was Superman. Superman was my hero too. We both had Superman costumes that, for obvious reasons, we couldn't wear at the same time. So David and I had to agree that when one of us was being Superman, the other had to be Clark Kent. Inevitably, this led to some tense and dramatic superhero moments that only our mum and dad could sort out for us.

When I asked David who was his hero in real life growing up, we both realized it was our dad. That's a tough one for us. We loved our mum, and we were both mummy's boys, but Dad was our hero. He was strong. He was our protector. He championed us. He fought in World War II. He'd traveled the world. He was kind. He was great fun. Most of all, he loved us. And none of us knew of his drinking problem until it was too late to save him. When a hero dies, you carry that wound for the rest of your days, and you must learn to use it somehow to press forward on your own hero journey.

When I got back home, I told Hollie about my hero conversation with Bo and Christopher. She already knew that she was their hero! Hollie's heroes growing up were her mother and her grandmother Dofi. Another of Hollie's heroes was her horse Typhoon, whom she kept from 10 to 16 years old. "Typhoon was always in his power, no matter what was happening," Hollie told me. "And he was the truest friend I could possibly have asked for during those years."

One of my first real-life heroes, other than my dad, was the England cricketer Sir Ian Botham. The way he played cricket was the way I wanted to live my life. *Beefy*, his nickname, was always in the action, never just standing on the boundary. He was cavalier. He played with imagination. He was always wholehearted. He competed fiercely, and he was great friends with many of his rivals. After he finished playing, he used his status to champion good causes. In 2007 he was knighted in the queen's birthday honors for his many services to charity.

I have a long list of heroes. Carl Jung is my hero of philosophy and psychology. Ernest Hemingway was my first writing hero. St. Francis of Assisi is one of my spiritual heroes. Another hero is my mentor, Tom Carpenter, a teacher of *A Course in Miracles*, my best friend for 25 years, and the most loving person I've met. Martin Luther King Jr., Thomas Berry, Mary Oliver, Maya Angelou, Joseph Campbell, and Matthew Fox are a few more of my heroes.

Heroes are people who inspire you. They show up in all manner of ways, in books, art galleries, theater, the TV news, and in your everyday life. They are part of your *Supernatural Aid*—a Joseph Campbell term—and they play a vital role in your hero journey. The timing of such meetings is always significant. For instance, I attended a dinner with Ian Botham, my cricketing hero, three days before I hosted my first Hero Journey Mastermind. My Angel of Synchronicity often arranges meaningful encounters like this one when I am starting something new.

Joseph Campbell observed that once a hero says YES to their quest, guides, heroes, and magical helpers will appear out of nowhere. They belong to your Supernatural Aid team. They appear only after you have crossed the threshold and begun your adventure. They breathe life into you. They offer divine assistance. They raise you up when you fall. Their influence is with you even when you feel lost and alone. They do everything in their power to make sure that you stay on purpose.

In *The Hero with a Thousand Faces,* Joseph Campbell wrote,

> We have not even to risk the adventure alone, for the heroes of all time have gone before us—the labyrinth is thoroughly known. We have only to follow the thread of the hero path, and where we had thought to find an abomination, we shall find a god; where we had thought to slay another, we shall slay ourselves; where we had thought to travel outward, we shall come to the center of our own existence. And where we had thought to be alone, we shall be with all the world.[10]

KICKED OUT OF ORDINARY

Your hero journey begins with an inciting incident that gets you *kicked out of ordinary*—another Joseph Campbell term. Most often, the inciting incident that summons you to your destiny is a wound or a shock of some sort. This is your wake-up call. You're not in Kansas anymore. You might as well throw away your old map. The future has changed, and you must too.

My first wound was a family wound. My dreamy childhood in Littleton, in the home called Shadows, turned into a nightmare. My mother was regularly taken away to a mental health hospital—a different one each time—where she was treated for her depression with a brutal concoction of electric shock therapy and drugs. When my father left home, I was unable to keep track of his whereabouts. He was often homeless, sleeping in church cemeteries to keep himself out of harm's way.

My family wound was the *inciting incident* on my hero journey. My studies in psychology and philosophy were a response to my parents' wounding and to the personal wounds I carried in myself. I've often said that Sigmund Freud would have had an easy time with my case file. My work with The Happiness Project is my open letter to my mum and her depression. My work with Success Intelligence is my open letter to my dad and his alcoholism.

Wounds are of an infinite variety. Just before I started writing this book, I had a profound conversation on dharma—the Buddhist philosophy of purpose—with Robert Thurman, formerly the Je Tsang Khapa professor of Indo-Tibetan Buddhist Studies at Columbia University and a close friend of the Dalai Lama for over 50 years. Bob told me, "I found my purpose by losing my eye in an accident when I was a wild youth. The accident was a deep shock. My life turned in an unexpected direction. I was introduced to mortality and suffering. I saw the world in a new way, and I went in search of wisdom and bliss."

Bob's recent book *Wisdom Is Bliss* was published on his eightieth birthday.[11] I interviewed him for the official launch. We talked more about purpose. "After I lost my eye, my pleasure-seeking life wasn't meaningful anymore," said Bob. "One of my first Buddhist teachers told me that the purpose of me losing my eye was to help me develop the sight of a thousand eyes! My accident was all part of a training in learning how to see. It's how I found the Dalai Lama, and also how I found wisdom and bliss." Perhaps there are no accidents on the path of living your purpose.

Sickness is another common wound. My friend Nina Hirlaender woke up one morning with a terrible feeling that something was devastatingly wrong with her. She was 24 years old, and apparently in good health, but she knew to trust her intuition. She immediately took herself to a nearby walk-in health clinic and demanded a full-body MRI scan. Sure enough, the doctor found a tumor that was hemorrhaging, and she was rushed to emergency care.

"Cancer led me to my purpose," says Nina. Her illness took her on a journey, both inner and outer. It was a journey that affected everyone in her family. At one point, her father, Horst, gave Nina a copy of a book on St. Francis of Assisi. Nina felt called to visit

Assisi, in Italy. There she fell in love with St. Francis and St. Clare. Together with her father, she founded Dancing Spirit Tours, offering spiritual pilgrimages to Assisi. One day I got a call from Nina inviting me to teach on a pilgrimage in Assisi, walking in the footsteps of St. Francis and St. Clare. This is how we became friends.

Everyone's personal biography has a traumatic inciting incident like the stillbirth of a child, the death of a loved one, the loss of a job, a divorce, a rape, an injustice, a prison sentence, bankruptcy, or a house burning down. Wounds like these cannot be written out of your biography or forgotten about. Indeed, you must be willing to include them fully in your story. "Your purpose is hidden within your wounds," wrote Rune Lazuli, the poet.

> *"If you want to find your purpose in life, find your wound."*
>
> — Rick Warren

Tragic events that affect many people at once happen every day on Planet Earth. Most of us struggle to keep up with the details of our own life, but a brief glance at the world news today will show you that happening right now are earthquakes, hurricanes, forest fires, floods, famines, droughts, pandemics, wars, mass shootings, and refugee crises. If you see the planet as your home, then all of this is happening in your neighborhood.

In recent times nothing has affected the whole world more than the COVID-19 pandemic. On March 11, 2020, the World Health Organization launched its largest ever global emergency response to the COVID-19 pandemic. In a few short weeks, we witnessed the death of normal. We were all kicked out of ordinary. This was our collective wake-up call. We experienced a shared inciting incident that meant we all had to rethink our lives. The future has changed, and we must too.

JOY IS YOUR COMPASS

Launching The Happiness Project was the start of a new chapter in my life. After five years of running my Stress Busters Clinic, I had written three books (including one called *Stress Busters*), I was lecturing across the country, I was presenting my weekly radio phone-in at BBC WM, and the BBC had broadcast a TV documentary on my work called *Stress Busters*. Everything was going great, but I was also feeling the strong pull of an invisible thread taking me in a new direction.

For the first year, I ran both The Happiness Project and my Stress Busters Clinic from the Health Shop in Handsworth, Birmingham. I had the full backing of the National Health Service to conduct research on happiness and run trial programs. Then came crunch time. A new director of public health was appointed, and her first task was to cut spending. She informed me that she had enough money to support only one of my programs, and that I had to choose between Stress Busters and The Happiness Project.

I had recently turned 28 years old, and I see now that I was at the start of a new seven-year cycle, according to Rudolph Steiner's biography work on life phases. The safe option was to keep going with my Stress Busters Clinic. It had a strong reputation, the work was growing well, and I saw a clear path ahead. The Happiness Project was still in embryo. The vision for it hadn't yet fully formed in my mind. In the end, the only way forward was to follow my inner voice, and so I chose to work full time on The Happiness Project.

The Happiness Project was my new call to adventure. I moved away from Birmingham, where I'd lived for 10 years, and set up a new office in Oxford. I funded the project largely by myself, with money I barely had. My brother, David, took a break from his work to help me recruit a new team and establish a new vision for my work. The more I thought about what true happiness is, the better I understood the causes of unhappiness, and I decided that the real purpose of my work with The Happiness Project was to help people *stop searching for happiness and start following their joy.*

My first task was to design an eight-week happiness program that became the signature event for The Happiness Project. One of my classes on the program was called Follow Your Joy, which was inspired by Joseph Campbell's mantra *follow your bliss.* In this class, I conducted an experiment called the 10-Minute Happiness Meditation. This simple meditation has had a deep and meaningful effect on many people, completely changing the way they relate to happiness and purpose.

The 10-Minute Happiness Meditation is easy to practice, and I encourage you, dear reader, to try it for yourself. The meditation has two parts to it. In the first part, I invite you to spend five minutes picturing yourself *searching for happiness* for the rest of your life. Notice how happy you feel about this scenario. Make a note of how your body responds, how your heart feels, and what specific thoughts arise. How excited are you at the thought of searching for happiness for the rest of your life?

In the second part, I invite you to spend five minutes imagining yourself *following your joy* for the rest of your life. What is this like for you? How do you imagine yourself following your joy? What images and thoughts come to mind? What are you saying YES to? Again, notice how your body responds, how your heart feels, and specific thoughts that arise. Overall, do you prefer a lifetime of *searching for happiness* or *following your joy?*

Most people prefer *following your joy* to *searching for happiness.* The thought of *searching for happiness* is exhausting, and it gives rise to anxiety and hopelessness because it places happiness outside you, and it turns happiness into a restless pursuit and an endless search for a needle in a haystack. Whereas *following your joy* locates happiness inside you; it makes happiness into a journey and not just a destination, you learn to follow your inner guidance, and your life is an adventure that you say YES to.

There really is a world of difference between *searching for happiness* and *following your joy*. You will experience your life in a completely different way depending on which choice you make.

THE CALL TO JOY

Inside everyone
is a great shout of joy
waiting to be born

— **David Whyte**

Placed in you is a call to joy, and much of the happiness and success you experience in your life will depend on whether you choose to answer this call or not.

What is joy? Joy is one of three types of happiness, the other two being pleasure and satisfaction. Pleasure is the happiness of your senses. It needs a stimulus. You can buy pleasure in a candy shop. Satisfaction is the type of happiness that most Western psychologists focus on for happiness research. Satisfaction needs a reason, e.g., *I'm happy because I like my life circumstances.* With both pleasure and satisfaction, they cease to exist when you remove the reason or stimulus.

Joy is different. Unlike pleasure, joy doesn't need a stimulus to make you happy. Unlike satisfaction, joy doesn't need a reason because it isn't dependent on external circumstances. Joy is an unreasonable happiness—an uncaused happiness—that lives in you and that arises from your Being, the essence of who you are. Bidden or not bidden, joy is always with you. Joy does not come or go; it is only your awareness of it that comes and goes.

Let's take a closer look at joy.

You are born with joy in you.

If you have spent time with a baby or an infant you know that this is true. "Thou Child of Joy / Shout round me, let me hear thy shouts, thou happy Shepherd-boy," wrote Wordsworth in "Ode: Intimations of Immortality from Recollections of Early Childhood." Joy is your life force. It runs through your veins, but it is not only physical. It lights you up from the inside out. It gives you your glow. It animates you. It brings you to life.

Joy is packed into your Godseed. The poet Rilke wrote about a "blank joy" that is untouched by the world and full of possibility: "Lovely joy left blank, perhaps you are / the center of all my labors and my loves." Joy is a creative spark within you. "Joy is a marvellous increasing of what exists, a pure addition out of nothingness," he also wrote.[1] By staying acquainted with joy, you will remember what Steiner called your "pre-birth intention," which is your higher purpose.

Joy is your compass.

Joy is not a goal; joy is your guide. When you follow your joy, it gives your life direction, it helps you get your life back on track, and it keeps you on your true path (and not someone else's).

Each new year, I set an intention to make this year my most enjoyable year yet. I give myself full permission to follow my joy. On my Success Intelligence Mastermind program, which always starts in January, I encourage everyone to live with this question: *If I were to enjoy myself even more this year than last year, what would I do more of, less of, or differently?* This living question sets up a great inquiry that stirs the imagination, stimulates great conversations, and sets new possibilities in motion.

Joy is intelligent.

The biggest thing I want you to know about joy is that *joy is intelligent*. There's a line in one of Rudolf Steiner's verses that goes, "I think with my thinking's best thoughts of joy." I see joy not as an emotion, but as a quality of your original mind. Steiner taught, "To be free is to be capable of thinking one's own thoughts, not the thoughts of the body, or of society, but thoughts generated by one's deepest, most original, most essential and spiritual self, one's individuality."[2] Following your joy helps you be free.

Joy is intelligent, but it is not always rational. When you follow your joy, you often have to make decisions that don't make sense to your rational mind. It's the same with living your purpose. Carl Jung described *vocation* as "an *irrational factor* that destines a man to emancipate himself from the herd and from its well-worn paths." Personally, when I answer the call to joy and let joy guide me, I often have to act on faith, not logic. Leaving Stress Busters to work full time on The Happiness Project is a good case in point.

Joy is moral.

Joy is wild and free; and it is also moral. Aristotle, the Greek philosopher, described a type of happiness called *eudaemonia*, which he contrasted with *hedonism*. Hedonism is pleasure seeking, and it has no other purpose than to feel good in the moment. Eudaemonia sets its sights higher. The etymology of *eudaemonia* is derived from the words *eu* ("good, well") and *daimōn* ("spirit"). Eudaemonia is a good daimōn, or angel, that guides you to your highest good and to the greater good of humanity. Eudaemonia is what you experience when you are following your joy and living your purpose.

When you listen to joy, you are listening to your conscience. "Joy is our original language," says Mardoche Sidor, a Harvard-trained psychiatrist, and a graduate of my Success Intelligence Mastermind program. Joy has its own vocabulary, and it doesn't use words like *should, ought,* and *must.* "Should is a cognitive error," says Mardoche. Joy doesn't want you to "be normal." Joy's main ethic is *Be true to yourself.* When you follow joy, you know in your bones that you are on the right path even if you can only see one step ahead of you.

Joy is resilient.

Following your joy doesn't give you a free pass to success. It takes you on a *road of trials*—a Joseph Campbell term— on which you encounter setbacks and sorrows, fears and frustrations, doubts and disappointments, just like everyone else. Joseph Campbell said, "Participate joyfully in the sorrows of the world. We cannot cure the world of sorrows, but we can choose to live in joy." When you follow your joy, you may stumble and fall many times, but joy—the good daimōn—has the power to lift you up and keep you going.

In the opening line of his triumphant poem "Ode to Joy," Friedrich Schiller describes joy as a "beautiful spark of divinity." Joy lights the way, helping us follow what Schiller calls "heaven's grand plan." He tells us,

> *Go on, brothers, your way,*
> *Joyful, like a hero to victory.*

"Ode to Joy" is best known for its use by Ludwig van Beethoven in his Ninth Symphony. What Beethoven did with "Ode to Joy" broke with convention. He was the first major composer to include a chorus and vocal soloists in the final movement of a symphony. The "Ode to Joy" comes as a great surprise, and with its heavenly powers it leads us on to victory. Beethoven's message to humanity is that pain runs deep but joy runs even deeper. Every pain ends in victory if you keep on following your joy.

Joy sees the bigger picture.

When you follow your joy, you sign up for a path of growth. Joy releases you from your chains of narrow self, and it sets you on your hero journey. Joy is always expansive, never wanting you to hide, shrink, or play small. Joy is all about the bigger picture. When you follow your joy, you are aligning yourself with something bigger than your ego. And you gladly allow the single grain of wheat to die so as to bear much fruit.

How can I follow my joy today? I ask myself this question each day in my morning meditation. I have lived with this question for many years now, and I always get an answer that is perfect for me. I love to share this inquiry with people I mentor and who come to my workshops. Following your joy connects you to your purpose on the personal level, the shared level, and the universal level. George Bernard Shaw said it like this:

> This is the true joy in life, being used for a purpose recognized by yourself as a mighty one. Being a force of nature instead of a feverish, selfish little clod of ailments and grievances, complaining that the world will not devote itself to making you happy. I am of the opinion that my life belongs to the whole community and as long as I live, it is my privilege to do for it what I can. I want to be thoroughly used up when I die, for the harder I work, the more I live. I rejoice in life for its own sake. Life is no brief candle to me. It is a sort of splendid torch which I have got hold of for the moment and I want to make it burn as brightly as possible before handing it on to future generations.[3]

SOWING SEEDS OF JOY

A few weeks after moving The Happiness Project to Oxford, I received an invitation to give a talk at the Bristol Cancer Help Centre, a leading charity in holistic cancer care, whose patron was HRH Prince Charles. It was here that I met Sue Boyd, the director of education. Sue gave me the warmest welcome. She made me a lovely cup of tea, and then she took me on a tour of the Centre, introducing me personally to everyone. She looked after me beautifully all day, and afterward we promised to stay in touch.

Sue has been my faithful friend for the past 28 years. Sue celebrated her eightieth birthday recently. We've been through a lot of life together. "Thrills and spills," she calls them. I sat at Sue's hospital bedside when she was in a five-day coma with encephalitis. She's been there for me in my darkest hours also. "How are you, deary!" she beams each time we speak. Sue has lots of names for me, like "deary," "darling," "lovely," "Bobby," and "Roberto."

Sue is my co-conspirator in joy. She attended the first eight-week happiness program I ran in London, at the Rembrandt Hotel in Knightsbridge, just down the road from Harrods. She was the first to sign up for a Teaching Happiness training program I taught at Oxford University's Worcester College. She's been an ever-present member of the team for my public events. If truth be told, Sue does sometimes fall asleep during my lectures. She insists she is "meditating." That said, Sue puts into practice everything I've taught, and she really does follow her joy.

One day Sue heard on the local grapevine in Westbury-on-Trym, the village she lives in, that there were to be no more flowers on display in the community. Sue didn't like the thought of this one bit. "Flowers mean joy, love, hope, and growth," says Sue. So she joined the Westbury-on-Trym Society, a small voluntary organization that has a mission "to look after the amenities, landscape and historic settings of our 1300-year-old village." After a couple of meetings, Sue came up with an idea she called Westbury in Bloom, WIB for short.

Sue's mission for WIB was to beautify the village. At first, she didn't have a clear plan for how to do this. "This is a *hold your nose and jump* job!" she told me at the time. Sue found it tough going to start with. She knocked on a lot of doors. Most people liked the idea but weren't convinced. "I don't think flowers make any difference," said one shoe-shop owner. Sue didn't give up, though, and after a couple of years that same person became a most generous contributor.

Sue and her team of volunteers gradually transformed Westbury-on-Trym into a natural beauty spot. Spaces outside the local library, the car park, and the shopping center that once were dull, unloved patches were turned into colorful beds of flowers and sustainable planting. Eventually there were 90 hanging baskets on lampposts, 36 large tubs of flowers around the village, and even an edible bus stop with a variety of vegetables growing in it—all sponsored by local businesses and residents.

In 2012 Sue was recognized as "an unsung hero" in her community and was awarded the Lord Mayor's Medal by the mayor of Bristol, which is the closest city to Westbury-on-Trym. The Royal Horticultural Society got news of Sue's adventures with WIB and awarded the village with an annual Outstanding Achievement medal each year from 2006 to 2016 (when Sue retired). Sue was also recognized for her work by the Happy City project, which made her one of their ambassadors of joy.

"It takes a village to transform a village," says Sue. Sue didn't try to follow her joy on her own. She shared her vision for beautifying Westbury-on-Trym with as many people as possible. Her purpose became a shared one. "It was a team effort," says Sue, who early on set up a small committee that included a retired gardener who knew everything about flowers. "I knew that the more people I got involved, the more flowers we would grow," Sue told me.

"The flowers brought us together," says Sue. The flowers also attracted tourists and visitors to the village. Businesses prospered and new shops opened as footfall increased. There have been many "spin-offs," as Sue calls them, from the WIB project, including a revamped summer fayre, an annual Christmas lights display, a Westbury-on-Trym heritage trail, and a theater project with live performances in local shops. Year by year Westbury-on-Trym grew into a happier, more cohesive, and more environmentally aware community.

Recently I asked Sue what she thought was the real purpose of her adventures with Westbury in Bloom. She told me, "Well, it was you, deary, who taught me that you don't have to fly to the moon to live your purpose; you just have to step out your front door. So I made it my aim to grow a little bit of heaven on earth right where I was. The flowers were our main focus, but I suppose it was really all of *us* who blossomed and grew along the way."

SWIMMING WITH JOY

In October 1997 I presented a one-day seminar with Dr. Wayne Dyer at the RAI Amsterdam convention center. It was called Manifest Your Destiny, after the title of Wayne's new book, and it was hosted by Angel Seminars. In the crowd were Winny and Kees van de Velden, a Dutch couple, who were big fans of Wayne Dyer. They had no idea who I was. During my talk, Winny had a vision of a rainbow over my head with a magical dolphin leaping out. Afterward, they introduced themselves to me. "Do you ever swim with dolphins?" Winny asked. "No, but I'd like to," I told her.

Our meeting felt like destiny. "From the moment you began your talk, we felt like we were old friends with you," recalls Winny. Somehow, Wayne Dyer, Angel Seminars, and what Joseph Campbell called "unseen hands" had arranged for us to meet that day. My talk was called Follow Your Joy. Winny and Kees's life changed dramatically soon after we met. A new call to adventure appeared in their life. "*Follow your joy* became our mantra for the next few years," recalls Kees.

Soon after Manifest Your Destiny, Winny attended a flower essence conference hosted by the Findhorn Foundation in Scotland. She had planned to go with a friend whose husband died suddenly just before the conference. "I nearly didn't go, but my friend and Kees encouraged me to," recalls Winny. When she got to Inverness Airport, she learned her luggage was still at Schiphol Airport in Amsterdam. The next seven days were full of mishaps and surprises and not like anything she had expected.

The flower essence conference was opened by Eileen Caddy and Dorothy Maclean, two cofounders of the Findhorn Foundation, an NGO associated with the United Nations and cofounder of the Global Ecovillage Network. Winny attended a lecture by flower expert Andreas Kortas, who gave her a dolphin necklace as a gift. She then went to a talk by Princess Irene of the Netherlands, whose new book, *Dialogue with Nature*, had been published by Findhorn Press. Princess Irene talked mostly about dolphins and whales and their vital role in our ecosystem and the future of our world.

"I went to Findhorn to deepen my interest in flowers, but instead I met whales and dolphins at every turn," says Winny. On the last day of the conference, a woman who Winny had met at the lost luggage counter at Inverness Airport told her about Fungie, a common bottlenose dolphin who was living in Dingle Bay on the southwest coast of Ireland. A year later, Winny and Kees and their children spent three weeks in Dingle swimming with Fungie.

Upon their return, Andreas Kortas, the flower expert, called Winny and Kees out of the blue and invited them to swim with whales and dolphins in the Canary Islands. "An invisible thread kept drawing us to the whales and dolphins, and the pull was enormous," says Winny. Whenever they tried to ignore or resist this mysterious pull, it didn't feel right. On their visit to the Canary Islands they went to the wrong island at first! By the end of that trip, though, they knew they had found their new home and said a hearty YES to their new adventure.

Winny and Kees located themselves at the port of Los Gigantes, on the southwest coast of the island of Tenerife. A few miles out to sea from Los Gigantes harbor is a rendezvous spot where Winny and Kees meet up to swim with the whales and dolphins. On Kees's birthday an envelope arrived addressed to Winny. Inside was a check made out to her for 9,000 euros. It was reparation money for her father's service in World War II. "We had no idea this money was coming, and it was the exact amount we needed to buy our boat, *Ocean Delight*," says Winny.

The locals at Los Gigantes were wary of Winny and Kees at first. That soon changed when they saw how Winny and Kees and their guests cleaned up the local beach, Los Guios, which was a rubbish dump full of plastic waste, old boilers, mattresses, and discarded car parts. They also heard stories of how Winny and

Kees rescued a bottlenose dolphin with a plastic bag over its head, and how they transported a turtle—found with rope and hooks around its neck—to the neighboring island of Gran Canaria for a lifesaving operation.

One day Hollie and I received an invitation from Winny and Kees to go on one of their sea pilgrimages and swim in the wild with whales and dolphins. The invitation arrived on Hollie's birthday. "Life is giving us a gift!" said Hollie. The dates they offered us were the last available dates for us to travel, as Hollie was pregnant with Christopher. Also, I had a book launch tour planned around that time that was fully booked except for those exact dates. We bought our tickets immediately, eager to accept what felt like a once-in-a-lifetime opportunity.

Holy joy! For four days, Hollie, who was heavily pregnant with Christopher by that time; our daughter, Bo, who was three years old; Lizzie, Hollie's sister, and I joined Winny and Kees and six other guests on board their eight-meter rigid inflatable boat, *Ocean Delight*. Each day we enjoyed blissful close-up encounters with whales and dolphins. We stayed on for three more days, and we've kept coming back ever since, bringing family and friends with us each time.

The Holden family has been on 12 sea pilgrimages with Winny and Kees, at last count. We've spent over 60 days at sea on the *Ocean Delight*. No two days at sea are the same. "You have to leave your plans behind and show up for the occasion," says Winny. Kees is our skipper, and Winny is our guide. Upon leaving the harbor at Los Gigantes, we clean up plastic waste in the sea. And then we venture farther out, up to 10 miles from shore, following Winny's intuition, paying attention to signs, and looking out for fins.

On my first swim, I went in the sea with Winny and Lizzie, and we were greeted by three pilot whales. They were standing upright in the water, each one about five meters tall, looking like an official welcome party—like Guardians of the Sea Council, in my imagination. They approached us carefully, so as not to frighten us. As they got closer, maybe four or five feet away, they turned on their sides, sang a beautiful whale song, and circled around us, while looking deeply into our eyes.

When I recall that first encounter, I can see vividly their big eyes, their smiling faces, and the detail of their long, beautiful grey bodies. Most of all, I remember feeling I was in the presence of truly intelligent beings. These are not just big fish; they are sapient beings that are conscious and aware. They are sentient beings who have a heart and a brain and demonstrate an intelligence that we can engage with and learn from.[4]

"Whales and dolphins are our greatest teachers," says Kees. "We rarely see a dolphin or whale on their own. They live together in community. We observe how each one has a unique purpose and also a shared purpose of looking after the whole pod. They also have an even larger purpose, which is to clean the ocean, balance the food chain, and maintain the ecosystem so that life on earth is made possible for us all."[5]

On our sea pilgrimages, the whales and dolphins mirror us in delightful ways. Our daughter, Bo, seems to attract the dolphins. They splash their tails with joy when they see her putting on her snorkel and flippers. Our son, Christopher, attracts the big whales. I remember the time when Winny sensed there was a fin whale near our boat. "If Christopher goes in the sea, the fin whale will appear," Winny told us. Sure enough, as soon as Christopher and I jumped in the water, a giant fin whale, about 18 meters long, surfaced and swam on its back beneath us.

> *"The destiny of humans and the destiny of whales and dolphins cannot be separated. We are on the same journey, and we share the same purpose."*
>
> — Winny van de Velden

One time the *Ocean Delight* was surrounded by a school of a hundred dolphins or more that were leaping and playing all around us. Winny sent me and Hollie out for a swim. As soon as we entered the water, the dolphins disappeared. The sea was empty. After a few moments, thousands upon thousands of bubbles appeared on the surface of the sea. Hollie and I both looked down into the water and we saw ourselves inside a vast column of dolphin bubbles. Hollie called it a cathedral of crystal bubbles.

Back on board our boat, I scribbled down a poem called "Ocean Delight." I shared it the next day with everyone. As soon as I'd finished reading it, two dolphins appeared by the side of the boat, serenading us with their song and with more bubbles of joy.

Joy is where the dolphins swim in
the sea and in your heart.
They appear and disappear into
the dark blue.

They send a line of bubbles
from the deep up
to you.

Bright angular bubbles roll across
your body as you float
on the ocean delight.
Fizzy water made of love.

Each holy bubble a dolphin's kiss.
Which bursts upon the surface,
crowning you from above
and below in
sovereign
joy.

A MEDITATION ON
SUCCESS

The planet does not need more successful people.
The planet desperately needs more peacemakers, healers,
restorers, storytellers, and lovers of all kinds.

— The Dalai Lama

On the eve of my thirty-fifth birthday, my life came to an abrupt halt. I had been experiencing a dull ache in my lower back for a couple of weeks. My instinct was to see a doctor and get it checked, but I had a busy lecture schedule, and so I pressed on. The dull ache got worse, and it soon turned into a sharp sensation like a bee sting. My body was telling me to stop, but I kept on going. Eventually, at the end of another lecture, my body seized up. I couldn't stand up straight. I couldn't drive home. I was later diagnosed with a prolapsed disc, and I had to stop.

Stopping was painful for me, especially given my fast genes, but it ended up being a blessing in disguise. I wanted a quick fix. My doctor recommended surgery. He told me I could expect to return to work after three weeks, but he also warned me about the possible side effects of surgery, which included reoccurring symptoms, nerve damage, and loss of mobility. This set off alarm bells in me. I was in a desperate hurry to get back to work, but my inner voice was telling me to slow down, to make time for my life, and to allow my body to heal naturally.

Stopping is a spiritual practice, I've since learned. There are two types of stopping: *voluntary stopping* and *involuntary stopping.* A voluntary stop is the healthiest option by far. It is a conscious decision you make to slow down, exhale, and enjoy the wisdom of rest when your life has become too hectic, too busy, and too laborsome. A short voluntary stop can be making time to meditate, taking a yoga class, walking in nature, enjoying an afternoon nap, a visit to the theater, and a date with your partner. Longer forms include a long weekend away, going on a retreat, and taking a sabbatical.

An involuntary stop is forced upon you. It is not a conscious choice. Examples of an involuntary stop include breaking a toe and having to slow down; a migraine that forces you to stop working; travel plans disrupted by severe weather; the end of an intimate relationship; a bereavement and time to grieve; a stressful event like a burglary or a house fire; a mental health issue that is telling to you change your life; and on a larger scale, a global crisis, like the COVID-19 pandemic, that forces everyone to stop what they are doing and rethink their lives.

My involuntary stop meant I had to cancel my lectures, take a break from writing, and leave the running of The Happiness Project to my team. A big space had now appeared in my busy schedule. At first I was too frustrated and impatient to see what a great opportunity this space was giving me. The truth was that I had been overworking for too long. I was saying yes to too many things. I was pushing through exhaustion. I'd lost my focus and was being "scattered into everydayness," a term used by Martin Heidegger, the German philosopher.

This was my chance to rethink my life. Up until now, I'd been running my life on the old work ethic mantra of *Success is 99 percent perspiration and 1 percent inspiration.* I was succeeding at everything I did, but I wasn't feeling successful inside myself. The rhythm of my heart had become hectic. I wasn't experiencing the fruitfulness of my work. I was lacking inspiration. I needed a new success mantra. Something like *Success is 98 percent perspiration and 2 percent inspiration.* Or better still, 10 percent inspiration, 50 percent inspiration, or even 99 percent inspiration.

For the next six months I lived in "slow time." I had to do everything more slowly than before. I got out of bed slowly, so as not to injure my back. I eased myself carefully into each new day. I moved about with the aid of a walking stick, which became a good companion. Living in "slow time" meant I had to do less, but I also had more time to think. I read books that I'd been meaning to read for years. I had rich conversations that I'd otherwise have been too busy for. And fate arranged a series of meetings with remarkable healers and teachers that spurred me on to a full recovery and a fresh start.

During my rehabilitation, I started a new journal. I ended up calling it my Success Journal. I began by acknowledging the pain I was in, writing down my frustration and anger, listening to my fears, and giving a voice to the "self" that believed it was dying a slow death. The more honest and compassionate I was with myself, the more open I became to exploring possible "hidden gifts" and surrendering to a bigger plan for my life. In one entry, I wrote this question: *What if this interruption in my schedule is really an invitation to a new way of living?*

Stopping gave me the space to do a lot of meditative thinking, as Martin Heidegger called it. I stumbled across Heidegger's work during my rehabilitation. "The most thought-provoking thing in our thought-provoking time is that we are still not thinking," wrote Heidegger in *What Is Called Thinking?*[1] Heidegger observed two kinds of thought: calculative and meditative. Calculative thought is technical, logical, and vital for practical activities like building a computer. Meditative thought is imaginative, and is used to ponder the purpose, meaning, and potential uses and misuses of a computer.

In my journal I recalled conversations with Freddie Frankl about the need to find a deeper meaning to help you grow through challenging times. *What meaning shall I give to my prolapsed disc?* I pondered. *What is the higher purpose of this involuntary stop I've been forced to make?* I wondered. I revisited some of the big life questions that I hadn't paid much attention to lately. I asked myself *What really inspires me?* and *What do I love?* and *How can I follow my joy more?* I also thought deeply about the times when I felt most *on purpose* in my life.

What is a successful life? This is the question I ended up focusing on in my journal. Hence why I called it my Success Journal. As a young boy, I dreamed of doing something "big" with my life and of being "a success." My ambition for success drove me on, but I rarely felt I achieved any great success. My success driver was a heavy cross to bear. This obviously had something to do with my dad. Maybe I was afraid that if I wasn't "saved by success," I'd end up trapped inside an empty whisky bottle. I always worked hard to be successful at what I did, but I hadn't ever stopped—until now—to think about what real success is.

My prolapsed disc forced me to stop chasing success. The athlete in me (from Carl Jung's Athlete Stage) had to stop racing. I had to face my *destination addiction,* a term I coined, which I wrote about in my next book, *Authentic Success.* Years later, I also gave a TED Talk called "Destination Addiction."[2] In short, destination addiction describes a mindset that believes happiness is over the rainbow, success is in the future, and that your purpose is somewhere you are not. This mindset causes you to live a manic, nonstop, busy lifestyle in which you are always "getting there" but never really getting anywhere.

As I questioned what success is, I began to think about success in more meaningful and inspiring ways. I challenged myself to break free from the conditioning of my culture and society about success. I changed the narrow lens through which I viewed success. I zoomed out from looking only at myself and focused more on the bigger picture. I thought carefully about Victor Frankl's advice about success. He wrote,

> Don't aim at success. The more you aim at it and make it a target, the more you are going to miss it. For success,

like happiness, cannot be pursued; it must ensue, and it only does so as the unintended side effect of one's personal dedication to a cause greater.[3]

Because of my destination addiction, my old thinking about success, purpose, mission, and legacy was mostly future focused. Was this the reason why I'd always been afraid of dying before I fulfilled my purpose? Slowly, but surely, I shifted my attention to the present moment. I meditated on happiness now, success now, and living my purpose now. I realized that *a successful life can only ever be the one you are living now.* Only in the here and now can you live your purpose. How you show up, and the way you go about your life, is your purpose.

I emerged from my rehabilitation with a new sense of self and a new way of thinking about my purpose. Looking back now, I believe I did die a death of sorts during that time. A bigger me—a more authentic self—was born, and my whole life shifted from that point on. Later I learned, in Steiner's biography counseling, that the mid-30s are when your *pre-birth intention*—Steiner's term for higher purpose—calls for your attention. If you are off track, you will need to make a voluntary stop, or an involuntary stop, as in my case, to reset yourself and live in a new way.

THE FOUR INTELLIGENCES

On my return to work, in the autumn of 2000, I launched a new company called Success Intelligence Ltd.[4] It was a small, boutique consultancy that offered leadership programs and coaching journeys both to individuals and organizations. My aim with Success Intelligence was to challenge the thinking of the day. One of my main messages was this:

The challenges we face today
do not require more effort;
they require more wisdom.

One of my early talks on Success Intelligence was at a conference called The Future Leader, hosted by the Leadership Trust. The audience was made up of leaders in government, business, education, science, and the arts. I gave the opening keynote, and the closing keynote was given by Danah Zohar, an MIT physicist and philosopher, and co-author with her husband, Ian Marshall, of *Spiritual Intelligence.*[5] Our talks focused on common themes, and we were invited back by the Leadership Trust to give a joint one-day Masterclass on Leading with Purpose.

Danah Zohar lived in Oxford, a 10-minute walk from my home. Danah liked to do her thinking late at night. After dinner I'd walk over to her home with an excellent bottle of Bordeaux wine in hand, and we'd talk past midnight and into the early hours of the morning. Her cat, Schrödinger, was often curled up on my lap as we shared our ideas about an expanded view of intelligence—a quantum intelligence, she called it—to help humanity enter the new millennium with a greater sense of vision, purpose, and hope.

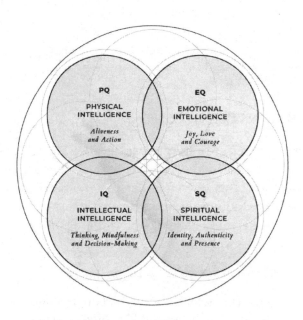

The Four Intelligences

With Danah's help, I designed a model of intelligence that underpinned all my work with Success Intelligence. The model is called the Four Intelligences, and the four intelligences are physical intelligence (P.Q.), intellectual intelligence (I.Q.), emotional intelligence (E.Q.), and spiritual intelligence (S.Q.) (see the figure opposite). These four intelligences are not separate types of intelligence; rather, they are four faculties, or innate skills, that a person can develop to live mindfully, to be wise, and to prosper.

The purpose of the Four Intelligences is to expand our idea of what intelligence is. Since the so-called Age of Enlightenment, also known as the Age of Reason, we humans have become so overly rational and intellectual that we use only 10 percent of our brain capacity, if that. What we need now is an Age of Enlightenment 2.0 that helps us to break free from our narrow view of intelligence and start thinking with our intellect and intuition, with reason and imagination, with heart and soul, and with logic and love.

By working with the Four Intelligences, we can hopefully experience a *metanoia*. Metanoia is an ancient Greek word, made up of *meta* ("after" and "beyond") and *nous* ("mind"), and translated it means "a complete change of mind and heart." Metanoia is a holy shift—a baptism in your being—that cleanses your lens of perception and plugs you into the Universal Intelligence—or Singular Consciousness, as Erwin Schrödinger named it his Nobel Prize–winning work on quantum theory—and thereby enables you to participate with reverence and awe in the greater purpose of creation.

P.Q.—Sense of Aliveness

In *The Power of Myth*, Joseph Campbell said something to Bill Moyers about aliveness that stopped me in my tracks the first time I heard it. Here's what Campbell said:

> People say that what we're all seeking is a meaning for life. I don't think that's what we're really seeking. I think that what we're seeking is an experience of being alive,

so that our life experiences on the purely physical plane will have resonances within our own innermost being and reality, so that we actually feel the rapture of being alive.[6]

Physical Intelligence (P.Q.) is about energy and the rapture of being alive. When I mentor people who want to get clear on their purpose, I ask them this question: *When do you feel most alive?* You shouldn't need much time to think about this. Your body will tell you straightaway. Another option is to complete the following sentence 10 times: "I feel most alive when . . ." A sense of aliveness, and feeling energized in your body, are good signs that you are on track, in the flow, and making authentic choices for your life.

A very practical way I work with people on their P.Q. is to help them manage their calendar better. P.Q. is about time and space. Your calendar is a faithful mirror that shows you how well you are using your time and space. Managing your calendar well is essential for living with vision and purpose. You must be brave and say no to chronic busyness if you are to follow your bliss. You must keep a space for your daily spiritual practice. You must make time for meditative thinking, for writing in your journal, for important meetings, and for what brings you most alive.

Taking enlightened action is another way I work with people's P.Q. Remember, P.Q. is about physical intelligence, and that includes translating wisdom into action. In my office I have a large and beautiful hand-painted Green Tara thangka that I brought home from one of my pilgrimages to India. The Green Tara represents embodied wisdom and enlightened action. She discerns between doing and nondoing, action and rest, busyness and purpose. When I gaze at her, I contemplate this question: *What is my most enlightened action for today?*

I.Q.—Time to Think

We live in an intelligent universe. "The total number of minds in the universe is one. In fact, consciousness is a singularity phasing within all beings," said Erwin Schrödinger. Note his words "all beings." "There is only one mind," said Schrödinger. "All beings" means every human, as well as every whale and dolphin, every bee and butterfly, every tree and flower, and Gaia, our Mother Earth. Surely, then, our great work is to make ourselves available to this infinite intelligence so we can play a part in the bigger story of life.

When I sit down to meditate, I like to imagine that I am participating in the thinking of the universe. I allow my body to become still, which is a good P.Q. practice. I breathe deeply, I empty my mind, and I make myself spontaneously available to inspiration, light, eurekas, and epiphanies. "I want to know God's thoughts," said Albert Einstein, the physicist and philosopher. I ask myself, *What is the highest thought I can think today?* Or, alternatively, the *most beautiful thought, most loving thought,* or *wisest thought.* I listen quietly. I take notes. I give thanks. And I act accordingly.

I often work closely with leaders in global organizations and big enterprises. One of my tasks is to help these people regularly make time to stop and think. "Leaders are not paid to be busy; they are paid to think," I tell them. One time I mentored a man who was overwhelmed by the size of his task. I came up with a mindfulness practice for him that I've shared many times since. The practice is to make one wise decision a day. The cumulative effects of this simple practice are often miraculous. Making one wise decision a day, my client soon became less busy and more impactful, and he led with a greater sense of vision and purpose.

Making the time to think is an enlightened action. In my Success Intelligence keynote, I show a *New Yorker* cartoon by Sam Gross. It's a single-panel cartoon with two men in suits standing in front of a billboard that says, "Stop and Think." One man says to the other, "It sort of makes you stop and think, doesn't it?" I have a framed copy of this cartoon that sits on a bookshelf by my desk. Right next to it is a framed quote by Saint Francis de Sales that reads,

> *Half an hour's meditation each day is essential,*
> *except when you are busy.*
> *Then a full hour is needed.*

E.Q.—A Path with Heart

It's a sign of how estranged we humans have become from our own hearts that we are only just beginning to realize that the heart is not only a physical muscle, or a repository for our emotions, but also a seat of intelligence. Emotional Intelligence (E.Q.) has many facets that include cultivating a wise and loving approach to your emotions, growing your capacity to be involved in conversations that are difficult but necessary, and listening to and following the wisdom of your heart.

On your hero journey you will encounter setbacks, disappointments, criticism, rejection, and betrayals. And you will meet fear, self-doubt, unworthiness, frustration, anger, envy, and every other emotion. You can't avoid fear and do what you love. And you can't play it safe and follow your joy. Remember, though, you don't walk alone on the road of trials. If you ask for help, help will appear. And when you meet your fears with honesty and love, the path becomes clear.

Your E.Q. helps you to recognize the conversations you most need to have, and with whom. We evolve through conversation. We must be willing, therefore, to be brave, honest, and vulnerable in these conversations. "Leaders are hosts to the conversations that matter the most," I tell my clients. When I mentor people on their purpose, I ask them, *What is the conversation that you most want to be part of?* What conversation is happening in your family, among your friends, in your workplace, and in the media, that brings you alive (P.Q.), inspires you (I.Q.), moves you (E.Q.), and makes you want to show up and take action?

When you work with your E.Q., you are learning to love yourself and to listen to the Voice of Love that resides in your heart. E.Q. helps you live your purpose by following what Carlos Castaneda called *a path with heart*. In *The Teachings of Don Juan: A Yaqui Way of Knowledge*, there is this famous passage about a path with heart. It reads.

Before you embark on any path ask the question: Does this path have a heart? If the answer is no, you will know it, and then you must choose another path. The trouble is nobody asks the question; and when a man finally realizes that he has taken a path without a heart, the path is ready to kill him. At that point very few men can stop to deliberate, and leave the path. A path without a heart is never enjoyable. You have to work hard even to take it. On the other hand, a path with heart is easy; it does not make you work at liking it.[7]

S.Q.—Living on Purpose

Danah Zohar began a conversation about spiritual intelligence (S.Q.) by writing her book *Spiritual Intelligence*. I believe that this is one of the most important conversations for our world today. It is a conversation that can help us humans, both individually and collectively, to live with a greater sense of oneness, wisdom, and love.

When I first started to talk about S.Q., I was worried that people wouldn't be as open to it as the other intelligences. I was afraid that they'd think spiritual means religious, which it doesn't. Fortunately, my audiences were intelligent enough to realize that S.Q. is not exclusively for people who attend a church, a mosque, or a synagogue; it is for everyone, regardless of religious persuasion, or none at all. Much to my joy, of all four intelligences, this was the one that most people wanted to know more about.

S.Q. invites you to meditate on your spiritual DNA—the essence of who we are—which is deeper than the color of your skin, your political affiliations, your nationality, or your religion and philosophy. S.Q. wants us to be true to ourselves and to connect to something greater than ourselves. S.Q. helps us remember that there is more to life than getting a job, earning a living, and paying the bills. S.Q. wants you to live with imagination, to find a path with heart, to be an instrument, and to participate in the great work of creation.

The best way to work with your S.Q. is to have a daily spiritual practice. For me, the best spiritual practices combine all four intelligences. They help you pay attention to your body's messages (P.Q.), listen to your heart (E.Q.), make wise decisions (I.Q.), and be authentic (S.Q.) in how you live your purpose. A spiritual practice can take any form you like, including meditation, contemplation, centering prayer, yoga, walking in nature, sitting by a pond, crocheting, painting, cooking meals, gardening, playing music, and journaling.

Here is how Danah Zohar and Ian Marshall summed up their thoughts on S.Q. in their book *Spiritual Intelligence*:

> High SQ demands the most intense personal integrity. It demands that we stand open to experience, that we recapture our ability to see life and others afresh, as though through the eyes of a child, to learn how to tap into our intuition and visualization, as a powerful means of using our inner knowing to "make a difference." It demands that we cease to seek refuge in what we know and constantly explore and learn from what we do not know. It demands that we live the questions rather than the answers.[8]

MORE MEANINGFUL SUCCESS

"Come to dinner! You need to meet Tex Gunning!" said Danah Zohar over the phone. The next evening, I met up with Danah and Tex at Claridge's Hotel in London. Over dinner Tex told us about his work with Unilever. Tex's position was business group president for Asia. His mission was to align Unilever—the world's third largest consumer goods company—with the UNICEF Millennium Development Goals project, whose goals include eradicating extreme poverty, reducing infant mortality, combating malaria and HIV/AIDS, and increasing global environmental sustainability.

Tex inspired us with his vision of how global business can be a force for good in the world when it embraces a higher purpose. After I told Tex about my work with Success Intelligence, he immediately invited Danah and me to speak at his three-day leadership conference in Singapore, starting the following Friday. The conference was called Journey to Greatness, and it was for his top 100 leaders. "I'll change the agenda right now if you both agree to come," Tex said. I told Danah, "I'll go if you go."

I booked my flight to Singapore first thing the next day. Two hours later, I got a call from Danah telling me she was double-booked for next Friday. She had managed to get hold of Tex, who said he was happy for Danah to give her keynote talk via satellite if I'd agree to extend my keynote into a three-hour Masterclass. Although I was disappointed not to be traveling with Danah, I felt certain that destiny was at work again. So I went to Singapore alone, and after my Masterclass Tex Gunning took me out to dinner with Sylvia Lagnado.

Sylvia Lagnado had recently been appointed president of Dove, the popular cosmetics brand owned by Unilever. She had enjoyed a very successful career with Unilever, working in Brazil, Argentina, the U.S., and now in the U.K. Tex Gunning was keen for me to coach Sylvia in her new role. Sylvia's main area of interest was in cultivating a greater sense of mission, purpose, and meaning in her work and life. Her interest in these matters had inspired her to create the Dove Real Beauty Campaign.[9]

Over the next four years, I worked closely with Sylvia both as her coach and as a consultant to the Dove Real Beauty Campaign. Together with my Success Intelligence team, I organized and hosted three annual Dove Planet conferences; I coached the vice presidents of Dove; I taught a Higher Purpose program for the global leadership team; and I presented Success Intelligence seminars to Dove teams in Tokyo, New York, Paris, Bologna, Hamburg, and many other cities. Everything we did had one main purpose: *to help more young people feel happy and beautiful every day.*

Sylvia Lagnado was inspired to create the Dove Campaign for Real Beauty after she read research that revealed 8 out of 10 girls around the world opt out of key life activities because they don't feel good about how they look. Sylvia commissioned a report, "The Truth about Beauty," which confirmed that even though we have more beauty products on the planet than ever before, we feel less beautiful and okay about ourselves. Another report on men found that the majority of men also don't pursue their dreams because of their self-image issues and low self-esteem.

Sylvia and the Dove global leadership team worked on a pledge for the Dove Real Beauty Campaign that promised to help reform the beauty industry with these three vows:

1. **We always feature real women, never models.** Models reflect a narrow view of beauty. Dove believes that beauty is for everyone and therefore features real women of different ages, sizes, ethnicities, hair color, type, or style.

2. **We portray women as they are in real life.** We never present the unachievable, manipulated, flawless images of "perfect" beauty which the use of retouching tools can promote.

3. **We help girls build body confidence and self-esteem.** The Dove Self-Esteem Project pledges to ensure the next generation grows up enjoying a positive relationship with the way they look—helping young people raise their self-esteem and realize their full potential.[10]

Looking back on my notes, I see that in my first coaching session with Sylvia Lagnado, I gave her a Success Journal, and I invited her to spend five minutes every day for the next 100 days with the question *What is success today?* At the end of our session, I gave her a poem to meditate on called "The Summer Day," by Mary Oliver. This poem begins with the question "Who made the world?" and it ends with another question: "Tell me, what is it you plan to do / With your one wild and precious life?"

My first big task was to help Sylvia ensure that every leader at Dove was on board with the Dove mission. To this end, I created a mission report called The Dove One Pager that was circulated every Monday to the Dove global leadership team. The report stated Dove's main purpose and key success measures. One measure was the number of talks given by Dove employees at local schools and community centers for the Dove Self-Esteem Project. By 2020, over 20 million young people had attended one of these events.

Sylvia wanted to make Dove a purpose-centered brand where everyone is encouraged to work with imagination and purpose. I helped everyone at Dove create their own Purpose Business Card. The idea was to replace the ordinary business card that has your title and position on it with a new card that also states your personal vision and philosophy. For example, on one side of the card you put your work title and a logo, and on the other side you state your personal mission statement, a quote that inspires you, or the main purpose of your work.

Sylvia also wanted Dove leaders to be ambassadors for a new conversation about beauty that celebrates cultural diversity. To help with this, I taught a Masterclass on The Enneagram of Beauty. Working with the wisdom of the Enneagram, we explored beauty through nine different lenses that focused on the beauty of courage, vulnerability, kindness, forgiveness, authenticity, and love. This was my first major piece of work with the Enneagram, and I followed it up with another program using the Enneagram called Living Your Purpose (see "The Enneagram Chapter" in Part III).

One of my favorite offerings by the Dove Real Beauty Campaign is its series of short films called *Real Beauty Sketches*. Each year, Dove releases a new film on YouTube that manages to be relevant and contributes to a major conversation or topic of interest in the world. During the COVID-19 pandemic, Dove released a film called *Courage is Beautiful* that featured portraits of frontline health-care workers who were battling with exhaustion and suffering to help save people's lives. It was a beautifully made tribute, a sincere thank-you, and very inspiring to watch.

I loved working with Sylvia Lagnado and the Dove Real Beauty Campaign. The work we did was innovative, courageous, and creative. Dove became the benchmark for creating purpose-centered brands. Dove sales jumped from $2.5 to $4 billion per annum inside 10 years. Dove soap bars became the number one preferred brand in the U.S. And a new wave of purpose-driven brands with ethical mission statements appeared in the world. Sylvia was promoted to a global vice president role, and I continued to work with her until she left Unilever.

My work at Dove led to many wonderful opportunities to work with leaders and organizations on purpose. I stayed on at Dove for two more years, working with the next Dove president, Fernando Acosta. I worked with Anita Roddick and The Body Shop, with IBM on its Intelligent Planet Campaign, and with Unilever on its initiative to make all its major brands more ethical, sustainable, and purpose-led. One of its newest brands is Love Beauty and Planet, which is an inspiring example of a new-era brand run by people who are passionate about living and working with a higher purpose.

DOING WHAT YOU LOVE

My retreat to Mount Athos, known as "the Holy Mountain," was a gift to myself. I'd recently celebrated my 40th birthday, and I wanted to stop and think, and to imagine what the future might be. This retreat was a voluntary stop, unlike the time when I was forced to stop with a prolapsed disc. Carl Jung is said to have observed, "Life really does begin at forty. Up until then, you are just doing research." Looking out over the Aegean Sea, I sensed another new beginning on the horizon.

With the rise of Positive Psychology, an initiative of the American Psychology Association, my work with The Happiness Project was more popular than ever. I had recently been a consultant for a new BBC documentary series called *The Happiness Formula*, a follow-up to the *How to Be Happy* documentary. With Success Intelligence, my team and I were working at capacity, and I'd just finished a book tour with *Authentic Success*. Now, more than ever, I had a strong sense that both projects were preparation for a greater work.

On Mount Athos I meditated on my life purpose. Each day I sat on a big, soft rock under an olive tree, a short walk from the monastery, and I recorded entries in my journal on what inspires me, following my joy, and doing more of what I love. When I returned from Mount Athos, I was fully rested, and I was ready to say a hearty YES to a new adventure. I reorganized my work—freeing up time, space, and energy for a new project, and a new conversation, this time on love. I called this project Loveability.[1]

My new project started quietly, without a fanfare. My first offering was a two-day public seminar that was attended by a handful of people at the Columbia Hotel in Central London near Hyde Park. I called it Love & Fear, and I based it on the work of *A Course in Miracles*. I first came across *A Course in Miracles* on my return from a pilgrimage to Bodh Gaya in India. Toward the end of that trip, I spent a day sitting under the Bodhi Tree at the Mahabodhi Temple, the place where Buddha is said to have attained his enlightenment. I prayed a big prayer that day, and I believe that finding *A Course in Miracles* was the answer to my prayer.

A Course in Miracles is the most beautiful teaching on love I know.[2] In short, the Course offers a practical training on the psychology and spirituality of love. It features a text of 669 pages and a workbook with 365 daily lessons. I'd been working with the daily lessons of the Course for several years by the time I gave my Love & Fear seminar. I'd also met Tom Carpenter, a much-loved teacher of *A Course in Miracles*, who became my mentor and dearest friend.[3] Tom was a great help to me in creating the syllabus for Love & Fear.

> *"Let yourself be silently drawn by the stronger pull of what you really love."*
>
> — Rumi

The Course teaches that love is your chief function, and that everyone on earth has been given the same assignment, which is to be a loving presence in the world. "Child of God, you were created to create the good, the beautiful, and the holy. Do not forget this," teaches the Course.[4] Love is our shared purpose. Our divine assignment is to be an instrument of love. We can express love in an infinite number of ways, like learning a science, being a kindergarten teacher, working in a café, having a passion for the arts, re-wilding nature, volunteering, and doing something you truly love.

After Love & Fear, I gave another two-day seminar called Love's Philosophy, named after a poem by Percy Bysshe Shelley. I shared my favorite teachings from philosophy and psychology on the wisdom and practice of love. On philosophy, we studied Bhakti Yoga, the path of love, which I first read about in *The Bhagavad Gita*; the Buddha's Metta Bhavana loving-kindness meditation; the Great Commandment by Jesus Christ to love God, ourselves, and our neighbors; and also poetry by two great Sufi love mystics, Rumi and Hafiz.

On the psychology of love, I began with Sigmund Freud and Carl Jung. Freud believed that love is the key to our mental health and well-being. "In the final analysis, in order not to fall ill, we must learn to love," wrote Freud.[5] Curiously, Carl Jung said very little about love in his lifetime. But privately, he wrote a lot about love in his journals, some of which was published in 2009, nearly 50 years after his death, in a work entitled *The Red Book*. "Thinking is hollow without love," he wrote. "[But with love] you will see how your soul becomes green and how its field bears wonderful fruit."[6]

After Freud and Jung, I gave special mention to Carl Rogers, Victor Frankl, and Erich Fromm. Fromm's work *The Art of Loving* was one of the books I had taken with me to Mount Athos. My mum had given me a copy as a present for my fortieth birthday. It's a short book, only 129 pages long. I expected to whiz through it, but there were too many brilliant and profound insights on every page. I started reading it on the first morning of my retreat, and I was still reading it on the plane back home to London.

"Without love, humanity could not exist for a day," wrote Fromm in *The Art of Loving*. He saw love as the "ultimate and real need in every human being" that helps you to grow, evolve and live your higher purpose. However, he also observed that in our modern society, "in spite of the deep-seated craving for love, almost everything else is considered to be more important than love: success, prestige, money, power—almost all our energy is used for this learning of how to achieve these aims, and almost none to learn the art of loving."[7]

I presented Love & Fear and Love's Philosophy a few times before I eventually designed a three-day seminar called Loveability. With Loveability, I encourage you to imagine living a love-centered life, in which you make love the central purpose of your life. Imagine how life would be if we put love at the center of our politics, our economy, our education, our work, our social justice programs, and our relationship with nature and Mother Earth. Why on earth would we not do this? What is stopping us, and what can we do to choose love?

I made up the word *loveability*. It doesn't exist in the dictionary yet. I chose it because, for me, loveability means your "ability to love and be loved." As Fromm rightly observed, love is natural, but we must learn how to practice it. I made sure that my Loveability seminar was both experiential and practical. In it I offer a creative mix of inquiries, practices, and tools to cultivate the necessary wisdom, healing, and courage it takes to become an instrument of love and a loving presence in the world.

The poet Rilke, in one of his letters to the young poet Franz Xaver Kappus, wrote, "For one human being to love another: that is perhaps the most difficult of all our tasks . . . the work for which all other work is but preparation."[8] I believe that the first 40 years of my life had been preparing me to teach Loveability. I felt truly on purpose writing, teaching, and lecturing on love. All of the good things in life, like happiness, success, friendship, and inner peace, increase as we learn how to love. Surely, then, learning how to love and be loved must be the true purpose of life.

LOVE IN ACTION

On the eve of the publication of my book *Loveability*, I was invited by the Findhorn Foundation to participate in a seven-day conference on Love, Magic, Miracles. I gave the opening keynote on Loveability and also facilitated two workshops later in the week, one on Love & Fear and the other on Love & the Enneagram.

The vision for this conference was working with love—as our most powerful natural resource—to create a future that is good for humanity and for the natural world. We had a stellar lineup of thought leaders that included Caroline Myss, author of *Sacred Contracts*; Andrew Harvey, founder of the Institute for Sacred Activism; Thomas Moore, author of *Care of the Soul*; David Spangler, author of *The Call*; and Dorothy Maclean, the oldest surviving founder of the Findhorn Foundation. And we were joined by an international crowd of 300 delegates, many of whom were leaders in their field.

Love, Magic, Miracles was a conference to celebrate the fiftieth anniversary of the Findhorn Foundation. From small beginnings on a barren sand dune in northeast Scotland, Eileen and Peter Caddy, their three children, and Dorothy Maclean grew a beautiful garden—known as the Original Garden—that attracted a diverse community of mystics, scientists, philosophers, gardeners, beekeepers, architects, educationists, ecologists, and artists. The Findhorn Foundation became a creative hothouse—a hive of activity—offering visionary ideas and initiatives for a better world.

The work at Findhorn is based on three root principles: 1) inner listening, 2) co-creation with the intelligence of nature, and 3) work as love in action. Eileen Caddy first heard an inner voice speak to her as she sat in a sanctuary in Glastonbury in 1953. "Be still and know that I am God," said the voice. The guidance Eileen received inspired the vision and purpose of the Findhorn Foundation in the early years. Her book *Opening Doors Within* is a collection of 365 daily inspirations from her inner listening. It has sold millions of copies worldwide, and it is one of my favorite books.[9]

The Love, Magic, Miracles conference was the first time Hollie, Bo, Christopher, and I visited Findhorn as a family. Findhorn is one of my favorite places on the planet, and the Universal Hall, which hosts the big conferences, is one of my favorite venues for teaching. Over the years, I've given two TEDx talks in the Hall, and many workshops, including Loveability and Living Your Purpose. By the end of the first day of the conference, Hollie was already looking for a house to buy. Four years later we built a beautiful home there that we share with family and friends.

To prepare for writing this chapter, I rummaged through my old files on Loveability, and I found the brochure for the Love, Magic, Miracles conference. Here's the blurb I wrote for my Loveability keynote:

> To know how to love and to be loved is the great miracle that helps you to live a life you love. The simple maths of love is: the more you love, the happier you feel; the more you love, the healthier you are; the more you love, the more successful you are at everything! Conversely, not loving enough is the root cause of every problem and conflict in your life and on our planet. In sum, your life works when you love; and it doesn't when you don't!

In my Loveability keynote, I began by making this key point: *Your destiny is not to look for love; it is to become the most loving person you can be.* I believe that love is your destiny because love is your true purpose. Therefore, to find your purpose, a good place to start is asking yourself, *What do I love?* The more attention you pay to what you love, and to what is sacred to you, the clearer you will be about your purpose. Another question to ask is *How do I like to express my love?* Love is not just a sentiment, or only a meditation; it is also a way of being in the world.

Love helps you live your higher purpose. When you do a thing with love, you are assisted by favorable forces that are far greater than your own willpower. Viktor Frankl described love as "the ultimate and highest goal" because it was love that sustained him during the hell of the concentration camps, and it was love that gave him the spiritual resilience to pursue his work after his release. In *Man's Search for Meaning*, Frankl shared his epiphany about love that saved his life. He wrote,

> *"All things done with love is your true purpose."*
>
> — Kyle Gray

A thought transfixed me: for the first time in my life, I saw the truth as it is set into song by so many poets, proclaimed as the final wisdom by so many thinkers. The truth—that love is the ultimate and the highest goal to which man can aspire. Then I grasped the meaning of the greatest secret that human poetry and human thought and belief have to impart: The salvation of man is through love and in love.[10]

Love is your highest purpose because it is the answer to humanity's worst problem. Humanity carries a wound, and that wound is our sense of separateness from each other, from heaven, and from the natural world. Thomas Berry, author of *The Great Work* and a great friend of the Findhorn Foundation, described our sense of separateness as "the central pathology of humanity" that causes us to act in unloving ways toward each other and our planet."[11] The universe is a communion of subjects, not a collection of objects to be used up," he taught. And as Dorothy Maclean observed, "What we do to nature, is what we do to ourselves."

In my Loveability keynote, I highlighted the eight Millennium Development Goals (MDGs) that were agreed by world leaders at the United Nations World Summit in 2000, and I asked the audience—and now I am asking you too—to imagine what good things would happen if today's leaders agreed to pour all their love into reaching these goals.[12] Here are the eight MDGs:

- To eradicate extreme poverty and hunger

- To achieve universal primary education

- To promote gender equality and empower women

- To reduce child mortality

- To improve maternal health

- To combat HIV/AIDS, malaria, and other diseases

- To ensure environmental sustainability

- To develop a global partnership for development

Is there enough money in the world to achieve these goals? I'm certain that there is, but if there isn't, we should print some more money! Do we have the brain power to meet these goals? Yes, I think so, don't you? Do we have the science and technology? Yes, we do, don't we? All the necessary resources exist. And love is our greatest resource because with enough love, we can mobilize every other resource we have for the greater good of humanity and the planet. But until we love enough, we will continue to suffer and these goals will not be achieved.

My big takeaway from the Love, Magic, Miracles conference was the realization that the fear for survival is not enough of a motivation to create a better future. Fear draws our attention to the problem, but it cannot create solutions that are sustainable. "Love is the moral sun of the world," wrote Rudolph Steiner. "Without the impulse of love . . . men will only increase their egoism [their separation]," he said. "When we practice love, cultivate love, creative forces pour into the world." Love is our true conscience. When we choose love, we naturally do what's right, and we make things right.

In my Loveability keynote, I paid tribute especially to Eileen Caddy and her teachings on love. I only met Eileen Caddy once, and I am so happy I did. Eileen was a true mystic in that she had had a direct experience of what she called the Voice of Love. She taught us that we each have a Voice of Love within us, and that when we listen to this voice, it will help us live our higher purpose. Her work was bringing heaven and earth together. She did it through inner listening, communing with nature, and love in action.

While I was writing this book, a new edition of Eileen's *Opening Doors Within* was published, with a new Foreword by her son Jonathan Caddy. Jonathan and I spent a magical evening together going through family photos looking for a picture of Eileen to use that showed off the light in her eyes. Later we were joined by friends and family, and we shared some of our favorite entries from *Opening Doors Within*. Here is one that focuses on love and on doing more of what you love.

> Whatever you do, do it with love; do it to My honour and glory; and never be concerned about it. When you do everything with the right attitude, it is bound to be done perfectly, so take this right attitude into everything you do. Keep ever before you the saying "Work is love made visible"; then you will work with joy and contentment, and work will never be a chore or something that has to be done. What a difference the right attitude to work will make to yourself and to all those souls around you! If you want to succeed in what you are doing, learn to love it and handle it the right way, with that right attitude. Often it is a question of changing your attitude from negative to positive which can uplift the most mundane job. Every soul feels in harmony with a different job. What do you feel in harmony with? Is there something you love doing? Then do it![13]

VIVA THE LOVE

I first met Viva while standing at the school gate at St. Michael Steiner School. It was pick-up time for children and parents. Bo had started her first year at the school, and Christopher had entered kindergarten. Viva's two boys were now in their second year. Our children, who were in four different classes, had gravitated toward each other and become good friends. It was our children who brought our families together.

What I first noticed about Viva was the light in her eyes. I couldn't stop looking at her eyes. It was the same light I saw in Eileen Caddy's eyes, in Findhorn, and in my mentor Tom Carpenter's eyes. What is that light that we see in each other? I'm sure it has to do with our spiritual nature. It's our life force, isn't it? Moreover, there is a light of recognition. When friends meet for the first time, it is the light in one that recognizes the light in the other.

Hollie saw in Viva what I saw. She and Viva had become friends on the first day at our new school.

One day I was standing at the school gate talking with Viva and Jasmine, another parent at our school. Jasmine had a copy of my new book *Life Loves You*, which I co-wrote with Louise Hay. We discovered we were all big Louise Hay fans, and that we had followed her work for years. Viva and I had talked many times by now, but I hadn't asked her what she did for work. I had no idea, and I'd never have guessed her answer. "I'm a bus driver," she told me. Jasmine then added, "Viva just won an award for London Bus Driver of the Year."

Viva's family are from Ghana. She was named Viva after her mother had an experience during pregnancy in which she heard a voice tell her, "Your girl is a bright light, and she will live vibrantly." Viva means "alive" and "to live." Viva told me, "I was raised to believe that God gives each of us a purpose. And it was my great-aunt who taught me that if you live your life to the full, you won't ever have to look for your purpose, because your purpose will find you."

Viva's mother was one of the first female police officers in Winneba, Ghana. She always encouraged Viva to live with imagination and to follow her joy. And her father taught her that *purpose is not what you do; purpose is who you are.* When Viva left school, she became a nurse. She cared for babies born with addiction to drugs such as cocaine. She nursed them through painful withdrawal symptoms called neonatal abstinence syndrome. For seven years, she looked after disabled children, including one child who was one of only three children in the world with a genetic disorder that prevented cartilage from forming into bones.

At 28 years old, Viva was pulled by her golden thread in a new direction. She trained as a makeup artist for fashion and film at University of Westminster. Once qualified, she went to Los Angeles. "I've felt guided spiritually all my life, and just when I'd established a career in Hollywood, I heard a voice inside me say 'Stop!'" Viva told me. Viva's life changed course again, and for the next seven years she worked and traveled all over the world. On her travels she met Esmond, her husband, and Grace, her best friend, who is now the administrator at the St. Michael Steiner School.

"So how did you become a bus driver?" I asked Viva. After she became a mother, Viva needed to find work that was flexible. She didn't want office work or office hours. She also knew in her bones that it had to be something she'd not done before. "Grace dared me to do it," Viva told me. Grace had learned to drive a bus in a previous employment. "I didn't take her seriously, but my soul said yes, and so I applied for a training to be a London bus driver." Viva failed her first test, but she managed to pass at the second attempt. She was now a fully qualified bus driver in London.

Viva works at a bus station in West London. Her hours are flexible. A short shift is seven and a half hours, and a long shift is 10 or 11 hours with a break. She often does the night shift so that she can take her boys to school in the morning. When she signs in at work, her first task is to inspect the bus assigned to her. She drives either a single-decker red bus or a double-decker that is 12 tons in weight and 36 feet long and carries a maximum of 120 passengers, allowing for wheelchairs. Viva has six different routes that include landmarks like Parliament Square, Big Ben, Westminster Bridge, Kensington Palace, Harrods, and the Royal Albert Hall.

When I asked Viva how she won London Bus Driver of the Year, she told me, "My manager nominated me!" After some pressing, I found out from Viva she was one of 56,000 drivers nominated. "I didn't give it any attention until my manager told me I'd made the list for the final twenty nominations," she said. Viva then received an invitation with 11 other drivers to go to the Bus Industry Awards. During the presentation for the final award of the evening, Viva's face appeared on a giant screen. "I thought to myself, *I know that face*, and then a lady next to me said, 'You've won!'" Viva told me.

So why did Viva win the award? Here are a few things I've found out from Viva about how she does her work.

"When I drive my bus, I silently bless all of my passengers. I pray that everyone will feel my love and have a good experience on their journey," Viva told me. Over the years, Viva has learned enough Spanish, French, Italian, Chinese, Polish, and other languages to be able to greet her passengers, to give them helpful directions, and to wish them a lovely day. "During the COVID-19 pandemic, when everyone was wearing a mask, I learned to smile and convey my love through my eyes," says Viva.

Viva never drives her bus alone. She always prays for guidance and protection before she sets off. "I've learned to pray as if it is already done," Viva told me. "So I say, 'Thank you, God, for keeping me focused today. Thank you, God, for keeping myself and my passengers safe today. Thank you, God, for keeping the other road users and pedestrians safe today.'" Viva experiences a heightened awareness while driving her bus. "I have full peripheral vision, and I can see everything happening in slow time," says Viva, who has a completely safe driving record after more than seven years.

Viva believes that everything in life happens for a purpose. So I asked her what she thought was the purpose of her learning to drive buses and winning awards. She told me, "To be a good bus driver, I had to learn to put my total trust in God. I am just the vessel that God uses to move the bus." Viva's mother and father taught her that we each exist for God's purpose. *"Do what you do, and do it with God's love, and what you do will be extraordinary*, that's what I was taught as a young girl in Ghana. And this is what I try to teach my boys too," says Viva.

Winning the award was challenging for Viva. Suddenly, she was in the spotlight. Her face was on posters all over London. "I didn't want people to think I won the award by myself or that I'm a better driver than my colleagues," said Viva. That night at the Bus Industry Awards, her manager won Manager of the Year and her bus station won Station of the Year. It was clearly a team victory. That said, Viva still had to get used to being seen. "My mother and father taught me that you cannot hide God's light in you *and* follow your purpose," Viva told me. "Our purpose is to shine so that more and more people can experience God's love in the world."

PART III

THE ORDEAL

MAKE ME AN INSTRUMENT

"St. Francis is calling for you, Robert!" said Caroline Myss in her characteristically emphatic way, waving her finger at me with a knowing smile.

Caroline and I were having dinner in a hotel in Edmonton, Canada. We were there for an I CAN DO IT! conference hosted by Hay House. Over dinner, Caroline told me about Nina Hirlaender and her company Dancing Spirit Tours that hosts spiritual pilgrimages to Assisi in Italy. I remembered meeting Nina briefly in Findhorn at the Love, Magic, Miracles conference. "I want to recommend you to Nina for the next pilgrimage to Assisi," Caroline told me. "I promise that you will love Assisi. All you need to do is say yes!"

Assisi is nestled into the hillside of Mount Subasio in Umbria. Down below is the valley of Spoleto. In the distance, some 12 miles away, you can see the city of Perugia. To get to Assisi, you exit the A1 Autostrada, which is the main motorway in Italy, and then travel through countryside with fields of red poppies and olive groves. You are transported back in time inside the walls of Assisi, with its narrow streets, cobbled paths, stone buildings, ancient wooden doors with ogival arches, balconies full of bright flowers, and rooftops with terra-cotta tiles.

Caroline was right, I loved Assisi. It offers the ideal setting for a spiritual retreat to contemplate your higher purpose. My first pilgrimage was called A Heart Full of Love, and on it I taught a three-day program on Love & the Enneagram. I enjoyed seeing how Nina and her Dancing Spirit Tours team move heaven and earth to offer an intimate and authentic experience, and how the people of Assisi have taken them into their hearts. I was also inspired by Nina's boundless love and appreciation for both St. Francis and St. Clare of Assisi. Before I left, I had already booked dates for a return visit.

The next pilgrimage to Assisi was called Living Your Purpose. Walking in the footsteps of St. Francis and St. Clare, we learned about how they lived their purpose-centered lives. Nina and her team created an itinerary that included attending Mass at San Damiano, where St. Francis received his calling; visiting the cloister of St. Clare; spending time at the tiny Porziuncola, the first HQ of the Franciscan Order; meditating at the St. Francis Hermitage of Carceri; dining and singing with Franciscan friars; and joining the procession of the stigmata on Mount La Verna.

The Living Your Purpose pilgrimage was a joy to teach, and our pilgrims raved about it so much that Nina and I decided to offer it as an annual retreat. When our pilgrimage in 2020 was cancelled because of the COVID-19 pandemic, we saw this as an opportunity to create an eight-week online inner pilgrimage called Make Me An Instrument that features live classes, interviews, films, podcasts, and meditations. These two offerings go together beautifully, like brother and sister, and many of our pilgrims take both journeys with us.

St. Francis and his spiritual sister St. Clare gave the world a practical blueprint for how to live an inspired life. St. Francis is honored by the world as the patron saint of ecology, but for me, he is my patron saint of purpose. St. Francis took a hero journey in his life. He searched for a higher purpose. He said YES to his calling. He experienced a dark night of the soul. He survived a terrible ordeal, and he showed the world, by his example, how to walk the Christ Path and become an instrument for love.

I call St. Clare my patron saint of vision. She is honored as a patron saint for many things including for eye disease, for extrasensory perception, and for remote viewing. Her name, Clare, means "bright" and "clear." She was a visionary and a pioneer. She was one of the first followers of St. Francis. She described herself as "the little flower of St. Francis," but she was his equal in many ways. She founded the Order of St. Clare and was the first woman to write a monastic rule. She spoke with popes, bishops, and cardinals, and she became a beacon of light for the world.

Both St. Francis and St. Clare lived in medieval times, and yet their teachings are especially relevant for modern times in which so many of us are suffering the effects of spiritual poverty, a lack of meaningfulness, working in a joyless economy, and living in a world teetering on the brink of environmental catastrophe. Meditating on both these saints' lives always helps me get clear on my personal vision and higher purpose. Each time I visit Assisi, I leave feeling realigned, rejuvenated, and ready to take the next step on my life path.

I could easily write a book on living your higher purpose with St. Francis and St. Clare, and maybe I will one day. For now, here are a few lessons I have learned from these two remarkable people.

EVERYONE IS CALLED

I have been all things unholy. If God can work through me, he can work through anyone.

— St. Francis of Assisi

You don't have to be a saint to have a purpose. Francis was not born a saint, nor did he ever consider himself to be one. He wished to be known simply as Brother Francesco. St. Clare, who was canonized in record time just two years after her death, had no interest in being a saint either. Most saints are not saints until well after their death. Indeed, it is important to note that most saints during their lifetime are disregarded as rebels, misfits, mavericks, and heretics who break with convention and go their own way.

Francesco was born with a great spirit of adventure. In his youth, he was a pleasure seeker. He was described by Thomas of Celano, who was his first biographer and a close friend, as being full of "youthful heat," showing "pomp of vainglory," and a "zealot in folly" who "strove to surpass the rest in frolics, freaks, sallies of wit and idle talk, songs, and soft and flowing attire."[1] Francesco's father, Pietro di Bernardone, was a wealthy silk merchant. He expected Francesco to succeed him in the family business. Meanwhile, Francesco was dreaming of a higher purpose.

Clare of Assisi was born into a noble family. In her youth, she did not display the same revelry as Francesco. She was a watchful young girl who quietly took everything in. She saw through the facade of nobility and was not impressed by the lavish balls and wearing of masques. At family dinners, she heard her father and uncle speak of their plans to groom her for marriage, hopefully into royalty. She was very beautiful, after all. Clare knew her own mind, though, and she cultivated within herself the qualities she would need to challenge the thinking of the day.

Francesco and Clare were willing to leave behind "normal" and get *kicked out of ordinary* to follow a more meaningful life. Francesco was like the Buddha, who left behind his family riches, and Clare gladly renounced her family privileges to join her spiritual brother, Francesco. Their path was not easy. Like any of us would be, they were often afraid, lost, and uncertain about what to do next. Francesco prayed constantly for guidance. Clare sat in meditation for hours on end. The way became clear to them one step at a time.

Francesco and Clare were two pilgrims inspired by something of great value—a pearl beyond price—that neither the life of a merchant or a noblewoman can purchase. They had both found their *chief point of inspiration*, a term I use to describe something so sacred that you would not exchange it for anything else in the world. For them, it was to follow the way of Christ and to live a life of love and service. They vowed not to sell themselves short. They did not betray their calling. They were faithful to the inner voice that guided them on their way.

In one of Clare's letters to Ermentrude of Bruges, she offered these words of encouragement to her sister pilgrim:

Our labor here is brief, but the reward is eternal. Do not be disturbed by the clamor of the world, which passes like a shadow. Do not let false delights of a deceptive world deceive you.

On both the Living Your Purpose pilgrimage in Assisi and the Make Me An Instrument pilgrimage online, I offer an inquiry that focuses on your own *chief point of inspiration.* The basic question you work with is *What inspires me?* After learning about Francesco's and Clare's early life, I invite you to reflect on what inspired you as a young child and young adult. What was your experience? Did you follow your bliss? Did you leave behind "normal"? Or did you refuse the call? And how about now? What most inspires you today? Are you living a life that inspires you?

Living an inspired life sounds lofty and unobtainable, but when you look closely at Francesco's and Clare's lives, you see that they gave up their thrones so as to access inspiration more readily. They took a vow of poverty to release themselves from the narrow chains of material wealth, social status, and worldly success. They opted to live a simple life, and this helped them find inspiration wherever they went and whenever they most needed it. When you simplify your life, the way ahead becomes clear.

Francesco and Clare answered the call that came directly to them from their heart. Neither of them had any formal qualifications for living their higher purpose. They were not scholarly. They were not theologians. There were not ordained by a church. "No one showed me what to do, but the Most High revealed to me that I was to live according to the Gospel," said Francesco. He also said, "I have done what was mine to do, may the Lord show you what is yours." In other words, you must first and foremost be true to yourself, and then the true way will appear.

DARK NIGHT OF THE SOUL

When Francesco was 21, a war broke out between Assisi and Perugia. Francesco signed up to the cavalry, and he set out for battle, dressed in shining armor and fine clothing, playing the part of a knight. Upon the bloody battlefield, Francesco was quickly outfought, and would certainly have been killed were it not for a Perugian soldier who recognized Francesco's fine attire and decided that he must be an officer or aristocrat who could be ransomed for a rich reward.

Francesco was thrown into an underground dungeon. He was plunged into total darkness and chained against a wall. Here he stayed for a year, until the war ended and his ransom was paid. It's impossible to imagine just how terrible it was inside the dungeon. His eyesight withered and his health deteriorated in the dark and septic conditions. One way he comforted himself was to gaze at the candlelight that shone from his prison guard's lanterns. There was something about this light that gave him hope.

> *"Et lux in tenebris lucet'— and the light shineth in the darkness."*
>
> — Viktor Frankl

This was Francesco's dark night of the soul. His dream of fighting for a higher cause had turned into a nightmare. Like Victor Frankl in the concentration camps, Francesco must have sensed enveloping gloom and imminent death. This was also Francesco's involuntary stop. His plans for his future were extinguished. Everything had faded to black. And yet his incarceration was also an inciting incident that sparked a search for a higher purpose. Here, in utter darkness, and emptied of all sense of self, he experienced an inner light he hadn't known before, and he received his first visions from God.

When Francesco's ransom was finally paid, he returned home severely malnourished, riddled with illness, and with no sense of what to do next. His mother nursed him slowly back to health, and he worked for his father for a time, but being a merchant still did not fit well with him. Where was Francesco's destiny? He couldn't see it yet. One night he had a strange dream in which he saw a huge hall full of knights' armor with holy crosses, and he interpreted this as a sign that knighthood was his true calling after all, and so he went off to war again.

This time Francesco went to fight with Count Walter of Brienne and his army. On his way to join Brienne, he stopped off at Spoleto, where he heard news of Brienne's death. Poor Francesco was terribly disillusioned by the news and developed a sudden fever. That night he had another dream, in which a voice asked him, "Who do you think can best reward you, the Master or the servant?" Francesco answered, "The Master." The voice then asked him, "Why do you leave the Master for the servant?" As Francesco picked apart the meaning of his dream, he realized that the higher purpose of being a knight was to serve not only a general or a king, but also God.

On both our pilgrimage to Assisi and our Make Me An Instrument online pilgrimage, I invite our pilgrims to live with the question *Who am I serving?* When I feel stuck or lacking in inspiration, I return to this question. *Who am I serving?* Meditating on this question helps me remember my chief point of inspiration. *Who am I serving?* Working with this inquiry helps me focus on the bigger picture and take my place in the grand scheme of things.

"REBUILD MY CHURCH"

The first place I visit when I arrive in Assisi is San Damiano church. This is where Francesco received his commission, and it is the first monastery of the Order of Saint Clare. Most days in Assisi, there is a long line of tourists waiting their turn to enter the Basilica of Saint Francis, which houses St. Francis's tomb. But here at San Damiano, just two kilometers out of town and hidden among olive groves, it is mostly quiet and peaceful. I've attended many masses here, and I happily meditate and pray here for as long as the friars allow me to.

Francesco's experience at San Damiano, and what unfolded thereafter, offers an excellent teaching example of how our own life purpose evolves through three distinct stages of development and ever-widening circles of love. Usually, purpose starts on a personal level and with small acts; then it grows, and we share it with a community of others; and eventually we fully embody our purpose, and we realize that we are part of something even more wonderful and universal.

One day Francesco was wandering aimlessly about in the Umbrian countryside when he stumbled across an abandoned old church. He was still very much in his dark night of the soul. He went inside and saw a wooden Byzantine-style crucifix hanging on the wall. Francesco fell to his knees, bowed his head, and began to pray. He prayed a prayer to find his higher purpose. This is the prayer he prayed:

Most High, Glorious Divine,
Cast your light into the darkness of my heart
Give me faith,
Give me hope,
Give me perfect charity,
And give me profound humility.
May I have the wisdom
To carry out what is truly
Your holy will.

After a while, Francesco looked up at the image of Jesus Christ, and he heard a voice say to him three times, "Francis, go and repair my church which is all in ruins." Francesco had received his instructions, and his work seemed clear enough, except that the voice had spoken to him three times and the word *church* has three distinct meanings and levels of experience.

The first meaning of *church* is "a building used for religious services," and this meaning is associated with the Greek word *kuriakon*. Francesco took his instructions literally at first, and he set about restoring the San Damiano church brick by brick. After he had finished, he rebuilt other dilapidated churches in the area. Franciscan spirituality is renowned for being practical and hands-on. "Let us not love in word or in tongue, but in deed and in truth," said Francesco. Living your purpose must include contemplation and action if it is to be lived fully.

The second meaning of *church* is an "assembly of people" who gather in worship, fellowship, and ministry, and this meaning is associated with the Greek word *ekklesia*. When Francesco was 28 years old and he was done repairing enough physical churches, he realized his purpose now was to set up the Order of Friars Minor, known simply as the Franciscans. And three years later, with Francesco's help, Clare set up the Order of St. Clare. Francesco and Clare fulfilled this stage of their mission by leading a larger community with a shared purpose.

The third meaning of *church* is more mystical, and it has to do with embodying the higher purpose of the teachings in your everyday life. "It is no use walking anywhere to preach unless our walking is our preaching," Francesco told his spiritual brothers and sisters. Deep down you realize that your purpose is not something you look for; it lives within you and you give expression to it. "What we are looking for is what is looking," said Francesco. You are your destiny. You are your purpose. You are the love you are looking for.

On our pilgrimages, we meditate on how it might look like to live your purpose on these three levels. For example, you love books, and so you open a bookstore so as to do something you love. Gradually you get to know your customers, your bookstore becomes part of the community, and you discover that you love serving your patronage. Eventually your presence becomes a blessing to everyone who enters your bookstore. Your customers could buy their books online or at another store, but they come to you because they enjoy your company and feel your love.

LIVING YOUR PRAYERS

The Prayer of St. Francis is the central focus of both the Living Your Purpose and Make Me An Instrument pilgrimages. Each day we pray the prayer, we meditate upon it, and we use it as a call to action. Here is the Prayer of St. Francis:

> *Lord, make me an instrument of your peace;*
> *where there is hatred, let me sow love;*
> *where there is injury, pardon;*
> *where there is doubt, faith;*
> *where there is despair, hope;*
> *where there is darkness, light;*
> *and where there is sadness, joy.*
>
> *O Divine Master,*
> *grant that I may not so much seek*
> *to be consoled as to console;*
> *to be understood, as to understand;*
> *to be loved, as to love;*
> *for it is in giving that we receive,*
> *it is in pardoning that we are pardoned,*
> *and it is in dying that we are born to Eternal Life.*

I've prayed the Prayer of St. Francis more than any other prayer. Avanti, my first spiritual mentor, introduced me to it when I was 19 years old, and I immediately included it in my daily spiritual practice. It was the first prayer that truly inspired me. Each time I prayed it, I felt hope. I believed that if I kept praying this prayer, I'd eventually find my purpose. I did not imagine, back then, that I'd visit Assisi one day and lead pilgrimages based upon this prayer. It's truly amazing what miracles the power of prayer can perform when you are open to it.

Praying a prayer, like the Prayer of St. Francis, activates the necessary inspiration and grace you need to live your purpose. To begin with, I used it as a simple petition prayer: *Lord, make me an instrument.* When I began to have experiences of being used as an instrument—when writing books, giving talks, mentoring people, being a friend—it became a prayer of gratitude: *Thank you, God, for using me as an instrument.* Over time, the prayer can become a holy affirmation for living your purpose on earth that is to bring light, faith, pardon, hope, joy, and love.

Francesco would often pray long into the night. One of his favorite prayers was "Who are you, Lord my God, and who am I?" This prayer was also his living question. He used it to take a pilgrimage from self to Self, to break free from the chains of narrow self and experience his soul's immensity. "I am who I am in the eyes of God. Nothing more, nothing less," said Francesco. He prayed so as to build his spiritual resilience, to overcome obstacles, to feel God's presence, to experience grace, and to connect with his higher purpose.

Clare of Assisi used prayer as a medium to tune in to the spiritual intelligence of the universe. For Clare, the purpose of prayer was to experience a *metanoia*—a holy shift in her psychology from fear to love. "God is love," she affirmed continually. Clare wanted to think the thoughts of God. "God is the light with which I see," she proclaimed. She taught those who came to her how to use prayer to experience divine inspiration and everyday grace. She said,

> *Place your mind before the mirror of eternity.*
> *Place your soul in the brilliance of glory!*
> *Place your heart in the figure of the divine substance!*
> *And transform your whole being into*
> *the image of the Godhead Itself*
> *through contemplation!*

The Prayer of St. Francis is a metanoia prayer that helps you give birth to your most creative Self. The most important line of the prayer is "it is in dying that we are born to Eternal Life." Remember the grain of wheat parable—a single grain of wheat must fall into the earth and die if it is to bear much fruit. To live your higher purpose, you must surrender to something greater than your ego. One way to do this is to make your ego into an instrument that is willing to serve a greater glory and universal inspiration.

I believe that the highest purpose of prayer is to help you become both fully human and fully divine. The Greeks call this fullness of living *anthropos*. A prayerful life helps you grow from a Godseed into someone who knows they have been planted here on earth for a higher purpose. Prayer helps you realize that you are what you are praying for. "We should seek not so much to pray but to become prayer," said Francesco. The highest purpose of prayer is to express yourself fully and thereby take your place in the greater story of creation.

> *"I am a hole in a flute that the Christ's breath moves through — listen to the music."*
>
> — Hafiz

On our pilgrimages, I encourage you to find a spiritual symbol or totem that helps you remember who you are and live your purpose. It might be a prayer, like the Prayer of St. Francis, or a mantra, a song, a psalm, a hymn, a proverb, or a poem. It might be a picture of Jesus or Buddha, or a painting of a butterfly or a rainbow. It might be a golden thread you wear on your wrist, or a rose quartz angel that stands on your bedside table. It might be a rose in your garden that you prune in late winter and that blossoms again in spring.

BRINGING THE LOVE

> *We become what we love and who we love shapes what we become.*
>
> **— Clare of Assisi**

One of my favorite experiences of the Assisi pilgrimage is a visit to the St. Francis Hermitage of Carceri. The Hermitage is built into the slopes of Mount Subasio and is surrounded by an ancient forest, a deep gorge, and nature trails. Francesco and his first followers came here to meditate. This is also where Francesco gave his famous sermon to the birds, telling them that "our Creator loves you dearly" and encouraging them to praise God with "every beat of your wings and every note of your songs." The birds listened tentatively to Francesco and "did bend their heads reverently towards the earth."[2]

The Hermitage is the perfect place to contemplate Francesco's love for the natural world. He believed that Jesus Christ's commandment to love one another included loving all of God's creatures. In Thomas of Celano's biography of Francesco, he wrote, "He was moved and fascinated by the working of bees and would often spend a day in prayer praising them and other industrious creatures of the Lord. In fact, filled with the Spirit of God, as Saint Francis was, he did not cease to glorify, praise and bless the Creator and Lord of all in all God's elements and creatures."[3]

Clare of Assisi taught her followers, "We are to become vessels of God's compassionate love for others." She believed, like Francesco did, that humanity's great work is to fulfill the Great Commandment to love one another and all of God's creatures. She shared Francesco's boundless love for Mother Nature, Brother Sun, Sister Moon, Brother Wolf, and Sister Lark. By making ourselves instruments of love, we access universal inspiration, we play a part in the big story of creation, and we live our highest purpose.[4]

We spend a long afternoon at the Hermitage of Carceri. I like to sit on a big rock in the middle of the forest, just behind the oratory. I take the first hour or so in silence, and after that I scribble down as many poems as time allows. My first book of poetry, *Finding Love Everywhere*, features 67½ wisdom poems to help you be the love you are looking for. The first poem of the collection is called "Bring Love." I wrote it at the Hermitage, and it is dedicated to Francesco and Clare. Here is "Bring Love."[5]

Good news!
I just got my invite, and I trust
you did too.
The world is throwing a party
again tonight.
Planets and stars will hang like
bunting from the ceiling.

Bees will bring honey.
Cows and goats will bring milk.
Flowers will bring perfume.
And each worm will bring a doily
made of silk.

Vegetables and minerals will sit
on every table.
Grapes will make wine.
Whales will recite sonnets from
the deep.
And dolphins will leap and play
And have a great time.

The wind and trees will make
music.
Birds, like the lark and dove,
will sing.
All God's creatures will bring a
little something.
And humans will bring love.

THE DEATH OF NORMAL

It was New Year's Eve, the last day of 2019, and we were about to witness the death of normal. People all around the world were full of cheer, busy observing their new year traditions, and looking forward with hope and optimism to the start of a new year and a new decade. My family and I were in Findhorn, Scotland. At the stroke of midnight, we raised our glasses and sang "Auld Lang Syne." None of us had noticed the news story earlier that day about a report from the Wuhan Municipal Health Commission, in China, of a small cluster of cases of a pneumonia-like illness.

The year 2020 had been heralded by thought leaders and elders as a make-or-break year in which we must come together to envision a better future for the world. The dominant metaphor for 2020 was 20/20 vision, the term used by optometrists for visual acuity and clear perception. I was looking forward to participating in some exciting 2020 initiatives around the world on climate change, spirituality, business, mental health, and education. We were busy reimagining the future, but none of us was ready for what happened next.

It all happened so fast. On January 23, Wuhan was quarantined by the government of the People's Republic of China. It was just a precaution, apparently. Eight days later, on January 31, the World Health Organization (WHO) issued a Global Health

Emergency and asked for solidarity and cooperation while the matter was being investigated further. On February 11, WHO officially named the virus severe acute respiratory syndrome coronavirus 2 (SARS-CoV-2) and the disease it causes as coronavirus disease 2019 (COVID-19). One month later, WHO declared COVID-19 a pandemic.

We had been hit between the eyes by a global medical emergency. What had started out as a foreign news story was now world news. COVID-19 wasn't just happening somewhere else in the world; it was everywhere. No one could afford to look away. This wasn't happening to someone else; we were all involved. We had to refocus our lives, but it wasn't easy. The news headlines were scary and at times contradictory and misleading. Conspiracy theories went viral. The blind were leading the blind. Many experts were voicing their opinions, but who knew what was really going on?

We were witnessing the death of normal, and I remember feeling overwhelmed and confused. What I wanted were some reliable *facts*. Digging around for trusted sources of information was difficult and perplexing. The media was a mixed bag of great reporting and fearmongering. On March 18, the WHO issued a statement entitled "Mental health and psychosocial considerations during the COVID-19 Outbreak," in which it recommended that we "minimize watching, reading or listening to news about COVID-19."[1]

> *"When you feel your life's too hard, just go have a talk with God."*
>
> — Stevie Wonder

The world went into lockdown. All our plans were put on hold. Suddenly hospitals were at capacity, and I was praying for two close friends who were fighting for their lives on ventilators with COVID-19. Schools were shut down, and Hollie and I were now homeschooling our children. The stock market crashed. Many of my friends were facing bankruptcy. My own income for the next year disappeared overnight. We were social distancing and missing our loved ones terribly. We were all in shock and in mourning. Nothing was certain anymore.

When I don't know what to do, the one thing I always do is commit more fully to my spiritual practice. Making time to stop and think, to do some inner listening, and to pray for guidance works well for me. One morning St. Francis of Assisi appeared to me in my meditation. *What advice would St. Francis offer about the COVID-19 pandemic?* I wondered. He is the patron saint of ecology, after all. That's when I got the idea to write a letter to Sister COVID. I'm pretty sure St. Francis would have addressed the virus as Sister COVID.

So I started to write a letter to COVID-19. In writing it I was exploring what kind of a relationship I wanted to have with this virus. A basic principle of medicine is *make sure the treatment doesn't kill the patient.* In other words, make sure your response to a condition isn't more damaging than the condition itself. What started out as a letter turned into a poem. No surprise there, really. At the time, I was on the final round of edits for my book of poetry, *Finding Love Everywhere.*

I called the poem "Spread the Love," and I published it in my newsletter on March 17, 2020. Here it is.

Dear Coronavirus,
I am waking up to a new world today.
Your presence has disturbed me
from my sleep.

You have kicked us out of normal.
We cannot keep on living the way
we were.

Wives, husbands, brothers, sisters,
have lost their loves and lives
to you.

What more will you take from us?
Our minds? Our hearts? Our love?
Too?

Very well then, I will accept your
terrible invitation, dear
coronavirus.

I, for one, will not squander this
hour of pain.
I'm going back to the drawing board.
With 2020 vision, I will live
with imagination.

I've been self-isolating for way too
long—cut off from reality by a
narrow self.

Self is not a singularity;
SELF is plural!

This morning, the sun also rises
as I come out of hiding.

I ask my heart—which is where
God lives—how I can start to
widen my circle of love.

I see the bigger picture now.
I'm all signed up and
I'm good to go.

I know what my work is.
I am here to spread
the love.

After I wrote "Spread the Love," I used it as a centering practice to help me think about how I could best respond to COVID-19. I asked myself questions like *What is my part in this?* and *How can I be useful?* and *How can I serve?* I'm not a medical doctor. I'm not a virologist. I'm not a director of public health. I had to think about the skills and talents that I did have, the resources and contacts that I had access to, and the most powerful actions I could take as fast as possible to help out and be of service.

The first thing I did was to reach out to both Reid Tracy, the CEO of Hay House, and Margarete Nielsen, the COO of Hay House. My idea was to help Hay House create an online library of free resources, with contributions from all the authors, to support everyone in their physical, mental, and spiritual well-being. I also offered to host a weekly live class called Spread the Love on Louise Hay's Facebook page. Louise's work began during the HIV/AIDS pandemic in the 1980s, and I was convinced that her teachings would be a great comfort and inspiration now. More than 50,000 people from over 50 countries tuned in for the first live class.

I also called up my friend Michael Neill and suggested we cohost a Spiritual Resilience Mastermind journey for the people we

> *"To find your purpose, ask, 'How may I serve?'"*
>
> — Wayne Dyer

coach and mentor. We talked about the purpose of the Mastermind and came up with three main aims for it: 1) Better Together—creating a community of support to help each other stay on purpose in challenging times; 2) Reimagining the Future—working with disruption so as to innovate and create something better; and 3) Death of Normal—creating a "new normal" and a "better normal" so as to emerge from the pandemic wiser, happier, and more on purpose than before.

A NEW LANGUAGE

Michael Neill and I began our Spiritual Resilience Mastermind by talking about the power of conversation. I told the story of how I created a business card for myself soon after I set up Success Intelligence Ltd. It was a white card, with words in black ink and a simple font. There wasn't a logo or design, just three lines of text. Line 1: Robert Holden, line 2: *Conversationalist*, line 3: my phone number. I didn't put my e-mail address on it. I believe we are all called to be conversationalists. The ability to hold a meaningful conversation about what matters most is the great work of our time.

In our first class, we drew up some rules of conversation to help each other be seen and heard, feel safe and respected, and be fully engaged and present. I talked about the power of language, how our use of words can make or break a conversation, and how the quality of listening influences the quality of speaking. I also talked about how we can use metaphors in conversation to explore the deeper meaning and higher purpose of our lives. I asked everyone this question: *What is the most meaningful metaphor you are working with in your relationship with COVID-19?*

> *"Speak a new language so that the world will be a new world."*
>
> — Rumi

The dominant metaphor used by world leaders with COVID-19 is that we are at war with an invisible enemy. "We are at war with a virus—and not winning it," declared UN Secretary-General Antonio Guterres at a G20 virtual summit on the COVID-19 pandemic on March 26, 2020. After that, President Trump gave himself a new title of "wartime president," Xi Jinping signalled a "people's war," and Boris Johnson told us he was now leading a "wartime government." The war metaphor steered the narrative toward "battle plans," "war campaigns," "lockdowns," "frontline workers," and being "under siege," and made for hostile talk between nations.

The upside of using a war metaphor is that it sounds a siren to wake everyone up, it creates urgency, and it galvanizes a fast response. The downside is that a war metaphor turns everything into a game of soldiers and enemies, and not all problems can be solved with a war mentality. You can't bomb a virus. Viruses are not terrorists. Viruses aren't trying to attack you. Your body is already a home to over 380 trillion viruses in its virome. Also, too much talk of war prevents us from learning about our so-called "enemy" and why it is here in the first place.

A war metaphor can encourage psychological traits like courage, teamwork, and sacrifice, but it doesn't do much for traits like openness, humility, and a willingness to learn. Working with new metaphors can help broaden and build our thinking and our conversations. For example, *let's not go to war; let's go to school.* Instead of defeating COVID-19 and labeling it as a "zombie-killer," let's learn from it. And while we're at it, let's learn about how our immune system works and how we can build a healthier society. With this learning metaphor, new conversations arise, and also new questions to live with, like *What is COVID-19 teaching us?*

The metaphor I've used for COVID-19 is the X-ray metaphor. As we all know, an X-ray enables you to look inside yourself. It helps diagnose maladies you can't see otherwise, like bone fractures, heart conditions, lung problems, and cancers. An X-ray also shows you where you are in good health and how well healing is progressing. I think the COVID-19 pandemic has been like a giant X-ray that is making us look within ourselves, at our society, and at the world we are making.

What has your COVID-19 X-ray shown you? On a personal level, how is your health, your lifestyle, your relationships, your happiness levels, and your sense of purpose? On a society level and a global level, economic inequality, systemic racism, and gender discrimination have been exposed for all to see. Unsustainable modern farming practices, unjust social welfare policies, the profit-led health industry, and global business pollution—with just 100 companies producing over 70 percent of global emissions—have all been exposed by the COVID-19 X-ray.

Another helpful metaphor for COVID-19 is from Suzanna Arundhati Roy, the author of the novel *The God of Small Things*. On April 3, 2020, Suzanna's article "The Pandemic Is a Portal" was published in the *Financial Times*. It's a thought-provoking piece that encourages us to take the conversation deeper, to explore new narratives, and to create a new and better normal. In conclusion, she writes,

> Historically, pandemics have forced humans to break with the past and imagine their world anew. This one is no different. It is a portal, a gateway between one world and the next.
>
> We can choose to walk through it, dragging the carcasses of our prejudice and hatred, our avarice, our data banks and dead ideas, our dead rivers and smoky skies behind us. Or we can walk through lightly, with little luggage, ready to imagine another world. And ready to fight for it.[2]

A DEEPER MEANING

COVID-19 stopped the world. This was an involuntary stop for all of us. No commute to work. No school run. No holidays. No international travel. No going anywhere. This was our moment to stop and think. It was a time for calculative and meditative thinking, as Heidegger put it. Michael Neill and I had begun our Spiritual Resilience Mastermind by looking at the metaphors and narratives. Next, we worked on our thinking to investigate the possible deeper meaning and higher purpose of the pandemic.

What is the meaning of the COVID-19 pandemic? This was the question I put on the table for our Mastermind group. Joseph

Campbell said, "Life has no meaning. Each of us has meaning and we bring it to life." The meaning you give to the events of your life influences greatly how you experience them and what you choose to do next. To explore how we create meaning in our lives, I shared with our Mastermind group my experience of losing my dad and what I did with that.

My father died a few days after my twenty-fifth birthday. I'd been mourning the loss of my father for a long time before his death. His alcoholism and nomadic life had already taken him away from me. Over the years I had lost my "hero Dad," my "fun Dad," my "sports Dad," my "strong Dad," and my "best-friend Dad." I'd grieved his demise for so long that I couldn't cry at his funeral. I tried to make myself cry, but I was not able to. Now that Dad was dead, I couldn't save him anymore, and this left a big hole my life.

> *"Every problem has a purpose."*
> —Rick Warren

For a long time after my dad's death, the question I lived with was *What meaning will I give to my dad's life and death?* I believed I had failed my dad because I did not save him. I was angry at God for not saving him. I was bitter at life and with my lot. After much inner work, I decided that my best option was to use my dad's life as a teaching and to learn the lessons from our time together. Most of all, I wanted to honor his life, and the best way to do that was by living my life fully.

We are meaning makers. Life happens, and then we give a meaning to what just happened. Hopefully, the meaning we bring to our life events—especially the scary and painful ones—will help us be brave, find a reason to keep going, and say yes to our life. For many of us, the COVID-19 pandemic meant we now had a chance to rethink our lives, hit the reset button, remember what is important, reboot our aspirations, and reengage with life in a more meaningful and fulfilling way.

Another question we examined on the Spiritual Resilience Mastermind was *What purpose will you give to the COVID-19 pandemic?* Early in the pandemic, I noticed how my friends and clients who already had a strong sense of purpose were using the pandemic as an opportunity to strengthen their commitment to their purpose. Along with the rest of us, they were being forced to adapt, diversify, cope with losses, and reinvent how they worked and lived. They were suffering too, but staying on purpose gave them the energy and resilience to rise to the occasion. Their purpose sustained them in their time of need.

I also noticed that many people were using the COVID-19 pandemic as an invitation to start questioning their purpose and live a more purpose-centered life. People everywhere were taking online courses, investing in retraining, learning to meditate, getting fit again, painting on canvases, reading novels, growing their gardens, re-wilding their neighborhoods, joining support groups, and participating in angel projects, and were determined to emerge from the pandemic in a positive way.

A BETTER NORMAL

Initially, we hoped that COVID-19 would come and go quickly so we could get back to normal. A short war campaign with a lockdown and a couple of jabs should kill off this virus by Christmas, right? But COVID-19 is still with us, and the healing is slow, and this is not a war. There is a larger story here. The virus is not the main protagonist; we are. It's not only about what the virus decides to do next; it's about what you and I, and humanity, decide to do. Yes, we will get through it, but will we grow through it? The dramatic question at the heart of this larger story is *What will humanity learn from this? And how will we grow?*

The death of normal must happen every now and then if we are to keep on evolving and create something better. The hero will get kicked out of ordinary, as Joseph Campbell put it. In every story there is an inciting incident that means we must leave the shire and set out on a new journey. Normal is not the end of the story. We are not meant to be preserved and pickled in a jar of normal. Normal is what we experience for a while before another new beginning.

"We long to return to normal, but normal led to this," wrote Ed Yong, a science journalist, in his article "How the Pandemic Defeated America," published in *The Atlantic*. He went on, "To avert the future pandemics we know are coming, we MUST grapple with all the ways normal failed us. We have to build something better."[3] The COVID-19 virus is not a terrorist; it's a messenger. And we will experience either victory or defeat depending on what we learn and how we grow.

"Nothing could be worse than a return to normality," wrote Suzanna Arundhati Roy in her piece for the *Financial Times*. She went on, "Our minds are still racing back and forth, longing for a return to 'normality,' trying to stitch our future to our past and refusing to acknowledge the rupture. But the rupture exists. And in the midst of this terrible despair, it offers us a chance to rethink the doomsday machine we have built for ourselves."[4]

Soon after the outbreak of COVID-19, I interviewed Pema Chödrön, the American Buddhist nun, for our Spiritual Resilience Mastermind, on her new book *Welcoming the Unwelcome: Wholehearted Living in a Brokenhearted World*. I began by acknowledging with Pema how all her books have a prophetic quality about them. She has her finger on the cosmic pulse, and she always manages to offer relevant and timely spiritual direction for the human soul in her writings. In her classic book *When Things Fall Apart: Heart Advice for Difficult Times*, she wrote,

> To be fully alive, fully human and completely awake is to be continually thrown out of the nest. To live fully is to be always in no-man's land, to experience each moment as completely new and fresh. To live is to be willing to die over and over again.[5]

Pema and I talked about how COVID-19 is a powerful teacher because it reminds us that life is transient and that normal is never normal for very long. In *Welcoming the Unwelcome*, she wrote,

"Every challenge presents an opportunity for spiritual growth, whether it's a small irritation or when everything as you've known it falls apart." In our conversation, Pema told me, "Nothing goes away until it has taught you what you need to know."

It's time for a new normal. The old normal was not reality. It had a short history, and it wasn't meant to last. The old normal was only good for 1 percent of the human population, leaving 99 percent of us out in the cold. The old normal was out of balance, and it wreaked devastation upon the natural world. The new rally cry on social media is *#Let's not go back to normal!* There are so many good things that could happen on our planet that haven't happened yet. Our purpose, both individual and shared, is to make these things happen.

Creating a better normal is the historical mission of our times. It's how we marry our personal purpose with the shared purpose of humanity and the higher purpose of creation. In our Spiritual Resilience Mastermind journey, the challenge we set everyone was this: *What is the better normal that I want to contribute to?* Your answer to this question is where your purpose lies. Here is your activism. Here is your great work. Here is the conversation that needs you. Ask yourself then, *What is my part in the better normal? What will I take responsibility for? How will I spread the love?*

IN A DARK PLACE

When I first met Liz, she was in the middle of a dark night of the soul. It was our mutual friend Anna, who had recently come through her own dark night, who suggested to Liz that a conversation with me might help. We met at my home, and Liz told me her story. "I've lost all sense of direction, and I don't know how to move forward," she said. Liz was in a dark place, feeling downcast and despondent, and she had absolutely no idea about the wonderful future that was before her.

Liz was a TV producer who had enjoyed a successful and busy career working on many drama series for the BBC. She was energetic and resourceful and had managed to juggle her career with raising her two young boys as a single parent. After her father's death, Liz also cared for her mother, who had dementia. And following a change at the BBC, Liz had become a freelance producer, which meant that instead of being assigned new projects, she now had to go out and find the projects herself. This was a new world, and it made Liz question the real purpose of her work.

In our first few sessions, Liz and I talked about the origins and purpose of the dark night of the soul. The phrase is commonly attributed to the 16th-century Spanish mystic St. John of the Cross, who wrote an untitled poem about a dark night that later acquired the title "Dark Night of the Soul." The poem is the story of a spiritual journey our soul takes through a dark night to experience "a sweet and delicious life with God."[1]

Everyone experiences a dark night of the soul in their lifetime, and some of us more than one. The dark night is triggered most often by a traumatic life event like a divorce, a bereavement, a job loss, or an illness, but it doesn't always happen that way. A dark night of the soul can happen after completing a big work project, after returning home from a meaningful journey, or after a great victory and success. At other times, a dark night of the soul appears when one chapter of life is ending and the next chapter has yet to begin.

Liz's dark night of the soul descended upon her around the time of her forty-second birthday. According to Rudolf Steiner's biography work, Liz was at the start of a new seven-year cycle, from 42 to 49, in which your inner work is to fathom the deeper meaning of your life, follow the bigger plan, and live your higher purpose. Likewise, Carl Jung wrote about "a night-sea journey" that we take in our midlife, often in our forties, in which we go through a passage of darkness that takes us from our former life into a much greater life.

> *"When we no longer know which way to go, we have come to our real journey."*
>
> — Wendell Berry

"I feel like a has-been whose life is over," Liz told me. My first task was to reassure Liz that what she was experiencing was not a mental illness, or a mistake, or a failure; but rather a rite of passage that was transitioning her from one life stage to the next. Thomas Moore, in his excellent book *Dark Nights of the Soul: A Guide to Finding Your Way Through Life's Ordeals*, describes the dark night as "a profound initiation into a realm that nothing in the culture, so preoccupied with external concerns and material success, prepares you for."[2]

A dark night of the soul is like a second puberty, with the same amount of awkwardness and uncertainty as the first time. It can be a hugely disorientating and painful time that feels like it will never end. Commonly, we experience a sense of feeling lost. We have little or no idea about our future and what is going to happen next. We cannot see a light at the end of the tunnel. We are "lost in oblivion," as St. John of the Cross says in his poem on the dark night.

Dante Alighieri, the medieval Italian poet and philosopher, also addressed this sense of being lost in his epic poem *The Divine Comedy*, which charts the soul's journey to God and eternal life.[3] The journey is in three parts: *Inferno* (Hell), *Purgatorio* (Purgatory), and *Paradiso* (Paradise). It is a hero journey, with a road of trials. Dante feels lost at each stage, but he discovers Supernatural Aid in the form of Virgil, the Roman poet, who offers reason; Beatrice, who offers divine revelation, and St. Bernard of Clairvaux, who offers spiritual vision. His epic journey begins with these three lines:

Midway upon the journey of our life
I found myself within a forest dark,
For the straightforward pathway had been lost.

During the dark night of the soul, you must allow yourself to be lost. When you admit that you are lost, you can accept that your ego-guidance system cannot take you any further. Now you can stop trying to navigate your life on your own. Here is your opportunity to be guided by a power greater than your ego. "It is an old and ironic habit of human beings to run faster when we have lost our way," observed Rollo May, the American psychologist and colleague of Victor Frankl. This is the temptation, for sure, but when you stop and do the inner listening, you will be guided in delightful and surprising ways into your new life.

Liz made a commitment to deepen her spiritual practice. She became a student of *A Course in Miracles*. She said a hearty YES to living a more guided life. Gradually she emerged from her dark night of the soul ready to meet her destiny. She showed up with a new sense of purpose, a determination to follow her joy, and a promise to herself only to accept work that she loved. One day Liz got an intuitive hit to call Frank McGuinness, a writer whom she had worked with on her first series as a producer. "I can't believe you called!" said Frank, who had been trying to find a way to contact Liz with an offer of an exciting piece of work.

> *"When everything is lost, and all seems darkness, then comes the new life and all that is needed."*
>
> — Joseph Campbell

One thing led to another, as it often does, and Liz was next asked to produce her first feature film, *From Time to Time*, written by Julian Fellowes and staring Maggie Smith and Hugh Bonneville.[4] Soon after that, Julian Fellows sent Liz a script he'd been working on for a new historical drama series set in England the day after the sinking of the RMS *Titanic* in April 1912. It was called *Downton Abbey*. Liz has worked on *Downton Abbey* ever since, producing all six *Downton* series and both *Downton* movies. Visiting Liz on set is always great fun, and it is a joy to watch her in her element, living her purpose, and doing the work she loves.

A TIME TO DIE

It was springtime, and Hollie and I and our daughter, Bo, who had just turned two years old, were living in New York for a few months. My cousin Juliet had kindly loaned her apartment to us. We were situated near Columbus Circle overlooking Central Park. We were having a great adventure, exploring the city, making new friends, and doing fun things together. The joys of spring were everywhere, but inside myself I was struggling. Nothing was wrong with my life; I just didn't feel right.

When Hollie asked me to describe what I was feeling, I told her, "Spring is here, but I'm still in winter." I felt like I was a hollow tree, with bare branches and no signs of new growth. A bleak midwinter was upon my heart. I was in the middle of a very happy time, but I was feeling like a piece of dead wood. I couldn't shake off the deadness inside, no matter how hard I tried. Hollie asked me to get some physical tests, just to make sure there was nothing terminal. I knew I wasn't dying, but I felt like something was dying inside me.

In the week before Easter, I experienced a sequence of events over three days that I still marvel at. On the first day, I got a call from a friend who had an unusual offer for me. She wanted to gift me a tarot card reading for later that day. She had booked her appointment weeks earlier but wasn't able to go now due to a work commitment. My first thought was that Hollie might like to go, but then I had the strongest feeling that I should say yes for me. So I gratefully accepted, and after having lunch with Hollie and Bo, I tootled off for my tarot card reading.

My tarot reader was a woman in her 50s, and she wore designer jeans, a blouse, a pearl necklace, and dark blue jacket. She didn't have a crystal ball, rainbow candles, or floaty scarfs, but I will tell you that she had the presence of an oracle. Her manner was very matter-of-fact, and she started the reading as soon as I sat down. The first thing she said was, "I see you are experiencing a dark night of the soul." *How could she see that?* I wondered. She shuffled her cards, and the first card she pulled was the Death card. "Not surprising!" she said.

The Death card had on it a skeleton in black armor riding a white horse over a dead king. "Don't worry; you're not going to die! It's not your time yet, and you still have work to do," she told me. Listening to her, I immediately recalled the incident I told you about in Part I when I was nine years old and nearly fell to my death, and I heard a voice tell me, "It's not your time yet."

"Completion! The Death card means completion!" explained my tarot reader. She then asked me if I had completed a big project recently. I told her I had just finished writing a book called *Be Happy*, and that I was about to go on a book tour. "Okay, this is why you are feeling dead inside," she told me. "Don't worry; your life force will return, but not yet," she said. She also told me that the Death card is about letting go of the past. "You must let the past go. You can only live your purpose in the present," she told me.

On the second day, I met up with Patty Gift, my editor at Hay House. We had brunch at the City Bakery, one of our favorite meeting spots. Patty was in the middle of decluttering her apartment after returning from a Buddhist retreat. "Do you have this book already? It's a spare, and I wondered if you might like it," she said, handing me a copy of *The Tibetan Book of Living and Dying*. This led to a deep and meaningful conversation about death and dying over a cappuccino and one of the bakery's famously large chocolate cookies.

The Tibetan Book of Living and Dying was heralded as a spiritual classic immediately after its publication in 1992. It was written by Sogyal Rinpoche, with the help of Andrew Harvey and Patrick Gaffney, and it explores the meaning of life. In Tibetan Buddhism, life and death are seen as one whole, in which death is always the beginning of a new chapter of life. Rinpoche writes,

> Normally we do not like to think about death. We would rather think about life. Why reflect on death? When you start preparing for death you soon realize that you must look into your life now . . . and come to face the truth of your self. Death is like a mirror in which the true meaning of life is reflected.[5]

Rinpoche observed that in the West we try to avoid death by not thinking about it. He's right. I remember giving a keynote talk on Success Intelligence for IBM at their headquarters in Yorktown Heights, New York. In it, I talked about our Busy Generation and how the real purpose of our life can get lost in too much busyness. I talked about chronic busyness, diversionary busyness, and terminal busyness. One of my PowerPoint slides read, "Busy, busy, busy, busy, busy . . . dead!" When I put this slide up, the word "dead" was missing. Afterward the HR director told me he had removed the word because he thought it sounded too negative.

Over a second order of cappuccino and cookies, Patty and I carried on talking about the relationship between dying and living. I shared with her about my tarot reading and the feeling I had that something was dying in me. "Every author dies a death when writing a book," she told me. The person who starts writing the book at Chapter 1 is not the same person by the time he or she writes the final chapter. When you take a journey, it changes you. Death allows for that change to happen. It also prepares you for your next journey.

Patty told me that in Tibetan Buddhism, you are encouraged to meditate upon your death. In her recent Buddhist retreat, her teacher had encouraged her to see that death is everywhere and is happening all the time. A question that arises from this awareness is *Knowing I will die, how shall I live?* In the *Tibetan Book of Living and Dying*, Sogyal Rinpoche wrote, "Living with the immediacy of death helps you sort out your priorities in life. It helps you to live a less trivial life." He also observed that "life is nothing but a continuing dance of birth and death, a dance of change."

On the third day, I received a package in the mail. It was a birthday present from my friend Elmer, a book called *I Hope You Die Soon* by Richard Sylvester. *Death really is everywhere*, I thought. It's a book about letting go of your ego's illusory ideas about itself (e.g., "I am separate from creation" and "I am too small to matter") so you can have a greater experience of being and living. One of its key messages is that you must let go of your self-image—and die to your old sense of self—if you want to keep growing and become more of who you really are.[6]

That night I went to the Barrymore Theatre along with Lizzie, my sister-in-law, to see a play called *Exit the King* by Eugène Ionesco.[7] I had no idea what the play was about. My cousin Juliet had highly recommended I get tickets. The play opens with King Berenger, then played by Geoffrey Rush, sitting on his throne in a throne room that is vaguely dilapidated and vaguely Gothic. Queen Marguerite, played by Susan Sarandon, informs the king, "You're going to die in an hour and a half, you're going to die at the end of the play."

Over the next 90 minutes, we watch King Berenger deny, resist, fight, and surrender to his own death. The play is layered with meaning. The motif of three days makes an appearance. The king's doctor tells him, "Your Majesty, several decades or even three days ago, your empire was flourishing. In three days, you've lost all the wars you won. And those you lost, you've lost again." Apparently, King Berenger has been alive for over 400 years, and he has not once contemplated the meaning of life or his higher purpose.

Queen Marguerite sees that time is ticking. Looking at her watch, she tells the king, in a matter-of-fact way, "In one hour and twenty-five minutes, you're going to die." Further into the play, with only an hour to go, the doctor tells King Berenger that it's not too late to live a well-lived life. He says, "A well-spent hour's better than whole centuries of neglect and failure. Five minutes are enough, ten fully conscious seconds are enough."

In the end, Queen Marguerite is by her king's side. She has no fear of death, for she knows who she is. Geoffrey Rush and Susan Sarandon play out the last scene that is full of tenderness and mercy. The queen escorts her king to his death. "This you is not the real you. It's an odd collection of bits and pieces," she assures him. Finally, as the stage fades to total darkness, she tells her king, "Now you can take your place."

This was the most thrilling night of theater. Surely, every person was changed by what they had experienced that night. We had all witnessed a death, and now it was time for us to take our place too. Nine years later, a production of *Exit the King* was put on at the National Theatre in London, directed by Patrick Marber and with Rhys Ifans as King Berenger. I bought plenty of tickets for several performances. "Come and die!" I told my family and friends. "You won't be sorry. Just come and die!"

THE THREE DAYS

> *Very truly, I tell you, unless a grain of wheat*
> *falls into the earth and dies, it remains just a*
> *single grain; but if it dies, it bears much fruit.*
>
> — John 12:24–26

At Easter time I like to host a talk or a workshop that explores the deeper meaning of the Easter journey and how it relates directly to our lives today. Each year I offer a mix of storytelling, meditations, poetry, and music to help us take the Easter journey for ourselves. Hollie and I often co-present together, and we also call upon our friends, like Liz, to make an offering. The Easter journey is not just a fable for ancient times; its symbolism and significance are timeless and essential for navigating the dark night of the soul that our world is now in.

The Easter journey takes place over three days, which is a recurring motif in Christian mysticism. In fact, there are more than 20 three-day journeys mentioned in the Bible. For example, Paul on the road to Damascus is blinded for three days; Jonah is swallowed and remains inside a whale for three days; and Moses leads an exodus from Egypt over "a distance of three days" to a land flowing with milk and honey. These three days are best understood as three stages, and they match the three stages of the hero journey that are Departure, Initiation, and Return.

Day One

On the first day, or stage one, of the Easter journey, a death is experienced. This is the day that Jesus dies. For us, we also experience a death. It may be the physical death of someone who means the world to you, like a parent, a child, a friend, an elder, or an inspirational figure. Or you may experience a metaphorical death due to the end of a relationship, a serious illness, a redundancy, children leaving the nest, a retirement, or the death of normal due to an ecological disaster, the COVID-19 pandemic, a war, or some other big life event. Suddenly day has turned to night.

In this first stage of the Easter journey, you are dying to your old self and your old life. Essentially, you are experiencing an ego-death, which Carl Jung described as a "psychic death." Due to a life event, you are suddenly labeled "widow," "divorcee," "unemployed," "cancer patient," "disabled," "diabetic," or "retired." Or perhaps you've turned 30 years old and are grieving because you've convinced yourself that you are now well and truly over the hill. The point is that something has happened that means you can no longer identify fully with your old self-image. The question you must live with now is *Who am I without my old self-image?*

Your ego-death feels fatal, but the real you does not die. St. Paul, in Corinthians, has words of assurance for us. He says, "I am telling you something that has been a secret. We are not all going to die, but we shall all be changed."[8] This terrible death you are experiencing is a change. "This you is not the real you," Queen Marguerite told King Berenger. Joseph Campbell, in his telling of the hero journey, often described our ego-death as the shedding of a skin. He quoted Nietzsche, who observed, "The snake that cannot shed its skin must perish."

Day Two

On the second day, or stage two, of the Easter journey, you enter the darkness. This is the day that Jesus descends into the underworld. What happens here is a mystery because it happens in the dark. This darkness is disorienting. We lose our sense of direction. We are suspended in what Mary Oliver described as "the sprawling darkness of *not knowing*." To our physical senses, it seems that nothing is happening and that there is no way out. We must be vigilant, though, for there is more to this darkness than meets the eye.

There is a purpose to this darkness. Something is developing here in the dark, though you know not what it is. The poet Rilke confessed a great love for the darkness. "I have faith in nights," he said. Instead of resisting the darkness, he would dialogue with the darkness, "You, darkness, of whom I am born—I love you more than the flame / that limits the world," he wrote. And in his poem "Let This Darkness Be a Bell Tower," he gives us counsel on how to meet the darkness. He tells us,

Quiet friend who has come so far,
feel how your breathing makes more space around you.
Let this darkness be a bell tower
and you the bell. As you ring,
what batters you becomes your strength.[9]

Here, in this dazzling darkness, we are learning to see with a new set of eyes. Soon we will come out of this darkness, and we will be guided by a light that comes not from outside ourselves but that shines within. Here, in the depths of darkness, "the vain emptiness of narrow self is filled with the fire of the cosmic Word," says Rudolph Steiner. This darkness is not death; it is a womb. It is a fruitful darkness.[10] It is a sweet darkness.[11] It is a holy darkness.[12] Here, in the darkness, your old self-image disappears, and a new sense of self is about to emerge.

Day Three

On the third day, or stage three, of the Easter journey you experience resurrection or rebirth. This is the day when Jesus is resurrected fully into the Christ Consciousness. For us, it is time to realize our I AM, which is the Christ that lives in all of us. Thomas Moore, in *Dark Nights of the Soul*, writes,

> Perhaps the dark night comes upon you from inside or outside to wake you up, to stir you and steer you toward a new life. I believe this is the message of most religions, and certainly it is the gist of Christianity and Buddhism. Your dark night may be a *bardo*, a period of apparent lifelessness that precedes a new birth of meaning. Maybe your dark night is a gestation, a coming into being of a level of existence you have never dreamed of. Maybe your dark night is one big ironical challenge, just the opposite of what it appears to be—not a dying, but a birthing.[13]

The Easter journey ends not in death but in rebirth and resurrection. And in my Easter offering, I often share the story of Nicodemus the Pharisee, who represents each of us on our journey.[14] Nicodemus makes three appearances in the Gospel of John. Remember, three is always significant. In the first appearance, he visits Jesus during the Passover "by night," which is also significant. Nicodemus is questioning his purpose and the meaning of life, and he has come to Jesus for guidance.

Jesus tells Nicodemus, "No one can see the kingdom of God unless they are born again." Nicodemus cannot grasp the meaning of this. He is far too rational and too identified with his narrow understanding of spiritual matters. He protests, "How can someone be born when they are old?" And he goes on, "Surely they cannot enter a second time into their mother's womb to be born?" Jesus answers him, "No one can enter the kingdom of God unless they are born of water and the Spirit." This rebirth is clearly not physical; it is emotional and spiritual.

Nicodemus appears two more times. The second time is at the trial of Jesus when he urges his fellow Pharisees to hear Jesus before judging him. This is a sign that Nicodemus has done his inner work and understands now what Jesus meant by being born again. The third time he appears is at the burial of Jesus when "Nicodemus, who had at first come to Jesus by night, also came, bringing a mixture of myrrh and aloes, weighing about a hundred pounds." Nicodemus is helping prepare Jesus for his rebirth and resurrection. Again, this a sign that Nicodemus is making himself ready for his own rebirth.

The psychiatrist Erich Fromm wrote, "Man's main task in life is to give birth to himself, to become what he potentially is." Birth is not a once-in-a-lifetime event; it is a lifelong process of growth and evolution. You are still being born, and you are being born right now, if you have the eyes to see it. Enfolded in each of us starting at birth is a purpose that unfolds as we say yes to the adventure of living, to dying to our old self-image, to shedding a skin, and to letting the grain of wheat be split open so it can bear much fruit.

In my talks and workshops on the Easter journey, I share a poem that Hollie, my wife, wrote for me when I was experiencing my dark night of the soul. I was in a dark place, feeling lost, and not at all sure what to do next. This poem was a healing balm for me. Inside this poem, there is a dramatic question, a meditation to sit with, and an invitation to step into the light and live your higher purpose. It's called "What Wants to Be Born in You, Beloved?"[15] Here it is.

I have become grateful for the moments
When I remember to stop
In order to listen
To what the earth has to tell me.

This morning it was a flower
Who took me by surprise
And shared her secrets with me.

She told me of her journey.
How it began in darkness,
In the quiet, cool embrace
Of the quiet, generous earth

She told me how the light called to her,
And how, slowly but solidly,
She began to unfold towards
The simple inevitability of her calling.

She told me of the exquisite cracking-open
Of all she knew herself to be;
The opening that felt like death
Until she realized it was her birth.

And then, with her open petals,
She asked me in the way
Only a full-bloomed flower can ask,
"What wants to be born in you, beloved?
What does the light want to call into being
From the quiet, generous earth
That waits patiently
In the cave of your heart?"

THE ENNEAGRAM
CHAPTER

One September afternoon in 2003, my friend Marika Borg took me out for a coffee at a café called Robert's Coffee in Helsinki city center, Finland. "I've brought you here for two very important reasons," Marika told me.[1] "The first reason is that I know how much you love good coffee, and this coffee is very good, and it has your name on it. The second reason is that I want to introduce you to the Enneagram."

I had no idea what the Enneagram was. At first glance, the Enneagram looks like another personality test, like the Myers-Briggs Type Indicator, which is based on Carl Jung's work. "It's more than just a personality test!" Marika told me. Marika began by drawing the nine-pointed Enneagram symbol on a napkin and then spent the next three hours telling me about it. As the café was closing and we paid our bill, Marika made me promise to explore the Enneagram more. She told me, "If you study the Enneagram, you will thank me for the rest of your life for introducing it to you!"[2]

About a month later, I attended a three-day workshop in London on the Wisdom of the Enneagram presented by Don Riso and Russ Hudson. It was held in a Victorian building that was home of the Study Society and owned by the Russian philosopher P. D.

Ouspensky, who bought it in the 1930s. There were about 50 people in the room. I didn't know what to expect; it was Marika who had told me about the event. The timing did feel auspicious, as Don and Russ were both based in New York and only made it over to England every couple of years.

Over the next three days, Don and Russ introduced us to the timeless wisdom of the Enneagram. It was billed as an introduction, but Don and Russ began with a deep dive into the higher purpose of the Enneagram. They presented the Enneagram as both an ancient and modern system for cultivating deep psychological and spiritual growth. For three days they conducted a continuous lecture full of eye-opening, jaw-dropping, heart-expanding, and mind-blowing material. I felt truly blessed to be there, and like I had the best ticket in town.[3]

So what is the Enneagram? The word Enneagram is derived from two Greek words *ennéa* (which means "nine") and *grámma* (which means "written" or "drawn"), and it is the name for a nine-pointed symbol. The precise origin of the Enneagram is unknown, but its teachings can be traced back to the work of Pythagoras and Plato, to Plotinus who wrote a book called *The Enneads*, to the Desert Fathers and Mothers of Egypt, and to ancient wisdom schools in northern Spain, Turkey, and Persia. In short, the Enneagram has been everywhere and has existed for a long time.

What we know for sure is that the Enneagram was introduced to Europe and America in the early 20th century by George Ivanovich Gurdjieff, the enigmatic Russian philosopher and mystic. Gurdjieff believed that humanity has a *Great Purpose*, a term he used, which is to participate in the evolution of creation. Every person is issued with the great task of doing what Gurdjieff called "The Work" or "Work on oneself." Doing this work enables you to live your higher purpose. The Fourth Way is another name for this work, and the Enneagram plays a vital part in it.

P. D. Ouspensky, the founder of the Study Society, met Gurdjieff in Moscow in 1915 while on a pilgrimage in search of ancient wisdom. Ouspensky worked closely with Gurdjieff for 10 years, and after that he taught The Work wherever he went. In Ouspensky's classic book *In Search of the Miraculous*, which was published in the same year as *The Hero with a Thousand Faces* by Joseph Campbell, he offers a summary of The Work by Gurdjieff as well as Gurdjieff's insights into the deeper meaning and purpose of the Enneagram. At one point, Gurdjieff tells Ouspensky,

> A man may be quite alone in the desert, and he can trace the enneagram in the sand and in it read the eternal laws of the universe. And every time he can learn something new, something he did not know before.[4]

Marika Borg was right when she said I would thank her for the rest of my life for introducing me to the Enneagram. Indeed, I wrote and thanked her again this morning before I started to work on this chapter! The Enneagram has been a great help to me in every area of my life, including my spiritual practice, my work, my health, my marriage, being a dad, and all my relationships. The Enneagram has been especially helpful to me in living my purpose, and I love teaching the Enneagram to help others live their purpose too.

My Purpose & the Enneagram program is one of my favorite programs to teach. When I teach the Enneagram, I work with it in three broad ways. The first way is to focus on the nine personality types of the Enneagram. Each Ennea-Type has a name that is a descriptor for a life outlook and a typical social role, such as the reformer, the helper, the peacemaker, the achiever, et cetera. By identifying your type, you can do the "Work on oneself," as Gurdjieff put it, so as to wake up to your true potential and follow your higher calling.

The second way of working with the Enneagram is to use it as a map for your spiritual growth. All nine Ennea-Types are on the same journey, but there are nine different ways to take the journey, like nine paths up the same mountain. The Enneagram helps you identify your chief motivation for living, for example, doing a good deed, being of service, finding a worthwhile cause, and creating acts of beauty. The Enneagram also helps you work with the inner blocks, the ordeals, the challenges, and the setbacks you will encounter as you live your higher purpose.

The third way is to use the Enneagram as a mandala that offers nine meditations—one for each Point on the Enneagram—to explore a theme like happiness, success, love, and purpose. This approach ensures a robust and rich inquiry that covers nine different angles or points of view.

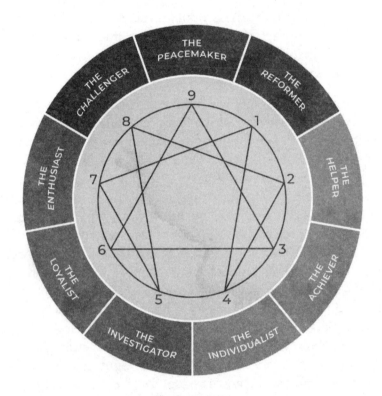

The Enneagram

We will now take a walk around the circle of the Enneagram symbol starting at Point One. I'd like you to imagine that each Point on the Enneagram has a meditation seat. While you sit on each seat, I'll introduce you briefly to the Ennea-Type, the path of spiritual growth here, and a spiritual practice that everyone can do no matter what Ennea-Type they are. This way we will do nine meditations on living your purpose.

POINT 1: DOING A GOOD DEED

The Ennea-Type One personality is called the Reformer or Perfectionist. Type One children are sensitively attuned to the basic goodness of human nature. They use it as a moral compass to be a good person and to do something good with their life. They uphold traditional values and at the same time want to make the world a better place. Silvia Lagnado, who I worked with at Dove and the Real Beauty Campaign, is a great example of an Ennea-Type One who works hard to reform the industry she works in, to create ethical brands, and to do purpose-centered work.

A challenge that Ennea-Type Ones often face is the impossibly high standards they set for themselves. The "Be Good" driver can, if unchecked, cause you to feel "not good enough" to fulfill your purpose. I once mentored a Christian minister, Claire, who told me how she put herself "through hell" to deliver the perfect Sunday sermon each week. "It's just never good enough," she wept. When I asked her if her congregation felt the same way about her "not good enough" sermons, she laughed out loud! "No! They tell me that they love my sermons!" she said.

At the end of our first session, I asked Claire to do some homework. I know how much Ennea-Type Ones enjoy homework and that they'll always do a good job with it. Her homework was to think carefully about this question: "What is even better than giving the perfect sermon?" A week later Claire came back with a revelation to tell. "I've been trying so hard to get everything right that I've been doing it all wrong!" she confessed. She then told me, "The purpose of a sermon is not to get it right or be clever; it's to feel God's love and to share that love with each other."

> **Point One Meditation:** "How far that little candle throws his beams! So shines a good deed in a weary world," says Portia in *The Merchant of Venice*. Because of our basic goodness, we all wish to do a "good deed" for the world. Our "work on oneself," so to speak, is to work out what that good deed is. A good question to live with is *What good do I want to do for the world?* When you keep faith with

your basic goodness, and stop putting unfair pressure on yourself, you see that your efforts are good enough and that your presence is a blessing to others.

POINT 2: BEING OF SERVICE

The Ennea-Type Two personality is called the Helper or Giver. Type Two children feel in their heart of hearts that we live in a thoroughly interconnected universe. Growing up, they try to hang on to this felt sense of connectedness by reaching out to others with offers of help, acts of kindness, and genuine caring. In adulthood, they are keen to deepen and widen their connectivity to feel at home in the universe. They take on roles in public service, charity work, the caring professions, and social ecology to make a meaningful contribution to the world.

"What really keeps me going is this transformation I see when a person realizes that they are connected to everything and that they matter in the universe," says Nassim Haramein, creator of the documentary *The Connected Universe* and founder of the Resonance Science Foundation.[5] Our connectedness calls us to give our all and to serve wholeheartedly. Of course, connectedness is also about receiving what life is giving us. Receiving is as vital as giving. This can be a challenge for Ennea-Type Twos, who often merge their identity with the role of helper and giver, and in doing so suffer unhealthy self-sacrifice, martyrdom, burnout, and the pain of their own unmet needs.

Point Two Meditation: This afternoon I took a break from writing to watch my daughter, Bo, perform her Eurythmy dance class at school. During the second dance, her teacher, Ms. Hunter, read a verse by Rudolf Steiner. It's a perfect meditation for Point Two, and a great reminder to stay open to extra help and inspiration when living your purpose. When you read this verse, make sure you receive the wisdom, the love, and the strength invoked by it. Remember, being a good receiver increases your capacity to be of service in a healthy and fulfilling way. Here is the verse:

May wisdom shine through me
May love glow in me
May strength penetrate me
That in me may arise
A helper for humanity
A server of sacred things
Selfless and true.[6]

POINT 3: FROM AMBITION TO MEANING

The Ennea-Type Three personality is called the Achiever or Performer. My Ennea-Type is Three, and as a young child I often pondered *What am I doing here?* and *What am I meant to do with my life?* and *When can I have a briefcase?* In my heart, I felt I was born to do a great work, but what was it? I was full of ambition. I had a strong work ethic. I dreamed of being famous. I played guitar in a rock band. I was a keen cricketer. At school, when I was about 15 years old, I got a detention for practicing my autograph in geography class.

I often show clips of Wayne Dyer's documentary *The Shift* when I teach about Point Three on the Enneagram.[7] The original title of the documentary, which was changed just before it was released in 2009, was *Ambition to Meaning: Finding Your Life's Purpose*. In this inspiring documentary, Wayne leads us through Carl Jung's four stages of life: Athlete, Warrior, Statement, and Spirit. Wayne tells us, "We can fulfill our greatest calling when we consciously undertake the journey from ambition to meaning. We can transform our individual lives and influence the destiny of our sacred planet as well."

Point Three Meditation: *What is the real work of my life?* Wayne Dyer tells us we must outgrow our ego-driven ambition if we are to fulfill our true purpose. He says, "Such a shift eliminates our feelings of separateness, illuminates our spiritual connectedness, and involves moving from the ego-directed morning into the afternoon of life where everything is primarily influenced by *purpose*." How do we do this? We shift from always trying to impress the world to living more from our own center. It's a shift from being *impressive* to being *inspired*. Wayne Dyer observes, "There is a voice in the Universe urging us to remember our purpose for being on this great Earth. This is the voice of inspiration, which is within each and every one of us."

POINT 4: CREATING SOMETHING BEAUTIFUL

The Ennea-Type Four personality is called the Individualist or Romantic. Type Four children arrive with a story that places them on the outside of the family constellation. They identify deeply with the role of the "odd one out," "misfit," and "loner." They are full of nostalgia, and act like they are "a troubled guest on the dark earth."[8] Most Ennea-Type Fours console themselves with an appreciation for beauty. The essence of beauty brings you home to yourself. Beauty saves you from your exile. Fyodor Dostoevsky, the Russian novelist, declared, "Beauty will save the world." Ennea-Type Fours know this to be true.

My friend Shawn Gallaway has an Ennea-Type 4 personality. We first met at a Hay House I CAN DO IT! conference in San Diego 2009. A friend had recently given me Shawn's *I Choose Love* CD. I listened to it on repeat each time I went for a run around the reservoir in Central Park. I had no idea Shawn would be at the conference. He was there as a guest of one of the speakers. I bumped into him at a book stall. We struck up a friendship, and he has played live music at many of my events over the years.

As a young man, Shawn experienced a dark depression and struggled to find meaning in his life. "It was music and art that helped me find my way back to myself," he told me. After the September 11 attacks on the Twin Towers in New York in 2001, when 3,000 people were killed and thousands more were injured and traumatized, Shawn did a lot of soul searching. "9/11 was a wake-up call for me," he told me. "I asked myself some big questions like *Why am I a musician?* and *What is my music really for?* I wanted to make a statement and create something beautiful to help lead us out of the darkness and into the light. That's when I wrote my song, 'I Choose Love.'"

> **Point Four Meditation:** Shawn's song "I Choose Love" became the inspiration for an album, a newsletter, an online program, and an I Choose Love movement.[9] Shawn says, "My mission and purpose is first and foremost to heal myself through the arts, and to help others do the same." The invitation to be creative and to appreciate beauty is here in every moment. A simple arrangement of flowers upon the dining table may be your work today. Sharing a poem that inspires you might be it. Or maybe it is to visit a museum or take a walk in your local park. Ask yourself then, *How can I enjoy more beauty and express my creativity today?*

POINT 5: WHAT REALLY INSPIRES ME?

The Ennea-Type Five personality is called the Investigator or Observer. Type Five children come into the world with their eyes wide open. They are watchful and inquisitive. They regard life with a curious mix of astonishment and suspicion. The mystery of life is both intriguing and unsettling. Why doesn't life come with an instruction book? The quest for knowledge and understanding helps Ennea-Type Fives feel less anxious and better equipped to face the task of living a life in a complicated world.

A lot of my closest friends, teachers, and mentors have an Ennea-Type Five personality. They are very interesting to be around, not least because they take a deep interest in life. They know that there is more to life than meets the eye. Their inner work is to cultivate a basic openness that helps them see life through a clear lens that is not distorted by fear, separateness, prejudice, or small-mindedness. Erwin Schrödinger put it this way: "The task is, not so much to see what no one has yet seen; but to think what nobody has yet thought, about that which everybody sees."

Point Five Meditation: When people come to me for help with discovering their life purpose, I encourage them to recognize what inspires them. "When do you feel most inspired?" I ask. Your purpose is to be inspired! Inspiration is a teacher, and you are the student. When inspiration grabs hold of you, don't resist. Follow the golden thread. Be open to what inspires you. Go on your own hero journey and experience your purpose in a way that no one else can.

Patanjali, the great Indian sage, offered this wonderful meditation on inspiration and purpose in his classical yoga text, the *Yoga Sutras*: "When you are inspired by some great purpose, some extraordinary project, all your thoughts break their bonds: Your mind transcends limitations, your consciousness expands in every direction, and you find yourself in a new, great and wonderful world. Dormant forces, faculties and talents become alive, and you discover yourself to be a greater person by far than you ever dreamed yourself to be."[10]

POINT 6: A WORTHWHILE CAUSE

The Ennea-Type Six personality is called the Loyalist or Skeptic. Type Six children are born with a question mark over their head. Why shouldn't they be? Think about it for a minute: This world is a big surprise, and who knows for sure what's really going on? Life is full of uncertainty, no two days are the same, everybody dies, and no one can predict the weather! Ennea-Type Sixes are looking out for what they can trust and depend on. They are also looking for a worthwhile cause to support and pledge their allegiance to.

I often refer to Louise Hay's work when I teach Point Six on the Enneagram. I co-wrote a book with Louise called *Life Loves You*, which is about cultivating a basic trust in life.[11] Ennea-Type Sixes sharpen their basic trust by working on their intuition, or sixth sense. For the first half of Louise's life, she "bumbled along," as she put it, without any real faith in herself or any sense of direction. When Louise was 49 years old, her husband left her, she was diagnosed with cancer, and she was in a dark place. This was when Louise began to pay attention to her "inner ding," which was her name for her intuition.

"I have learned to trust my 'inner ding' with my life," Louise told me while we were writing *Life Loves You*. Louise's "inner ding" connected her to what she calls "the infinite intelligence" of the universe. "I believe that everyone is blessed with an internal guidance system and that the purpose of our life unfolds as we learn to trust and follow this guidance."

Point Six Meditation: After Louise passed away in August 2017, I compiled, edited, and wrote the Foreword for *Trust Life: Love Yourself Every Day with Wisdom from Louise Hay*.[12] It features 365 daily entries that include affirmations and meditations from her major works. Here's one entry that is a good practice for Point Six on the Enneagram.

I Am Safe in the Universe, and All Life Loves and Supports Me

The stars, the moon, and the sun are all operating in perfect Divine right order. There is an order, a rhythm, and a purpose to their pathways. I am part of the Universe; therefore, I know that there is an order, a rhythm, and a purpose to my life.

Sometimes my life may seem to be in chaos, and yet in back of the chaos I know there is a Divine order. As I put my mind in order and learn my lessons, the chaos disappears, and then order comes back. I trust that my life is really in perfect Divine right order. All is well in my world.[13]

POINT 7: FOCUSING ON NOW

The Ennea-Type Seven personality is called the Enthusiast or Producer. Type Seven children are filled with natural *joie de vivre*. They have a big appetite for life. They are hungry for adventure. They dream of many possibilities for their future. It is not uncommon for an Ennea-Type Seven child to dream of being a scientist and a fashion designer, a belly dancer and an astronaut, a rock star and a firefighter when they grow up. These adventure seekers are often future focused, always in a big hurry, and have a "don't stop me now" attitude. Hidden beneath the surface of these venturesome explorers is a "purpose anxiety," which is the fear of not finding and missing out on their true purpose.

> *"To live will be an awfully big adventure."*
>
> — Peter Pan

The journey of growth for Ennea-Type Sevens is to make a shift from *searching for your purpose* to *recognizing that your purpose is right where you are.* My friend Liz Trubridge, the producer of *Downton Abbey*, whom I told you about at the start of the "In a Dark Place" chapter, has an Ennea-Type Seven personality. She says, "The Enneagram helped me to see that I don't have to chase the future to find my purpose. My purpose is always with me, whether I am on set filming, at home with my boys, or out walking my dog, Raffy. My purpose is who I am, not something to find. And

I trust that when I stay open to my purpose in any situation, my purpose will always find me."

Point Seven Meditation: The discipline of focus is a great meditation for Point Seven. To find your purpose, you must shift your focus from the future to the present. If you take a few minutes each day to focus on your purpose, your purpose will become clear. It might not be clear straightaway, so it's important that you hold your focus, and that you don't panic or distract yourself. It can be helpful to work with an affirmation like *My purpose goes with me wherever I go.* A prayer that Liz carries with her on set and through the day is *Dear God, show me what my purpose is here.*

POINT 8: A HIGHER POWER

The Ennea-Type Eight personality is called the Challenger or the Boss. When I think about Type Eight children, I immediately hear DA-DA-DA-DUM!—the famous four-note motif of Beethoven's Fifth Symphony. Much has been written about the possible meaning of these first four notes. They certainly convey power, purpose, and a sense of providence. Beethoven's secretary and biographer, Anton Schindler, tells the story that when he asked the composer what these notes stood for, Beethoven replied: "This is the sound of fate knocking at the door."

Young Ennea-Type Eights tend to have a big life force. Their physical circuits hum with energy. Their larger-than-life presence is something they must learn to live with. Like Type Seven children, they want to grow up quickly. Being in a small body can be frustrating. They want to be strong, to be independent, and to test their powers. They look for a challenge to bring them alive and to announce their presence in the world. "Let's make a dent in the universe," said Steve Jobs, sounding the rallying cry of the Ennea-Type Eight.

The Ennea-Type Eight person wants to play big in the world. But what does *play big* really mean? You might be king of the hill in your neighborhood, but is that all you were made for? Martin Luther King Jr. said, "An individual has not started living until he can rise above the narrow confines of his individualistic concerns to the broader concerns of all humanity." In other words, you must be willing to surrender your independence if you want to take your place in the larger story and bigger picture.

Martin Luther King Jr. took on the challenge of living his bigger purpose. "Injustice anywhere is a threat to justice everywhere. We are caught in an inescapable network of mutuality, tied to a single garment of destiny. Whatever affects one directly, effects all indirectly," he wrote in his "Letter from Birmingham Jail" on April 16, 1963.[14] To live his higher purpose, Martin Luther King Jr. had to call upon a power far greater than his own ego. He anchored himself in the Christ. He declared, "Love is the greatest force in the universe. It is the heartbeat of the moral cosmos. He who loves is a participant in the being of God."

> **Point Eight Meditation:** If you really want to play big, you can either keep on inflating your ego until it pops, or surrender to a power greater than your ego. Too much self-reliance turns a strength into a weakness. Independence can take you only so far. What will you decide? Here is your DA-DA-DA-DUM moment. Your fate is to surrender to a higher power so you can fulfill your higher purpose. Ask yourself then, *What is my higher power?* Align yourself with this higher power and allow it to guide you, direct you, and inspire you today.

POINT 9: THE PRESENCE OF LOVE

The Ennea-Type Nine personality is called the Peacemaker or Dreamer. Type Nine children come down to earth with a bump. Every family has its own story of ups and downs, good times and bad, rises and falls, and all this can be very disturbing for a child who wants to hold on to their equilibrium and balance. Typically, an Ennea-Type Nine child decides to withdraw from others to "keep the peace," so speak. They disappear into themselves. They hang out on cloud nine. They don't want to cause any trouble, but their lack of engagement upsets their chances of enjoying real peace and harmony in the world.

> *"I am a place where God's love turns up in this world."*
>
> — M. Basil Pennington

The journey of growth for Ennea-Type Nines is to offer the world what they most want for themselves. This is everybody's journey, really. For the Peacemaker it is to help create peace on earth. Peacemakers often work as mediators, activists, environmentalists, diplomats, and healers to create heaven on earth. Winny and Kees van de Velden, the founders of Ocean of Love, both relate to Point Nine on the Enneagram. Winny once told me, "The purpose of our work with the whales and dolphins is to show the world that we can all live in harmony, as above and so below, and that we can create heaven on earth together."

Point Nine Meditation: Your home is not on cloud nine. You are meant to be here on earth. Your destiny and the destiny of the world are not separate from each other. Your great work, therefore, is to engage with a story that really matters to you. Remember that your presence really matters to the rest of us. Ask yourself then, *Where is my presence most needed in my life today?* Trust that your presence is what helps create more wholeness, harmony, and unity here on earth. To help you remember this, get a pen and paper and complete this sentence a few times, "One way my presence makes a difference in this world is . . . "

PART IV

THE VICTORY

A COMMENCEMENT
SPEECH

I am sitting with Ron and Mary Hulnick in the greenroom backstage at Royce Hall, UCLA. We are drinking tea and munching on sandwiches, dressed in our graduation robes complete with tassels. The hall is nearly full now. Over 1,700 family and friends have gathered to celebrate the graduation of 250 students who have completed their degree and M.A. programs in spiritual psychology at the University of Santa Monica (USM). Ron and Mary are hosting the ceremony in their joint role as co-directors of USM, and I am here to give the commencement speech.

I am struck by how calm Ron and Mary are. This is the biggest day in their calendar. There is no offstage anxiety, only genuine excitement for what is about to unfold. "This is a day of great joy," says Mary, who looks radiant and serene. "It is indeed," says Ron as he takes her hand. Ron and Mary often hold hands; it's how they are with each other. Faculty, board members, staff, the official photographer, all pop in and out of the greenroom as we are getting ready. Everyone is focused, happy, and on purpose.

Ron and Mary have hosted 36 USM graduation ceremonies so far. More than 6,500 students have graduated from one of the USM programs. USM was founded in 1976 by John-Roger Hinkins, a philosopher and mystic, who was also the founder of the Movement of Spiritual Inner Awareness. In 1980 John-Roger invited Ron and Mary, who were serving on the faculty of New Mexico State University at the time, to be USM president and academic vice president, respectively. In 1981 students were admitted to the first M.A. program in spiritual psychology.[1]

Ron began his welcome address by sharing the vision and purpose of USM. "From the start, our purpose was to put the soul back into psychology and into modern life," he tells us. Ron points out that the word *psyche* means "breath, principle of life, soul." He explains that the original purpose of psychology, as taught in ancient Greece, was to acquaint you with your soul, which is your true nature, so that you can live a life full of inner direction, inspiration, and purpose.

My psychology studies at university were based on a curriculum without a soul. Nowadays, most universities have redefined psychology as "the science of mind and behavior." The lectures I attended focused on the ego and on cognitive behavior. There was also a reluctance to study the soul, or even mention the word *soul*, in my philosophy lectures. Furthermore, "soul" is disappearing from modern Bible translations. For example, in the New Revised Standard Version of the Bible, "soul" is replaced by "life" in the Gospel of Mark 8:36.

For what will it profit a man if he gains the whole world,
and loses his own soul?

— **King James Version**

For what will it profit them to gain the whole world
and forfeit their life?

— **New Revised Standard Version**

The aim of every program offered by USM is to help people be soul-centered in their life and work. One USM program I've worked on is the Soul-Centered Professional Coaching Program. My role is to teach the six-day summer lab that happens at the end of the program. In my classes, I acknowledge that the soul is impossible to define, but that this does not mean we should ignore it. The soul is immeasurable, *and* it exists. Everyone possesses the ability to recognize the soul's presence. We can all tell when a musician, a chef, a gardener, a barista, or a teacher puts their heart and soul into what they do. We know when someone has "got soul."

"To be soul-centered is to live from your own center," explains Mary in her opening address at the graduation. As Mary talks about the soul, we perch on the edge of our seats, eager to hear more. She tells us, "The soul is your inherent nature. It is your life force. It is your inner light. It is the presence of love in you." She goes on to say that being soul-centered is a daily practice that helps you live a more creative and inspired life. "The purpose of soul-centered living is that it brings forth your inherent talents and helps you fulfill your purpose," she tells us.

> *"Education is not the filling of a pail, but the lighting of a fire."*
> — William Butler Yeats

When Ron and Mary teach about purpose, they make a distinction between the "Goal Line" and the "Soul Line." The Goal Line is a horizontal line. It moves from the past to the future. Ron explains, "On the Goal Line, your purpose is *what* you do. For example, you work as a doctor, a lawyer, or as a musician, and you enjoy material success that is measured by status, reputation, and money." The Soul Line is a vertical line. It represents your antenna, or spiritual aerial, that attunes you to the grace and inspiration you need to live your purpose. "The Soul Line is not about what you do; it's about how you do it. It's the Soul Line that gives your life a deeper meaning and a higher purpose," says Ron.

Ron and Mary teach their students to be loyal to their soul. Their book *Loyalty to Your Soul* is a modern classic of spiritual literature.[2] By being loyal to your soul, your personality becomes an instrument for your higher purpose and you are able to take your place in the greater story of creation. This is how Ron explains it in his introduction to spiritual psychology:

> As Spiritual beings, our primary goal is not to change life on this earth. Rather, life on this earth exists the way it does to provide us with experiences through which we can transform ourselves—meaning learning to express the essence of who we are in fuller and deeper ways. And the best description of our inherent nature is that we are, at our core, comprised of the energy we call Loving. So Spiritual Awakening is about becoming more and more aware of our nature as Loving beings. The irony is that the only way life on this earth transforms is when enough people transform themselves. It's from this place of inner transformation that we can make a meaningful contribution in our world.[3]

BEING READY ENOUGH

Giving a commencement speech is always a thrill. I have been fortunate enough to have given a few, including two for the University of Santa Monica.

The purpose of a commencement speech for the listener is twofold. First, it is to honor the journey you have taken up until now. You do this by acknowledging the calling that inspired you to begin; by recognizing your courage in navigating the ordeals and challenges you have faced; and by giving thanks for the learning and support you have received along the way. Second, it is to prepare you for the journey you will take starting from now. Now is the time for another new beginning. Life is full of new beginnings.

New beginnings are full of excitement and fear. Cast your mind back to when you were a child walking through the school gate on the first day of term. Remember how you felt on the first day of a new job or a new leadership position at work. Think about the last time you went on a first date. It doesn't matter what age you are; everyone feels barely 18 years old on a first date. Any new beginning, such as opening a shop, writing a book, going back to school, or signing up for online dating is both rousing and scary.

"I love all beginnings, despite their anxiousness and their uncertainty, which belong to every commencement," wrote Rilke in his poem "I Choose to Begin." Learning to love new beginnings is vital for living your purpose. Meeting your anxiety with honesty and love is a necessary skill for each new chapter or stage you encounter on your journey. A new beginning cannot happen unless you say yes. You must affirm, as Rilke did, "I choose to begin" to get your journey started.

> *"Your strongest message, by far, will be your example."*
>
> — Ron Hulnick

No one feels 100 percent ready for a new beginning. We each have a voice inside our head that tells us, "You are not ready." This is the voice of your ego, or narrow self. It pleads for more time. It tells us, "You are nearly ready" and "You are almost ready" and "You will be ready soon." Before we can begin, according to our ego, we need one more qualification, we need a foolproof plan, our life must be better organized, we must have more money and resources, and oh, a supernatural talent would come in handy.

Personally, I rarely feel completely ready to begin a new project. This is especially true for writing a book, including this one. "You need to do more research!" my ego tells me. "Move your deadline back six months," my ego advises. Normally, it takes a nudge from the universe to help me begin.

I remember I'd been stalling for weeks on starting my book *Loveability*. "Love is too big to write about," I kept telling myself. Then, one morning, my friend Shawn Gallaway (whom I told you about in "The Enneagram Chapter") sent me an e-mail with a demo of his new song. "Hi brother! Here's my new song. Enjoy!" he wrote. The song is called "Begin." Sure enough, life was sending me a message, loud and clear, and I made a start soon after. Here's a verse and the chorus from Shawn's song.

> *Get on out, of your own way*
> *Let your spirit, lead the way*
> *Allow, the nature of your truth*
> *To shine right now.*

> *With a little shot of courage*
> *From the fire within*
> *Move into your heart*
> *Let your dream begin.*

New beginnings are a risky business. "To live your purpose, you sometimes have to be half-a-shade braver than you want to be," Mary Hulnick once told me. The road ahead is uncertain. The destination is not yet clear. There are no guarantees that you will succeed. Indeed, you may well stumble and fall many times. It's always a risk to follow your joy and to do what you love, but it's even more of risk *not* to. To live a life of purpose is a risk worth taking. And it's a risk you don't have to take alone.

In my commencement speeches, I always share this message with the graduates:

> *The ego is never ready to do the soul's work,*
> *but that's okay, because it is the soul that does the work.*

The ego-voice that tells you, "You are not ready" is the same voice that will say one day, "You are too old." Always remember, though, that your ego is only an instrument. Your purpose is already with you. With God's help, you are ready to begin. "Unfurl yourself into the grace of beginning" and "awaken your spirit to adventure," says John O'Donohue in his poem "For a New Beginning." Once you begin, you activate the grace and inspiration—what Joseph Campbell calls *Supernatural Aid*—you need to help you live your purpose.

To live your purpose, you don't have to be entirely ready, just *ready enough.* Your work is to reassure your ego that if you say YES, inspiration will appear. *A Course in Miracles* encourages us to offer "a little willingness" to activate a flow of miracles, providence, and grace. It teaches that only a little willingness is necessary to do God's work because it is God that does the work through us. "Living your purpose is a *hold your nose and jump job,*" is how my friend Sue Boyd put it when she launched her Westbury in Bloom initiative. Sue is also a student of *A Course in Miracles.* "I've learned to trust that miracles happen after I begin, but not before," she says.

You don't have to be ready for the whole journey, just the first step. Take the first step, and the next step will be revealed to you.

Start with
the ground
you know,
the pale ground
beneath your feet,

writes David Whyte in his poem "Start Close In."[4] That first step might be a small step. Most new beginnings are small. Ron and Mary Hulnick at USM started with only 11 students on their first M.A. program on spiritual psychology. A community of 11 graduates swelled into over 6,500 graduates over the years because Ron and Mary chose one day to begin.

BEWARE DYSFUNCTIONAL INDEPENDENCE

In my commencement speeches, I address what I believe is the most common block to finding your purpose and living an inspired life. My name for this inner block is *dysfunctional independence.*

As a young man, I was a bit too independent for my own good. Being independent accommodated my shyness. It also suited my introverted personality. I had a small circle of friends, some of whom I lost touch with after university. I was extremely self-disciplined in my work. I didn't need anyone to motivate me. When

I wasn't working, my time was mostly spent caring for my mum and dad. My independence gave me freedom, but at a cost. I became increasingly lonely. Intimacy and vulnerability weren't easy for me. Inspiration was hard work. I grew tired of the struggle that comes with self-reliance. Too much independence cuts you off from life.

It was Chuck Spezzano, a psychologist and teacher of *A Course in Miracles*, who made me look at my relationship with independence. On the eve of my twenty-eighth birthday, I attended a three-day public workshop he gave in London. On the first morning, Chuck picked me out of the crowd and asked me to join him at the front of the room. He asked me about my life. He talked about Carl Jung's four stages of life. He then looked me in the eyes and said, "Robert, you're a great athlete and you've run a great race until now. But you won't be able to run much further by yourself. It's time to ask for help."

The secret that every independent person carries in their heart is that they are hiding an old wound. My family has a long line of unhealthy or dysfunctional independence. My mum was the misfit, the outsider in the family, haunted by depression. My father was a loner, the rock of the family, who suppressed his feelings with alcohol. The baton of independence was handed to my brother, David, and me. We didn't have to grab it, but we did. Being self-reliant is how we both coped with the trauma of our parents' pain. Self-reliance helped us to function and get by, but, as Chuck Spezzano pointed out, it only gets you so far.

Independence is not all bad. There is such a thing as healthy independence. The psychologist Abraham Maslow pointed out that if a person is to self-actualize, they must be willing "to be independent of the good opinions of others." Healthy independence enables you to live from your center, to make authentic decisions, to not sell yourself short, and to follow your true vocation. Maslow said of self-actualized people,

> They have become strong enough to be independent of the good opinion of other people, or even of their affection. The honors, the status, the rewards, the popularity, the prestige, and the love they can bestow must

have become less important than self-development and inner growth.[5]

Healthy independence helps you with inner listening and with becoming your true self rather than simply being a copy of someone else. Maslow observed,

> A musician must make music, an artist must paint, a poet must write, if he is to be ultimately at peace with himself. What a man can be, he must be. This need we may call self-actualization . . . It refers to man's desire for self-fulfillment, namely, to the tendency for him to become actualized in what he is potentially . . . to become everything that one is capable of becoming.[6]

Healthy independence *does not* mean, however, that you must do life all by yourself. Trying to be entirely self-sufficient is unhealthy independence, and it is unwise and not necessary. Too much independence—what I call dysfunctional independence—is not sustainable in the long run. Dysfunctional independence increases the sense of separateness, which, if unchecked, leaves you feeling utterly alone, too small, and not able to live the bigger purpose of your life.

Erich Fromm's theory of biophilia recognized that we humans have an inherent tendency to seek connections with each other and the whole of life. Yet Fromm also recognized that our sense of separateness is "the problem of human existence." Along with psychologists like Otto Rank, he cited our sense of separateness as the root cause of all our suffering and all human destructiveness. Dysfunctional independence compounds this problem of

> *"Each of us carries a unique spark of the divine, and each of us is also an inseparable part of the web of life."*
>
> — Viktor Frankl

separation, and, therefore, we must be willing to grow beyond it if we want to participate in the greater purpose of life. Fromm wrote, "The deepest need of man, then, is the need to overcome his separateness, to leave the prison of his aloneness. The absolute failure to achieve this aim means insanity."[7]

Albert Einstein described our perceived sense of separation as an "optical delusion." He, too, saw that our main task in life is to see through our separateness in order to escape the confines of a narrow self and a distorted worldview. In a letter that Einstein wrote in 1950 to a rabbi, Norman Salit, who was seeking guidance after a tragedy in his family, he said,

> A human being is a part of the whole, called by us "Universe," a part limited in time and space. He experiences himself, his thoughts and feelings as something separated from the rest—a kind of optical delusion of his consciousness. This delusion is a kind of prison for us, restricting us to our personal desires and to affection for a few persons nearest to us. Our task must be to free ourselves from this prison by widening our circle of compassion to embrace all living creatures and the whole of nature in its beauty.[8]

Thomas Berry, the twentieth-century geologian, described our sense of separateness as a "fatal flaw" and as the "central pathology" of the human condition that sets up a "human versus nature" outlook. "The destiny of humans cannot be separated from the destiny of earth," he wrote. "We lose our souls if we lose the experience of the forest, the butterflies, the song of the birds, if we can't see the stars at night." Our work, therefore, is to overcome and repair the "radical discontinuity" that we have inserted between us and the universe. In *The Great Work*, Berry writes,

> The universe must be experienced as the Great Self. Each is fulfilled in the other: the Great Self is fulfilled in the individual self, the individual self is fulfilled in the Great Self. Alienation is overcome as soon as we experience this

surge of energy from the source that has brought the universe through the centuries. New fields of energy become available to support the human venture. These new energies find expression and support in celebration. For in the end the universe can only be explained in terms of celebration. It is all an exuberant expression of existence itself.[9]

Each year I host a series of Mastermind programs for small groups of people on Success Intelligence, The Hero Journey, and Higher Purpose. A Mastermind program gives individuals the chance be together in community, to support each other, to cheer each other on, and to enjoy the BIG successes that are only possible through cooperation. When we meet for our first class, I start with a prayer to wish everyone the greatest success on their journey. I tell everyone that *every new level of success requires a new level of collaboration and partnership.*

In my Success Intelligence Mastermind program, I ask everyone this question: *Are you too independent to be truly successful?* We address dysfunctional independence as a block to living your purpose. I encourage everyone to identify how they can be less self-reliant and more successful. In one inquiry, I ask everyone to complete this sentence 10 times: "One way I could be less independent and more successful is . . ." On the other side of dysfunctional independence is a whole new world of inspiration and adventure.

On my Mastermind, I issue everyone a virtual Help Card. Each person is encouraged to post their Help Card on our online forum when they have a specific need or request. Interestingly, everyone loves this idea but not everyone uses their Help Card. Why not? One reason is that it is so countercultural for those of us raised in individualistic societies where the emphasis is on self-reliance. Some of us need help with asking for help. I've certainly needed a lot of help with my own dysfunctional independence over the years—it's a hard habit to break—and so it is especially meaningful to me when I can help others be more okay with asking for help.

A THREAD YOU FOLLOW

At a graduation ceremony or ordination, it is the tradition to dress up in fine robes and gowns, to wear a stole, or to carry beads on a thread, for example. At first glance this pomp and circumstance may seem somewhat trivial and unnecessary, but when you take a closer look, you discover that this tradition is layered with symbolism and has a deeper meaning and purpose.

Historically it was the custom for people attending their own commencement—be it religious, academic, knightly, or professional—to participate in the making of their ceremonial garments. Basically put, weaving is the interlacing of vertical threads, called the warp, with horizontal threads, called the weft. When weaving is practiced as a meditation, you can contemplate both the vertical axis and horizontal axis of your life. You can reflect upon the Soul Line and the Goal Line that Ron and Mary Hulnick teach about. You can bring together heaven and earth.

When a person weaves as a conscious spiritual practice, they may use it to connect with their lineage and ancestry, to affirm their tie with all that is sacred, or to weave a wonderful prayer or intention into the fabric. Many people use weaving as a mindfulness practice to explore their inner self, to balance the right and left hemispheres of the brain, and to cross over into a liminal space that is most conducive for meditative thinking, inspiration, imagination, and new beginnings.

The metaphor of weaving is commonly used by both mystics and scientists to explain and describe our basic relationship with each other and with the universe. Theoretical physicists now use the term *quantum entanglement*—or "spooky action at a distance," as Albert Einstein called it—in their observation of how the fates of tiny particles are linked to each other even when they appear to be separated by huge distances. Another theory, called *string theory*, recognizes that particles are not separate little balls of matter that bounce off each other; rather, they are more like the cross section of a piece of string that is part of the basic fabric of the universe.

William Blake, the painter, poet, and printmaker, was one of the first mystics I really paid attention to. He was baptized at St. James's Church in Piccadilly, London. My family on my mother's side has a long connection with this church. The memorial for my great-uncle Derek Hill, the artist, was held there. St. James's hosted the first ordination of ministers for the OneSpirit Interfaith Foundation, an organization I helped to set up with Miranda Macpherson in 1996.[10] Every year since then, I have been invited back by Alternatives, which is based at the church, to give a talk for their Monday night lecture series.[11]

William Blake's final and most epic poem, called *Jerusalem*, is written in four parts and is illustrated with 100 fine prints.[12] In one part, which is addressed "To the Christians," Blake writes,

I GIVE you the end of a golden string;
Only wind it into a ball,
It will lead you in at Heaven's gate,
Built in Jerusalem's wall . . .

The American poet William Stafford picked up on Blake's "golden string" metaphor and used it as inspiration in his own poem "The Way It Is."[13] This great poem is a perfect offering to share at commencement ceremonies. Here is the poem in full:

There's a thread you follow. It goes among
things that change. But it doesn't change.
People wonder about what you are pursuing.
You have to explain about the thread.
But it is hard for others to see.
While you hold it you can't get lost.
Tragedies happen; people get hurt
or die; and you suffer and get old.
Nothing you do can stop time's unfolding.
You don't ever let go of the thread.

Following a thread is how you find direction, meaning, and purpose in your life. It is especially helpful when you are traveling through dark passages in your journey. Or when you are lost in a maze or a labyrinth, like in the ancient Greek myth of Theseus, son of King Aegeus, who is given a ball of red thread by Ariadne, daughter of Pasiphae and the Cretan King Minos, to help him navigate the dark, narrow passages that take him deep into the center of the labyrinth, where he slays a Minotaur with his trusty sword and then finds his way back out into the world again.

Following the thread is what connects you to your destiny. Rainer Maria Rilke used the thread metaphor in one of his letters to Franz Xaver Kappus in *Letters to a Young Poet*. He wrote, "Destiny itself is like a wonderful wide tapestry in which every thread is guided by an unspeakable tender hand, placed beside another thread and held and carried by a hundred others."

All my life I've been pulled along by a thread. Initially I had barely any idea what the thread was or where the thread was leading me. Along the way, I began to join up some of the dots. One thing I've learned is that my thread belongs to the Christ lineage. As a child, I knew nothing about the Christ story. My family was not religious. We went to church only twice a year, once at Christmas to visit Santa Claus and once at Easter to visit the Easter Bunny! It wasn't until I left home and met Avanti, my first spiritual mentor, that I was properly introduced to the Christ Path.

Avanti introduced me to Jesus Christ, the mystic. He told me about a Cosmic Christ that belongs to all of life, not just humans. He also taught me about Christ Consciousness, which is, essentially, the One Mind that we share with God and all creation. He gave me a book to read called *Autobiography of a Yogi* by Paramahansa Yogananda. He then gave me another book by Paramahansa Yogananda called *Second Coming of Christ: The Resurrection of Christ Within You*. This really was a revelation. I was being introduced to the Jesus Christ story not by the church, but by mystics.

After that, the Christ became my thread, even though I often didn't realize it at first. When I began my studies of Western psychology, I didn't expect to find the Christ anywhere. There was certainly no mention of Christ in my lectures. That changed as I became better acquainted with Carl Jung's work. Jung saw the Christ archetype as the perfect symbol of the individuated whole Self in all of us. He wrote, "The Christ-symbol is of the greatest importance for psychology in so far as it is perhaps the most highly developed and differentiated symbol of the self, apart from the figure of the Buddha."[14]

When I bought a copy of *A Course in Miracles*, I didn't know it was a Christian mystical text. After studying the Course for a year, I met Tom Carpenter, who has taught me as much as anyone about the Christ by his loving presence. When I found the Enneagram, I discovered that it was entwined with the teachings of the Desert Fathers and Mothers of Egypt, who were Christian mystics. When I came to Findhorn for the first time, and I met Eileen Caddy and Dorothy Maclean, I learned that the guidance they both received emanated from the Christ Consciousness.

When Hollie and I were researching school options for our daughter, Bo, we found out about a Steiner Waldorf Kindergarten School in Richmond, London. Hollie's godmother, Barbara, had sent her children to a Steiner School. Neither of us knew that Rudolf Steiner was a Christian mystic. After kindergarten, Bo settled in very happily at St. Michael's Steiner School, which had recently relocated from Central to West London. Once we were established at the school, we began to take classes in Rudolf Steiner's teachings. One of the first books I read was a series of lectures by Rudolf Steiner called *From Jesus to Christ*.[15]

When I met Ron and Mary Hulnick at the University of Santa Monica, we soon discovered that we shared an interest in Christian mysticism. We talked at length about our favorite gospel, the Gospel of John, which is often referred to as the mystical gospel. We discovered that we had made pilgrimages to Assisi, Jerusalem, and Galilee, and that we had been in these places at the same time but in different groups. We also learned we share a love of William Wordsworth's poetry. The golden thread of fate had been weaving us closer and closer together until the time was right for us to meet.

Following the thread is how we find each other. Fate uses the threads of our basic relatedness to draw us together. These threads are like invisible telegraph wires that send out a signal to arrange a time and place for our meeting. Speaking of this phenomenon, Carl Jung said, "I call it, to myself, the Golden Thread." We all know that feeling of being deeply entwined with each other. I smile when I think of how many times our daughter, Bo, and son, Christopher, have made special love bracelets for Hollie and me. I've often worn several of these many-colored threads on both wrists at the same time because the agreement is that they can't come off until they fall off.

> *"I recognize a thread of creativity that has been running through my life since forever."*
>
> — Mary Hulnick

In my program called The Golden Thread, I give each of my students a piece of golden thread to wear on their wrist. The idea is to use the golden thread as a mindfulness practice to pay attention to your life and recognize the moments when you are being pulled by a thread. Most often, you experience this unmistakeable tug when you are following your joy, doing something you love, and engaged in something that feels meaningful and worthwhile. The golden thread is a physical anchor that reminds you that you don't have to do life on your own, that guidance and support are always available, and that your personal purpose is connected to a purpose you share with others and with all of creation.

NOT SELLING
YOURSELF SHORT

"Oprah Winfrey loves your book *Happiness NOW!* and she would you like you to be a guest on her show." The person speaking to me on the phone was Brian Piotrowicz, co-producer of *The Oprah Winfrey Show*. Brian had been given my number by Ian at my office, who thought it best that I speak to him straightaway. I got the call while I was taking Bo for an afternoon walk in our local park. Bo was fast asleep and strapped to my chest in a sling. I remember Brian and I conducted our conversation in a whisper, with soft voices and low tones, so as not to wake her.

Bo woke up as soon as my call with Brian ended. I sensed she had been listening to us the whole time. "How was your walk?" asked Hollie when we got back home. I told Hollie that Bo had slept for 90 minutes and that I'd just been invited on *The Oprah Winfrey Show*. "That's amazing!" said Hollie, referring to Bo's 90-minute nap. Bo was only six weeks old. The focus of our life was on sleeps, feeds, and nappies. "What was that about Oprah?" asked Hollie.

The Oprah show was called *How Happy Are You?* and it was to be filmed live with an audience at Harpo Studios in Chicago.[1] The broadcast date was two days after my forty-second birthday. In Rudolf Steiner's theory on biography work, 42 is the start of a new seven-year life cycle in which you commit more fully to the real work of your life. The aim is to align yourself more closely with your spiritual values and to tie the various threads of your life together into a single, unified purpose. This is your time to step forward, to take a lead, and to serve a higher purpose.

The night before the show, I went to the Cadillac Palace Theatre to see a preview performance of *The Color Purple*. The musical is based on Alice Walker's Pulitzer Prize–winning novel. Oprah Winfrey was one of the main producers, and she also starred in the film version of the book, directed by Steven Spielberg. When the main character, Celie, sang her final song, "I'm Here," which is about showing up fully for your life, it rearranged the molecules of my body, my heart swelled, and I burst into tears. Great theater can transform your experience of yourself and the world. It was the ideal preparation for the show the next day.

I had the strongest feeling of déjà vu as I stood in the wings waiting to be introduced by Oprah. I knew deep down that appearing on Oprah was in accordance with the larger plan that my life belongs to. I noticed on the teleprompter that it read, "and his new book is *Happiness NOW!*" In fact, *Happiness NOW!* had first been published nine years before. It had never been a bestseller. The annual royalties were modest. After the show that day, *Happiness NOW!* went to number 4 in all book categories on Amazon. A biography of Einstein and two Harry Potter books kept it off the top spot.

As a writer, you are full of hope when you send your book out into the world, but you never really know where it will go, who will read it, or what effect it will have. Books have a life of their own, and they are part of a bigger plan. They fall off the shelf, they land on your lap, they get given as a gift, and they appear in your life at the right time. My book *Shift Happens!* had been published for 12 years already when I got a call inviting me to do a PBS special on it.[2] The big plan arranges everything according to its own design and timing.

The original plan for my appearance on the Oprah show was that I would appear on three of the eight segments. That didn't happen. Each time the stage manager came to take me off, Oprah insisted that I stay. Oprah went way off script, and I ended up staying on for the whole show. We covered a lot of subjects in a short space of time. We talked about the pursuit of happiness, the destination addiction trap, the perils of dysfunctional independence, and the danger of leaving yourself out of your own life.

"Could you be happy after taking a ninety percent pay cut?" Oprah asked her audience. She then introduced Liz Heinrich, a former banking executive on Wall Street, who left her lucrative job in order train as a full-time trapeze artist. Liz told Oprah, "I was about to turn thirty, and I realized it was time for me to live the life I wanted for myself, not the life other people wanted for me." She went on to say, "I felt like I had to stifle parts of myself in order to be what Wall Street wanted from me. I felt like I was playing a corporate character, like it wasn't coming from who I really am."

Coincidentally, I had worked on Wall Street when I was in my 20s. I had a job at Bear Stearns investment bank. The pay was lucrative, the career track was well mapped out, and I was good at what I did, but, just like Liz, I didn't feel any passion for the work. I tried to convince myself to stay. I gave my inner guidance several chances to change its mind. *I can do what I love later in life,* I told myself. Saying yes to the money looked good on paper, but in real life I knew that I'd be selling out on something far more valuable.

I didn't realize at the time what a big deal appearing on Oprah would be. I was still in the bubble of being a new dad. Bo was all I could think about. Her happy face was a permanent screen saver in my mind. Changing her nappy was the first thing I did when I arrived back home after my flight. However, all my friends and family were keen to know what it was like to have met Oprah. Interestingly, I was mostly asked, "Is Oprah genuine?" "Is she the real deal?" and "Is she authentic?" Upon reflection, I think what people really wanted to know is if it's possible to be a big success in the world without selling an image of yourself and putting on a show.

Here's what I experienced being in Oprah's company. First, the show was recorded live, and each time we went to a commercial break, Oprah carried on talking in just the same way as when we were on air. I never felt that she was playing a role. I didn't feel interviewed. It was one continuous conversation. She also kept me on for the whole show because she wanted to learn more about my take on happiness and living your purpose. "I do this show because I want to live my best life, and I want to help others to do the same," she told me when we talked after the show.

What I experienced next is commonly called the "Oprah Effect." The phone rang off the hook, and I was very grateful to my team for fielding all the calls. Soon after, I was in Los Angeles and New York meeting with agents. At the first agency I went to, I sat around a table with seven agents dressed in suits. They told me that they wanted to develop a commercial strategy for my work, to conduct extensive market analysis, and to catapult me into stardom. I noted that I wasn't asked any questions about the purpose of my work, what it means to me, and why I love it.

When I met Jennifer Rudolph Walsh at the William Morris Agency in New York, it was a different vibe. The first question Jennifer asked me was "Have you recently had a baby?" She asked to see a picture of Bo. When I asked Jennifer how she knew, she told me that she got an intuitive hit the moment she saw me. "Babies bring blessings into our lives on many levels. Her arrival and you being on Oprah are part of the big plan," she told me, with a knowing smile.

Jennifer became my agent, and, along with her WME team, she pitched my work to every major U.S. publisher. The offers came in thick and fast. "I'm determined to find the publisher that is the perfect fit for you, Robert," Jennifer said. Once all the bids were in, we went through them together. "Intuitively, I get that Hay House is the perfect home for you," Jennifer told me. Hay House wasn't offering the most money, but after I spoke to Reid Tracy, the CEO and president, and heard about Louise Hay's mission and vision, I knew without a doubt that Hay House was right for me, and, sure enough, they've been my publisher ever since.

THE USES OF FAILURE

Avanti Kumar, my first spiritual mentor, was a yogi and a talented writer. His first play was broadcast on BBC Radio when we were at university together, and he earned a regular income as a BBC script editor. Avanti's love of literature and writing was inspiring to me. Along with classic texts of spiritual literature, he gave me books to read like *Leaves of Grass* by Walt Whitman, *A Moveable Feast* by Ernest Hemingway, *Death of a Salesman* by Arthur Miller, and *The Catcher in the Rye* by J. D. Salinger. We spent many hours together exploring the subtle narratives and hidden meanings of these great works.

After university, I committed myself to my writing. I wrote a daily entry in my journal in longhand, which I still do today. For articles and proposals, I worked on my black Imperial Good Companion typewriter. I submitted articles to magazines, wrote short stories for *Reader's Digest*, and sent comedy scripts to my favorite TV and radio shows. I also took on bigger projects, like a play for radio and three books on spiritual psychology, holistic healing, and inner happiness.

In the first four years of writing, I was in regular contact with commissioning editors, producers, and agents who told me I had potential, but I received no acceptances, no credits, and no royalties. I was a successful unpublished writer. I kept on writing, though, because I didn't want to be a writer who didn't write anymore. Eventually, I got a break. I was invited by Sarida Brown to work for *Caduceus*, a quarterly holistic health journal. After working on two editions of the journal, Sarida offered me the position of assistant editor. It was unpaid work, but I loved it, and I was finally given the chance to write interviews and articles published in my name.

I didn't earn a single penny for my writing for six years. I spent a lot of money on reams of recycled paper, typewriter ribbons, and Tipp-Ex correction fluid in that time. My dream was to write a book. I interviewed lots of people. I did masses of research. I wrote several synopses and three full manuscripts that never made it to print. This was in the olden days, as my son, Christopher, says, before e-mails and PDF files, and I learned to recognize the heavy thud of another returned manuscript pushed through my mailbox and hitting the floor. To keep my spirits up, I made sure I had at least five manuscripts out in the world at any one time.

I received approximately 70 rejection letters before I was offered my first book deal. Each rejection letter was about three lines long. I'd examine these letters thoroughly, looking for a sign of encouragement and any hint of hope. Failing so regularly was most despairing for a young man like myself who was desperate to make his mark upon the world. With hindsight, I see now that these failures had their uses. With each rejection, I had to ask myself, *Why do I write?*

I've taught many writing classes over the years, including for the Hay House Writer's Workshop, which has a terrific track record of helping publish many first-time authors. I've also served as a mentor in the Hay House Diverse Wisdom writing school. One of the first exercises I give my students is to work with this sentence: "I write because . . ." Most writers feel compelled to write. We write because we must. We are following our joy, but it's not all fun. We work in solitude and often meet fear, doubt, rejection, and loneliness along the way. Knowing your "because" makes you resilient and keeps the inkwell from running dry.

On my writing desk, I have a pink quartz angel with outspread wings, about three inches tall. Bo gave her to me as a gift on the day I started to write my book *Loveability*. She was five years old at the time. "Here's your writing angel, Daddy," she said, handing it over to me. I think she "borrowed" it from Hollie's office. Each time I sit down to write an article, a blog, a newsletter, or a book, I ask Bo's writing angel to help me tune in to the highest purpose of what I am writing about so that inspiration will flow freely and easily.

Each week I write a newsletter called *Shift Happens!* Writing my newsletter is a spiritual practice for me. I rarely know in advance what I will write about. However, when I pay attention to my life—the one that is happening right now—a thread appears, and I make sure I follow the thread until the newsletter is written. Writing my newsletter helps me be present, do my inner listening, appreciate my life, and commit to my purpose.

One of my favorite writing projects is called *Love Notes* for my Instagram page. *Love Notes* are a series of short meditations on the nature of love. I write each love note by hand using my favorite fountain pen. I take a picture of each one on my smart phone, and then I post them on my Instagram account. There's no flashy design. I don't have a marketing plan. I'm not selling anything. I'm simply posting love notes out into the world. I like to think that if everyone sent one love note out to the world—one love note per person—our world would be transformed by love.

> *"We write to taste life twice, in the moment and in retrospection."*
>
> — Anaïs Nin

Writing is an act of love. It can be that if you want it to be. And, hopefully, in the process of writing, the writer becomes an instrument of love, not just when writing but in their whole life. In my writing classes, I recommend Natalie Goldberg's book on writing called *Writing Down the Bones*. In it she writes, "The deepest secret in our heart of hearts is that we are writing because we love the world." She goes on to say, "And why not finally carry that secret out with our bodies into the living rooms and porches, backyards and grocery stores? Let the whole thing flower: the poem and the person writing the poem. And let us always be kind in this world."[3]

In my first book of poetry, *Finding Love Everywhere*, I include a poem called "Love's Instrument."[4] It's a poem, a prayer, an affirmation, and a meditation all in one. I recite it to myself before I write. Along with my writing angel, it helps me set an intention to be an instrument for a higher purpose when I write. Here is "Love's Instrument."

I am a pencil in God's hands.

I am here to write Love Letters from God to everyone in the world.

God is ready to write and therefore so am I.

I sit patiently before God and listen for the thoughts of God.

I ask God to remove any imagined blocks to writing now.

I meet every fear with love.

I find it easier than expected to write because God does the work.

All I do is listen.

And take notes.

And enjoy the process.

WORTH GETTING CRITICIZED FOR

It takes a lot of courage to fully show up for your life, to speak your truth, and to live your purpose.

When I sit at my desk to write, I am often met by a big temptation to do something else first. I get the urge to open my e-mail, to check a sports result, to book theater tickets, to call a friend, to water a plant, to unstack the dishwasher, to give the oven a deep clean, or to book a holiday to somewhere far, far away. This temptation, which has a thousand forms, masks a terrible fear that there will be no inspiration today. The point is, though, that whatever your work is, you must show up for inspiration to appear.

Sitting before the blank page is mirror work. It's not always pretty. Most mornings what I see first are my fears projected back at me. The lead story in my mind is *I'm not ready to write*, which is followed by thoughts like *I've got nothing to say* and *I'm not in the right mood* and *The energy is not right* and *I need better lighting in this room* and *Is Mercury in retrograde?* and *It's the wrong time of year* and *I should wait until spring to begin.*

Anyone who expresses themselves creatively, and who follows their joy, will meet internal and external criticism along the way. When writing, I hang out with my inner critic a lot. My inner critic's first language is judgment. On some mornings, my inner critic shows up with a bunch of noisy friends, like the perfectionist, the doubter, the editor, and the accuser. My mind is occupied by a bunch of squatters—imaginary figures—holding up placards on poles that say, "You're not Shakespeare!" and "You're not a real writer!" and "It won't be a bestseller!"

The best bit of advice I've read on writing is by Ernest Hemingway in *A Moveable Feast*. There's a passage in which he shares his own struggles with trying to write something worthwhile. He writes,

> I would stand and look out over the roofs of Paris and think, "Do not worry. You have always written before and you will write now. All you have to do is write one true sentence. Write the truest sentence that you know." So finally I would write one true sentence, and then go on from there. It was easy then because there was always one true sentence that I knew or had seen or had heard someone say. If I started to write elaborately, or like someone introducing or presenting something, I found that I could cut that scrollwork or ornament out and throw it away and start with the first true simple declarative sentence I had written. Up in that room I decided that I would write one

story about each thing that I knew about. I was trying to do this all the time and it was good and severe discipline.[5]

Hemingway's words "write the truest sentence that you know" encapsulate the highest purpose of writing for me.

No matter what your purpose is and how you choose to express yourself, you will encounter your inner critic, and you will also have to deal with criticism from others. Inevitably, there will be times when you are tempted to edit yourself, to dumb yourself down, and to play it safe. But don't sell out! And don't betray yourself. The poet Rumi said, "They say I tell the truth. Then they ask me to do a puppet show of myself in the bazaar. I'm not something to sell. I have already been bought!"[6] In other words, stay true to your higher purpose and your reward will be greater than any amount of money or prestige can buy.

Over the years I've received my share of one-star Amazon book reviews, thumbs-down ratings for my TED Talks, cruel comments on my Facebook page, unsubscribes from my newsletter list, and so on. It can be very painful and disheartening at times. That said, I believe that *living your purpose is worth getting criticized for.* Criticism offered constructively can help you raise your game. And the other sort of criticism, which is not constructive, is a useful training in staying true to your purpose by remembering that you do your work not to be loved but in service to a greater love.

PRESENCE OF LOVE

I had the honor and good fortune to interview Maya Angelou three times. The first time was on Valentine's Day in 2013. I was a little giddy, I must confess. The interview was a big surprise. It was arranged by a friend with only three days' notice. Most unexpectedly, here I was in conversation with one of the most beloved and celebrated voices of our day, and on this special day, which also happened to be the official publication date of my new book *Loveability*. When Ms. Angelou signed off by saying, "Thank you, Mr. Holden, for being my happy valentine today," I did wonder if I had dreamed the whole thing.

In our first interview, we talked mostly about love and how learning to love and be loved is the highest purpose of life. I began by quoting Maya Angelou to Maya Angelou. "Thank you for remembering these words," she said afterward, with gentle humility and grace. She told me that she still stood by these words and that her greatest aspiration was to be a voice for love in the world. Here are the words that I quoted to her:

Love builds up the broken wall
and straightens the crooked path.
Love keeps the stars in the firmament
and imposes rhythm on the ocean tides.
Each of us is created of it and
I suspect each of us was
created for it.

Maya Angelou issued an urgent challenge to the human family through her writing and activism to embrace love as our shared purpose. She saw love as the perfect antidote to our sense of separateness that is the root cause of fear, poverty, prejudice, racism, and war. She also saw love as a higher power that, when we truly align ourselves with it, can help us overcome the ordeals and challenges we face in our world today. "Love recognizes no barriers. It jumps hurdles, leaps fences, penetrates walls to arrive at its destination full of hope," she said.

Maya Angelou told me, "Be courageous every day and you will succeed at living your purpose." She described courage as the most important of all virtues. "Without courage, you can't practice any other virtue consistently," she said. When I asked Maya where she got her courage from, she quoted Wordsworth to me. She said, "Knowing that I am a child of God, and that I come trailing wisps of glory, has given me the confidence to know that I am always in the right place at the right time. And knowing that with God's love, all things are possible, I find the courage I need to say yes to my life."

When Maya Angelou gave a Masterclass for the *The Oprah Winfrey Show*, she told us that our life's purpose is to be a blessing to each other and to be a rainbow in somebody else's cloud. She sang a couple of lines from a gospel song "God Put a Rainbow in the Sky," which is inspired by Genesis 9:13: "I have set my rainbow in the clouds, and it will be the sign of the covenant between me and the earth."[1] And then she told us of another way she finds the courage to do her work and live her purpose. She said,

> One of the things I do when I stand up on a stage, when I stand up to translate, when I go to teach my classes, when I go to direct a movie, I bring everyone who has ever been kind to me with me. Black. White. Asians. Spanish speaking. Native American. Gay. Straight. Everybody. I say "Come with me! I'm going on the stage. Come with me, I need you now." Long dead. You see. So I don't ever feel I have no help. I've had rainbows in my clouds. And the thing to do, it seems to me, is to prepare yourself so that you can be a rainbow in somebody else's cloud.

"I want to be a representative of my species," Maya Angelou told me in our third interview, shortly before her death. To be in Maya's presence was to experience someone who fully embodied her purpose. Not only did she represent the human family so beautifully, but she was also the perfect ambassador of her message. "Preach the Gospel at all times. When necessary, use words," is a saying often attributed to St. Francis of Assisi. When Maya Angelou talked about love, you experienced love as it really is. To be with Maya Angelou was to be in the presence of love.

A few weeks after Maya Angelou's death in 2014, the NASA spacecraft *Orion* made a test flight more than 3,600 miles into space in preparation for a much greater voyage to new destinations in our solar system. On board the *Orion* were commemorative items that symbolized *Orion*'s mission and humanity's true endeavor. One of the items was Maya Angelou's poem "A Brave and Startling Truth," which she composed for the fiftieth anniversary of the United Nations in 1995.[2] Maya Angelou dedicated her poem to "the hope for peace, which lies, sometimes hidden, in every heart."

In her poem, she describes three journeys that we are all participating in. They are the journey of the cosmos, the journey of humanity, and our own personal journey. All three journeys are entwined with one another. They are the golden thread of life. On these journeys, we discover a power that Maya says "pulls the stars in the firmament" and "pushes and urges the blood in our veins." This power is God's love, and it is the greatest truth of our lives. In the final stanzas, Maya tells us,

When we come to it
We, this people, on this wayward, floating body
Created on this earth, of this earth
Have the power to fashion for this earth
A climate where every man and every woman
Can live freely without sanctimonious piety
Without crippling fear

When we come to it
We must confess that we are the possible
We are the miraculous, the true wonder of this world
That is when, and only when
We come to it.

OUT OF THE CAGE

One of my favorite possessions is a signed copy of *I Know Why the Caged Bird Sings* by Maya Angelou.[3] It's a first edition, in hardback, with a striking cover of a golden sun with ever-widening circles, a red-orange sky, and the silhouette of a bird soaring high. I've kept this copy in pristine condition. My intention is to hand it on to my daughter, Bo, on a special birthday or maybe a graduation. I expect I'll know when the time is right.

I Know Why the Caged Bird Sings was published in 1969, and it has often been described as a "coming of age" book. This is true on two counts. First, it tells the story of Maya's traumatic childhood in which she endured rape, poverty, racism, and prejudice of every kind. The narrative begins when three-year-old Maya and her older brother, Bailey, are sent to live with their grandmother in Stamps, Arkansas, and it ends when Maya becomes a mother at the tender age of 16.

Second, it introduced Maya Angelou to America as a powerful new voice in the civil rights movement. Her book was catapulted onto the *New York Times* bestseller list, where it remained for two years. It was the catalyst for her future work as a memoirist, an essayist, a poet, a playwright, a theater director, a TV producer, and furthermore as a university professor and mentor. With each new offering, her message and influence stretched out across the globe, and she was heralded as a true humanitarian who offered a new vision of hope and possibility for us all.

When Maya was eight years old, she was sexually abused and raped by her mother's boyfriend, Mr. Freeman. She told her brother, Bailey, who then told the rest of the family. Mr. Freeman was arrested, held in custody, tried in court, and sentenced to one day in jail. Four days after his release, he was murdered. No one was officially charged for his death. Perhaps it was one of Maya's uncles who took the law into his own hands. On hearing the news of Mr. Freeman's death, young Maya became mute, and she didn't speak again for almost five years.

In our first conversation, Maya told me, "After I was raped, and the man was killed, I thought my voice killed that man. If I hadn't spoken his name, he would still be alive. So my voice has the power to kill, and so I had better stop speaking." With that, Maya withdrew into herself. She became an invisible child and the forgotten daughter. She lived inside a cage, which she dared not come out of, for fear that she might cause further harm and violence.

The symbolism of a caged bird is powerful because we can all relate to it. There is trauma in everyone's biography. We have all been wounded. History is full of acts of oppression. Everyone has been silenced at one time or another. The temptation to withdraw and hide is commonplace. We learn how to survive in the cage, and even make it comfortable, but eventually we must try to free ourselves. As Carl Jung observed, there is an impulse within each of us "to follow nature's own striving to bring life to the fullest possible fruition in each individual, for only in the individual can life fulfill its meaning—not in the bird that sits in a gilded cage."[4]

When I asked Maya what the symbol of the caged bird meant for her, she said, "Mr. Holden, I would like to recite for you the poem which inspired my work." She then recited "Sympathy" by Paul Laurence Dunbar, the African American poet and novelist, the son of a farmer's slave, who lived for 33 years at the turn of the 20th century.[5] Maya recited the three short verses of "Sympathy" with such reverence that I imagined I was sitting in church listening to a sermon or a prayer. Here is the final verse of this most soul-stirring poem.

I know why the caged bird sings, ah me,
When his wing is bruised and his bosom sore,—
When he beats his bars and he would be free;
It is not a carol of joy or glee,
But a prayer that he sends from his heart's deep core,
But a plea, that upward to Heaven he flings—
I know why the caged bird sings!

Maya told me that "we create our own cages, and our own prisons, out of fear, and out of not knowing what tomorrow brings." And yet, just as the sun shines, the wind stirs, the river flows, and the first buds open—all images from Dunbar's poem "Sympathy"—we humans must sing out our prayers, sing of our wounds, sing our hopes and fears, and sing the song that is our true offering to each other. As Maya observed in her poem "A Brave and Startling Truth," from our mouths which issue such "cankerous words" at times, also "come songs of such exquisite sweetness / That the heart falters in its labor / and the body is quieted into awe."

When I asked Maya about her five years of self-imposed silence, she told me, "I'm not sure I would have left my cage without my brother, Bailey, and my grandmother's love." Maya told me that her grandmother would say, "Sister, Mum don't care what people say, that you must be a dummy. I know that when you and the Good Lord are ready, you will become a teacher, and you are going to teach all over the world." Maya's grandmother was her Supernatural Aid, the one who saw the hero journey that Maya was preparing herself to take.

The self that lives inside a cage is not the Self you are destined to be. At some point you must come out of hiding and set yourself free. It's a journey that begins with a choice. "You may not control all the events that happen to you, but you can decide not to be reduced by them," said Maya. I have quoted these words of Maya's many times in my lectures and workshops. They remind me of what Viktor Frankl said in *Man's Search for Meaning*: "Everything can be taken from a man but one thing: the last of the human freedoms—to choose one's attitude in any given set of circumstances, to choose one's own way."

"Turn your wounds into wisdom," says Oprah Winfrey, who credits Maya Angelou as her mentor. That's exactly what Maya did. Through the writing of her autobiographies, seven in all, Maya found a way to honor her wounds but not be defined by them. At the same time as she was honoring her wounds, she also discovered a bigger presence waiting inside her, and she became reacquainted with her true Self. In telling her story, Maya Angelou was able to proclaim, "I am not my biography; I am what God made me!"

Maya Angelou stepped out of her cage, she found her voice, and she became the world's most visible Black female leader and teacher of her generation. On January 20, 1993, Maya became only the second poet in history to read a poem at a presidential inauguration.[6] The poem was called "On the Pulse of Morning," and it was read for President Bill Clinton's inauguration. The recording of her poem won the Grammy Award in the "Best Spoken Word" category.

"On the Pulse of Morning" is an invitation to accept our destiny. Maya put her whole self into this poem. She wrote it with the voice of an elder, a shaman, a priestess, and also a nature mystic. I can't help but think of Wordsworth's "Ode: Intimations of Immortality" when I read it. Her poem is an address to all of us to sing the songs that our Creator gave to us "when I and the / Tree and the rock were one." In the course of her rousing poem, she tells us,

> *You, created only a little lower than*
> *The angels, have crouched too long in*
> *The bruising darkness*
> *Have lain too long*
> *Face down in ignorance,*
> *Your mouths spilling words*
>
> *Armed for slaughter.*
> *The Rock cries out to us today,*
> *You may stand upon me;*
> *But do not hide your face.*

THE USES OF FORGIVENESS

The last time I talked with Maya Angelou was to pay tribute to Nelson Mandela and his life. Shortly after his death, Maya had put pen to paper and written a poem to commemorate her dear friend, who had faced brutal apartheid, savage racism, and unjust imprisonment and yet somehow emerged triumphant to become one of the most inspiring leaders of our times. She called her poem "His Day Is Done."[7]

I began our conversation by saying, "Ms. Angelou, you once said, 'I've learned that people will forget what you said, people will forget what you did, but people will never forget how you made them feel.' You knew Nelson Mandela very well. How did he make you feel?" Once again, I was quoting Maya Angelou to Maya Angelou. I remember she responded with a big smile and a happy laugh. "I was amazed at his kindness," she said softly. Since the first time they met, which was in Cairo in 1962, she observed in Nelson Mandela a capacity to offer love and respect to everyone equally.

In "His Day Is Done," Maya begins by recounting a few of the terrible ordeals Mandela faced in the lead-up to his imprisonment in 1964. "Would the man survive? Could the man survive?" Maya asks. Nelson Mandela was locked away in a cage—a prison cell on Robben Island—and here, in his darkest hour, he found inspiration. One source of inspiration was the poem "Invictus" by the British Victorian poet William Ernest Henley.[8] Mandela recited this poem to himself often. It begins,

> *Out of the night that covers me*
> *Black as the pit from pole to pole,*
> *I thank whatever gods may be*
> *For my unconquerable soul.*

Maya and I talked about Nelson Mandela's leadership, and how, like many great leaders, his life became his message. "What would you say is Nelson Mandela's message to us?" I asked her.

Without any hesitation, she replied, "To learn to forgive." She went on to say, "When he walked out of the prison after twenty-seven years of being unjustly imprisoned, people were wondering, *What is he going to be like?* Will he shout? Will he be angry? No! He came out smiling, and he offered the world a chance at reconciliation!" This noble gesture was Nelson Mandela's personal victory and a truly great act of leadership.

Maya Angelou attended Nelson Mandela's inauguration as South Africa's first democratically elected president on May 10, 1994. Also in attendance were Nelson Mandela's former prison guards, who were seated in the front rows. Nelson Mandela was teaching forgiveness and reconciliation by his words and actions. He was offering the world an example of a bigger love—a love that exists inside all of us—that has the power to overcome all our grievances. Every argument, every conflict, every war, ends in love, but first we must choose love as our teacher, our path, and our purpose.

Maya's poem "His Day Is Done" is the story of a man who fulfilled his purpose. The words *His Day* refer not just to a passage of time but to a mission on earth. By fulfilling his mission, Nelson Mandela inspires us to fulfill our mission. This is his legacy. "Yes, Mandela's day is done," writes Maya Angelou in her tribute, "yet we, his inheritors, will open the gates wider for reconciliation, and will respond generously to the cries of Blacks and Whites, Asians, Hispanics, the poor who live piteously on the floor of our planet." Maya finishes her tribute with, "We will not forget you, we will not dishonor you, we will remember and be glad that you lived among us, that you taught us, and that you loved us all."

I think of Maya as my angel of forgiveness, as someone who showed me by her presence and example what is possible when we choose to forgive. We talked especially about the purpose of forgiveness and the blessings that forgiveness offers us. "Forgiveness is the greatest gift you can give yourself. Forgive everybody," Maya told me. She said, "Without forgiveness, we will not make our friendships, our family, our communities, and our countries into everything they could be. And we will not accomplish the work we have been sent to do."

Forgiveness is at the heart of all my work. I believe that forgiveness is humanity's greatest need. I have written about forgiveness in every book. I talk about forgiveness in all my lectures, especially the ones on love, leadership, and purpose. I teach classes on forgiveness in every Mastermind and retreat. I believe that forgiveness is an essential spiritual practice that we must be willing to learn. A good living question is *What do I need to forgive today?* "Each day we have a chance to be more forgiving," Maya told me.

The most helpful teachings I have learned about forgiveness are from *A Course in Miracles*, my favorite book. The Course teaches that forgiveness is our main function here on earth. One of my favorite lessons in the Course workbook is entitled "Forgiveness is my function as the light of the world."[9] "All forgiveness is a gift to yourself," teaches the Course, because forgiveness helps you escape the prison of your isolation and overcome your suffering. "It is your forgiveness that will bring the world of darkness to the light," teaches the Course. It is what sets the bird free from its cage.

Perhaps the chief purpose of forgiveness is that it helps you remember who you truly are. Another teaching from *A Course in Miracles* is "Through your forgiveness does the truth about yourself return to your memory. Therefore, in your forgiveness lies your salvation." Forgiveness is for the forgiver. No one benefits more from forgiveness than the one who forgives. "I am willing to practice forgiveness in every situation because forgiveness is always for my highest good," said Maya. With forgiveness, you are not a victim, you are not defeated by circumstances, and you remember your unconquerable soul.

Forgiveness is a miracle because it changes your relationship with the past. Forgiveness can't change the events of the past, but it can change the meaning you give to the past. Forgiveness helps you honor your wounds, learn from your mistakes, grieve your losses, and give a new meaning to what happened so as to release you from the prison cage. Every single experience in your biography, including the most shameful and painful ones, can help you fulfill your purpose if you allow it to.

Forgiveness helps you live in the present tense. "The present is forgiveness," teaches the Course. Forgiveness is a new beginning. With forgiveness we can proclaim triumphantly, *I am not my past. I am more than that. I am not my heartbreaks. No single failure is an entire biography. Mistakes are lessons, not nameplates.* The past is not the final chapter in your life. With forgiveness you can have a better past (because you have given it a new meaning) and a better future. "In my country, we go to prison first and then become President," wrote Nelson Mandela in *Long Walk to Freedom.*[10] He also wrote,

> As I walked out the door toward the gate that would lead to my freedom, I knew if I didn't leave my bitterness and hatred behind, I'd still be in prison.

One of the greatest miracles of forgiveness is that when you forgive, not only do you heal but you also open yourself up to a whole new level of inspiration and grace. I've witnessed this miracle in myself and in others time and time again. Whenever I am struggling, tired, stuck, lost, in pain, or in the dark about something, I ask myself, *What do I need to forgive here?* I ask to be shown the fear, judgment, criticism, or grievance that I am holding on to. I trade in my psychology for grace, I exchange my grievances for miracles, and I ask that I might be guided and inspired by a higher power that is greater than my ego.

Forgiveness opens you up to what Caroline Myss calls a COSMIC-SIZED love in her book *Intimate Conversations with the Divine.*[11] This great love offers an atmosphere of miracles. It helps

> *"When I have forgiven myself and remembered Who I am, I will bless everyone and everything I see."*
>
> — *A Course in Miracles*

you step out of the darkness and into the light. Louise Hay, with whom I co-wrote the book *Life Loves You*, once told me, "I would not be the Louise Hay that I am today without forgiveness. There was a time when I did not love myself because of my past. Forgiveness helped me to love myself. By loving myself, I changed my past, and I painted a new future for myself."

Forgiveness is our greatest victory. "It liberates the soul, and it removes fear," said Nelson Mandela. With forgiveness, you can show up more fully in your life. You are more open to guidance, available to inspiration, and ready to be employed by the COSMIC-SIZED love that overcomes separation and suffering. Forgiveness gives you wings. You live a more expanded life. You enter a new level of consciousness. You see things from outside your cage and from a new vantage point. And your presence is a blessing to others and to the whole world.

SING THE WHOLE SONG

"Daddy, if I'm going to sing, I've got to sing the whole song," said Bo, my daughter, who was 11 years old at the time.

It was the third day of a workshop that Hollie and I were teaching in the Universal Hall at Findhorn. The workshop was called Love, Relationships and Miracles, and it was based on the teachings of *A Course in Miracles*. We had over 150 participants, a truly international crowd with people coming from faraway places such as Lebanon, Israel, New Zealand, Syria, Peru, China, and Russia. This is typical for a Findhorn event and a big reason why I love to teach at the Universal Hall.

Hollie and I were on a lunch break. We were sitting at our kitchen table while Bo and Christopher were busy buzzing around us. We had just finished a morning session on The Function of Forgiveness. The focus was on forgiving the past so as to step more fully into the present. This was our third day, and by now the group felt safe and whole, and so the work we did together that morning was especially transformative, healing, and inspiring.

For the first two days of Love, Relationships and Miracles, Hollie and I had taught pretty much without a script. We had witnessed such profound sharings and synchronicities between people that we happily put aside our notes and went with the flow. Our role as teachers was to be fully present and *spontaneously available*—my mentor Tom Carpenter's favorite term—to whatever wanted to happen next. All the while, we both felt that the Angel of Findhorn and other unseen hands were pulling the strings.

Now, on day three, we still had three sessions to go after lunch, and we were unsure about what to teach next. In our event timetable, the first session was entitled Teach Only Love: Committing to Love as Your Spiritual Purpose. The second session didn't have a title other than Finish and Farewells. And the third session was an evening *ceilidh*—a traditional Scottish dance—in the Universal Hall, starting at 7 P.M. We love to finish our workshops in Findhorn with a ceilidh, and fortunately for us, Jonathan Caddy and his ceilidh band are always on hand to lead the dance.

"So what shall we do now?" Hollie asked me. I had no idea. "Something will happen," I told her.

Unbeknown to us, Bo had been eavesdropping in on our conversation. She is a great eavesdropper. Eavesdropping on her parents is one of her talents.

"I can sing a song for you!" Bo said, trying to sound casual, as she glided past the kitchen table.

"Thanks, Bo!" I replied, thinking little of it.

"I want to sing 'Hallelujah'!" she told us.

"'Hallelujah'?" asked Hollie, making sure she'd heard her right.

"Yes, 'Hallelujah'!"

"Bo, that's a big song," I said.

"Are you sure that's the song you want to sing?" asked Hollie.

"Yes!" insisted Bo.

"Okay, we'll think about it," I said.

"Why do you need to think about it?" replied Bo.

We were both surprised, and a little nervous, that Bo wanted to sing this song in front of a crowd of people. Bo has a natural ear for music. She sings beautifully and she plays the guitar well. But Bo had sung only once before in public. It was at the St. Michael Steiner School summer fair, over a year ago. She sang her own version of the Jason Mraz song "I'm Yours," and I accompanied her on guitar. Hollie and I had heard Bo practicing "Hallelujah" in her bedroom over the last few days. She hadn't performed it for us yet.

"Daddy, I need you to print out the lyrics for me," Bo told me. As we sat in front of the computer, looking up "Hallelujah," I was thinking to myself, *Is this really a good idea?* Hollie was thinking the same thing. We found several versions of the song; most had four or six verses and plenty of lyrics. I suggested to Bo that maybe she'd like to sing just a couple of verses. That's when Bo looked me in the eye and said—as if she were a Zen priestess—"Daddy, if I'm going to sing, I've got to sing the whole song."

Over at the Universal Hall, the tech team set the stage for Bo with a chair, a microphone, and a music stand for the lyrics. Hollie introduced Bo to everyone, and then Bo sang her song. After a couple of bars strumming her guitar, and just before she started to sing, Bo got a croak in her throat. She had a sip of water and took a moment to compose herself, and then she started again. After that, Bo transfixed us with the melody of her voice and sensitive playing. Everyone joined Bo for the final chorus of "Hallelujah," and we rose to our feet spontaneously as one to give Bo a standing ovation.

> *"If you have a song to sing, who are you not to open your mouth and sing to the world?"*
>
> — Maya Angelou

Bo delivered us her own hallelujah. I watched the recording of it again just now. It's even better than I remembered it. I'd like to think that Leonard Cohen, Jeff Buckley, Bono, Bob Dylan, k.d. lang, Yolanda Adams, and everyone else who has ever hummed or sung this song in their bedroom would appreciate how Bo made it her own. She wasn't concerned with making it a perfect offering. She didn't even have a full rehearsal of the song in the hall. She did what the lyric of the song says. She stood before the Lord of Song, with nothing on her lips but Hallelujah. And she gave us her song of praise.

After Bo's song we all went down to the Original Garden at Findhorn. We stood in a ring of three circles. I recounted how Bo had said to me, "Daddy, if I'm going to sing, I've got to sing the whole song." And how those four simple words "sing the whole song" are vital if we are to teach only love and live our purpose fully. I then took a moment to read the Greatest Commandment in the Gospel of Mark 12:30 that encourages us to love God and each other with "thy whole heart, and with thy whole soul, and with thy whole mind, and with thy whole strength."

Bo's words, "Sing the whole song," have become an anthem for me. They often appear spontaneously in my mind when I am about to give a talk, do an interview, write an article, or start a new chapter for a book. I imagine I must have an angel on my shoulder who politely but persistently says, "Ahem, do please remember to sing the whole song." When I hear these words, I am reminded to tune in to the infinite, to remember the Oneness, and to allow myself to be supported and guided by the universal spirit of inspiration—the Holy Spirit—that is everywhere.

For me, to sing the whole song is an invitation to be my whole authentic self, to be open and vulnerable, and honest and true. It's a call to practice self-acceptance and to embrace my human needs, admit my fears, recognize my weaknesses, come out of hiding, ask for help more, and show up fully in my life. One thing I know for sure is that it's in the moments when we dare to be fully present and be our true self that we feel most on purpose with life. This is also the greatest act of love we can offer ourselves, each other, and the world.

THE PURPOSE OF A BEE

This morning Christopher and I went with our friend John Willoner to visit the Findhorn beehives. We dressed up in our all-in-one white cloth bee suits, with round hoods and fencing veils, and our long beekeeper gloves. Looking like spacemen, we then walked through the pine forest, past the windmills, and on to a clearing in the gorse where the beehives are situated. The sun was out, there was a light breeze, and the temperature was about 20°C: the perfect conditions for stopping by and saying hello to the bees.

John Willoner came to Findhorn in the 1960s. He was among the first people to join the founders of the Findhorn Foundation. As a young man, John watched in awe as Dorothy Maclean, one of the founders, communed with the bees. She demonstrated a natural affinity with them, as if she spoke the language of bee. John has been a beekeeper ever since. He is dedicated to the care of the Findhorn bees, as are Jonathan Caddy and Martin Harker. John's home, which he built here on the Field of Dreams, is called Honey Pot.

As we approach the beehives, we are met by the guard bees, whose job it is to protect the hive from unwanted intruders. At this point, John likes to stop and take a moment to do an attunement with the bees. "I like to let the bees know that we are here for a visit, and that we come as friends," John tells me. The attunement helps John be present to the bees, get a feeling for the well-being of each bee colony, and identify the specific needs of each hive. John always offers a simple prayer of thanks for the bees. He treats the bees with reverence and love.

When I wrote the proposal for this book, my first thought was about the bees. Bees are central to the story of our planet. Mother Nature relies on bees to create life on earth. Without bees, the history of flowers would be a blank. There would be no milk and honey. Bees have clocked up more than 100 million years of evolution so far. The bee population are our elders in many ways, and they have much to teach us about how to live our purpose.

Bees are a wonderfully diverse species. As well as the honeybee and the bumblebee, there are carpenter bees, mason bees, mining bees, and more than 20,000 other varieties. Bees are also a beautifully complex society in which every bee is committed to a threefold purpose that I have explored throughout this book. When you spend time with bees, and study how they live, you see that each bee has 1) a personal purpose, which is unique; 2) a shared purpose, which supports a colony; and 3) a universal purpose, which helps the evolution of the planet and creation itself.

A colony of bees is made up of between 20,000 and 80,000 bees. Inside each colony, there are three castes of bee: worker bees, drone bees, and the queen bee. Worker bees take on many different tasks in their brief life span, and they do so with a singleness of aim, which is to serve the colony. For example, the female worker bee will happily work as a cleaner, a nurse, a chef, a guard, and a forager. By contrast, the male drone bee has only one task on his mind, which is to mate with the queen bee. Every bee is essential to the colony, and it goes about its individual business to help the colony survive and prosper.

Bee colonies are a matriarchal society. The leader of every hive is a female. How, I wonder, would the human civilization have evolved if there had been more female leaders? And how might humanity fare if we believed in a Mother-Father God and also treated Mother Nature with reverence and awe? The queen bee doesn't rule over her subjects; she is in service to them. One of her main jobs is to lay approximately 2,000 eggs a day. She also emits a queen mandibular pheromone that gives the colony its identity and supports optimal functioning around the hive.

Every bee fulfills the first two levels of purpose by making its unique contribution to the collective well-being of its colony. Beyond that, bees fulfill the third level of purpose by serving Mother Nature. Bees are the top pollinators on our planet. This is true of both social bees, who live in colonies, and solitary bees, who hang out on their own. In fact, bee lovers have observed that solitary bees do more pollinating than another kind of bee. So whether you are an extrovert or introvert bee, you are always participating in the great song of creation.

The presence of a single bee, which may live for just a few days or weeks, plays a vital part in the whole cycle of life on our planet. They are intimately involved with how the flora of Mother Nature blossoms and blooms. "A bee is an exquisite chemist," said a royal beekeeper to Charles II. They are natural scientists who humbly serve every other species on our planet. Spring would not be spring without bees. Crops would not grow the way they do if it were not for bees. Humans would not drink coffee, eat jam on toast, or enjoy the fruits of the earth if bees were not as generous as they are.

Rudolf Steiner advocated that we study bees to help us live our purpose and experience a greater kinship with the cosmos. He gave a series of nine lectures on the life of bees, which has become a most valuable resource for ecologists, farmers, and beekeepers. Rudolf Steiner was a scientist who observed what he called "a collective wisdom [that] is unfolded by the bees in their external activity." He described the activity of the bees in terms of love. He said, "What we only experience when love arises in our hearts is to be found, as it were, in the whole bee-hive, as substance. The whole hive is in reality permeated with love."[1]

Steiner went on to say, "One only begins to understand the life of the bees when one knows that the bee lives in an atmosphere completely pervaded by love. On the other hand, the bee is quite especially favoured by the fact that, in its turn, it feeds upon just those parts of the plants which are also wholly pervaded by love." In other words, bees do what they do because of a higher love for all of life. Imagine if we humans behaved the same way.

Today a major part of humanity's work is to care for bees. Bees have offered us everything out of love. "Not a single bee has ever sent you an invoice," said Pavan Sukhdev, in a United Nations report on the Economics of Ecosystems and Biodiversity. "And that is part of the problem—because most of what comes to us from nature is free, because it is not invoiced, because it is not priced, because it is not traded in markets, we tend to ignore it."[2] But we cannot afford to ignore it. Bees and humans belong to each other. The future of the bees is our future too.

Just like the human civilization, the bee civilization is now in decline. Bees, along with every other species, have always had their predators and threats. And, as for most other species, the main problem is humans. The catastrophic collapse of bee colonies—called colony collapse disorder—has been caused by climate change, urbanization, loss of habitat, pesticides, and other human influences. Bees have also had to face their own equivalent of a global pandemic with varroa mites. Performing a varroa check is one of the jobs we always do when we visit the Findhorn beehives with John Willoner.

"We are the bees of the unseen," wrote Rainer Maria Rilke in a letter to his Polish translator Witold Hulewicz. He saw that the purpose of his work was to "passionately gather the honey from the visible and invisible worlds" and offer it to each other. He described the universe as "the great golden beehive of the unseen." Imagine that! If we weave the mythology of bees together with our own human story, we can find a way out of our lonely existence. By loving the bees, and learning from the bees, we can save the bees, we can save the planet, and we can save ourselves.

VOICE OF LOVE

Dorothy Maclean lived to be 100 years old. She was one of the cofounders of Findhorn and a much-loved and respected spiritual leader around the globe. Hollie, Bo, Christopher, and I were present at her birthday celebration held in the Universal Hall. Three hundred of us gathered in person, and many more joined on the livestream to offer messages of congratulations and thanks. Jonathan Caddy compered a jubilee of song, dance, readings, and meditations, and a short play with an actress dressed up as a bee.

I was asked to give a reading at Dorothy's birthday celebration. I read an excerpt from her wonderful autobiography, *Memoirs of an Ordinary Mystic*.[3] Afterward I told everyone how each time my family and I return to Findhorn, Dorothy magically appears to greet us. She is always one of the first people we see. She might be taking a walk with one of her carers, or sitting on a bench, or even passing by our house. This has happened so often that Bo and Christopher tell us it must be the angels who let Dorothy know we are here.

For the first six years of the Findhorn story, Dorothy Maclean lived with Peter and Eileen Caddy and their three sons in a small light-blue caravan that is still in the same spot in the Original Garden today. When I step inside the caravan, I can't imagine how they managed to live together in such a small space. Dorothy lived in Findhorn for 11 years before she returned to Canada and then traveled the world with her work and her message. She came back to Findhorn in 2009 and lived the rest of her days in a small bungalow next to the Original Garden. She passed away in her sleep a few weeks after her hundredth birthday.

I visited Dorothy for tea in her small bungalow many times. Each visit was arranged by John Willoner. To be in her presence was a joy. She always had a twinkle in her eye and a radiant smile. She had a rainbow-colored walking stick and matching rainbow gloves and hat; that was her motif. We enjoyed many luminous conversations, and sometimes we were just quiet together. Her short-term memory had begun to fade, but it didn't bother her. She once told me, "I gave my mind to God a long time ago, and if there is something I really need to know, God will tell me."

In her autobiography Dorothy describes her small-town upbringing in Guelph, 60 miles west of Toronto, Canada. She writes, "I have often been asked if I had any spiritual experiences in my youth. No, I was excessively ordinary." Dorothy was a shy girl who enjoyed the company of nature, her daydreams, and a good book. Most significantly, she tells us, "What I did have, from an early age, was one abiding question: 'what is the purpose of life?' This question was always on my mind."[4]

What is the purpose of life? was Dorothy's living question. She lived with this question throughout her life, and she used it as an oracle and a guide for making important decisions and life choices. In the Second World War, Dorothy worked in the British Secret Intelligence Service in New York, and she traveled extensively. The world was in crisis. Dorothy's boyfriend, Jim, was killed at war. It was around this time that Dorothy met her first spiritual mentor, a lady called Sheena. Now Dorothy had someone to talk to about living her purpose.

Dorothy dedicated herself to a study of the wisdom of the ages. She studied the major sciences, spirituality, and metaphysics. She attended lectures at the Study Society, in London. She read books by Ouspensky, Gurdjieff, Steiner, Krishnamurti, and Alice Bailey. She worked for a while at a Quaker center called Friends House near the Euston train station. I've given many talks there over the years. She also began to practice meditation, and one day she heard a voice within that said to her, *"Come closer."*

After some initial misgivings, Dorothy learned to trust that voice and to follow its direction and guidance in good faith. She described the voice that said, "Come closer" as the most loving voice she had ever heard. Dorothy once told me, "Eventually, I realized it must be my voice that I was listening to, but not just my voice, *all our voices.* I was listening to the Voice of Love, which is the one true voice of humanity and the one true voice of God. Love was speaking to me."

By paying attention to the Voice of Love, Dorothy developed a natural affinity with nature, with bees and trees, with angels and devas, and with all life. She learned to respect the laws of nature, which are the laws of creation and of God. She realized that nature is fully conscious, and that love is the great intelligence of the universe. She saw that humanity must be transformed by love if we are to survive. She said, "There is no doubt that the planet is going through a transformation where all of us are learning to recognize our wholeness. The soul is being grounded in a new way. As we bring love into all things, we transform the planet into a higher vibration."

Dorothy described love as "the home of all virtues and gifts." She believed that love is our greatest resource, and that with enough love we can overcome our aloneness, dissolve all barriers, and solve every problem. She encouraged every one of us to put love first in all our endeavors. In one of Dorothy's books, *Messages from God*, which features daily inspirations from her journals, there is an entry that begins,

If you put love first and do even the most ordinary thing with love, elements of wonder, openness, purpose or rightness are present. With love the most ordinary event takes on completely different colours. So, practice love's presence all day long whatever you do and every event will be lit up with a hitherto unknown radiance.[5]

Dorothy always insisted she was an ordinary person who simply put God first and offered herself as an instrument of love. Her conviction was that the willingness to be ordinary is the essential qualification for living a life of purpose. By being willing to be ordinary—and just like everyone else—we can tap into a shared and greater purpose. "Let love work through you, and give all the glory to love," Dorothy said.

When you live a love-centered life, you are making "a submission towards the infinite," as Kahlil Gibran put it. Love becomes the chief inspiration. Love is your life's Star. Love is your moral compass. Love is the golden thread. Love is your Supernatural Aid. Love is the way and the truth and the life of all things. When Dorothy was asked on her ninety-sixth birthday, by her friend Geoff Dalglish, if she had any remaining ambition for her life, she replied, "Only to be more loving."

A NEW KIND OF POLITICS

Love is our one true purpose. It is the universal purpose we share with each other and with Life Itself.

The truly great thing about love is that *all acts of love are maximal*. There really is no such thing as a so-called "small" or "big" act of love. The love that inspires a seemingly small or big act of love is the same love. There are no grades of love. Every act of love has the same purity of love in it. It has the same golden thread. And there is no separation in love. Therefore, when you do anything with love, you are drawing from the same source of love that all love comes from. Thus, every act of love has effects that are immeasurable and endless.

A great example of *all acts of love being maximal* is the story of the Love Button Global Movement, set up by two medical doctors, Dr. Habib Sadeghi and Dr. Sherry Sami.[6] I first met Habib and Sherry after I gave a commencement speech at the graduation ceremony for the University of Santa Monica. Both Habib and Sherry are USM graduates. As we got to know each other, we realized we had much in common, and we have collaborated on several projects since, including my Mastermind on Love-Centered Living.

"The Love Button Global Movement grew out of the crucible of my trauma and healing," Habib told me as we got to know each other. As a young medical student, Habib was suddenly diagnosed with cancer. This was his death of normal, his inciting incident, and his call to adventure for his hero journey. "I was terrified and directionless," said Habib. "As I was rolled into surgery, I wrote *God is Love* on my hand."

As Habib recovered from his cancer, he thought deeply about the meaning of life and his true purpose. "After graduating medical school, I wore a love sticker on my lab coat to remind me of the healing that happens when we choose love," recalls Dr. Habib. Habib's patients kept asking him about his love sticker. One day Habib and Sherry had the idea to make a Love Button, something they could hand out to their patients. The design for the Love Button came to Habib in a flash of inspiration at a fundraising dinner for a charity they supported. Their first order of Love Buttons soon ran out, so they ordered some more.

"It started with a simple act of love," recalls Sherry, "and it inspired countless more acts of love." The Love Button caught the imagination of friends and family who volunteered their time to distribute Love Buttons at airports, train stations, hospitals, shopping malls, and other hot spots in the local community. "The Love Button was no longer just an object; it had become a grassroots community," said Sherry. "We were like a beehive of human beings that was sending more and more love into the world with each Love Button we gave away."

What began as an idea—*God is Love*—became a sticker, and then a Love Button, and then a grassroots community, and eventually a global movement. The tipping point came when Chris Martin, the lead singer of Coldplay, arranged for 75,000 people in Levi's Stadium in Santa Clara, California, to have Love Buttons and to hold up colored placards during the halftime show at Super Bowl 50 to reveal a **Believe in Love** message that filled the stands and featured the Love Button logo in its resplendent, multicolor design. Over 100 million people saw the Love Button on TV, and after that, the Love Button went global.

So far, over 7 million Love Buttons have been distributed worldwide. Of course, the Love Button Movement is not just about buttons; it's about people making a stand for love. With proceeds from their nonprofit organization, Habib and Sherry have partnered with UNICEF, with Doctors Without Borders, with the University of Santa Monica, and with many other organizations to spread their message of love. "The Love Button Movement teaches us every day that we are the love," says Sherry, "and that by being a loving presence we all can make a difference in the world."

I am happy to be an ambassador for the Love Button Movement. I give out Love Buttons at my talks and workshops, and when I run the coffee stall at the summer fair at St. Michael Steiner

> *"Love's in need of love today."*
>
> — Stevie Wonder

School. Last week, John Willoner and Sylvia Black gave out over 100 Love Buttons at a meditation event held in the Universal Hall at Findhorn. I like telling people the story of the Love Button Movement because it teaches us that *with love all things are possible.*

Love is the greatest activism of all because everyone can participate in it. Love is the heart of activism. Activism is love in action. A true activist performs acts of love through their presence and their work. Whatever form your activism takes, what matters most is that you do it with love. Through love in action, you can connect with the universal purpose of life, with the shared purpose of humanity, and with your unique purpose.

Every act of love is an act of leadership. Remember, leadership is not a position; it is a way of being. Each time you act with love, or simply introduce love into the conversation, you are leading with love. It doesn't have to be a super big thing you do. "One small garden can help to change the world," said Dorothy Maclean. "It takes one seed to create a forest," Dr. Habib Sadeghi once told me. This world will be transformed by millions of acts of love that are not recorded in a hall of fame or in a newspaper. A true leader is happy to be among the nameless ones, and for their acts of love to be offered as a gift to the world.

It is love that sent you into this world trailing clouds of glory, and it is love that makes you into a happy warrior. Another of my favorite William Wordsworth poems is "Character of the Happy Warrior."[7] It begins,

> *Who is the happy Warrior? Who is he*
> *That every man in arms should wish to be?*
> *—It is the generous Spirit, who, when brought*
> *Among the tasks of real life, hath wrought*
> *Upon the plan that pleased his boyish thought:*
> *Whose high endeavours are an inward light*
> *That makes the path before him always bright.*

Wordsworth tells us that the happy warrior is one who "keeps faithful with a singleness of aim." When we are on purpose, we are sustained by the love that is our mission. Love is love's own reward. And therefore, the happy warrior "does not stoop, nor lie in wait / For wealth, or honours, or for worldly state." We cannot be bought. We will not sell out. We will remain faithful to our calling and to the greater glory that we honor and serve.

Every act of love is a tipping point! This is the most marvellous thing about love. Every act of love joins forces with every other act of love—because there is only One Love—and therefore the "R number" of love is so infectious that there really is no telling how big, wide, deep, and far the effect of a gentle smile, a message of love, or an act of kindness will travel. This is why Maya Angelou encouraged everyone who has been tempted to give up on love (which is all of us, isn't it?) to "have enough courage to trust love one more time and always one more time."

Love is the flowering of humanity. "May my soul blossom in love for all existence," wrote Rudolph Steiner. This was his simple prayer, and look how he is still serving the world a century or more after he left his mortal body. "From the heart's unbounded love / The vain emptiness of narrow self is filled / With the fire of the cosmic Word," wrote Rudolph Steiner in another one of his verses.[8] Each time we choose love, we are transforming ourselves from a single grain of wheat into living spirit that can bear much fruit.

You are here to love the world. This is your business. Everything you do must be in service to this. Love is "the longest stride of soul men ever took" says Christopher Fry in his poem "A Sleep of Prisoners."[9] Love is the metanoia—the holy shift—that changes everything. Love is here to stir humanity, who has taken "so many thousand years to wake." We are here to love humanity into a new stage of existence. With enough love, we can each participate in a new kind of politics, in which each one of us is an activist, a leader, and a happy warrior.

In closing, I will leave you with a poem called "A New Kind of Politics," which I wrote one early morning while sitting on my favorite bench in the Original Garden in Findhorn.[10] The sun was out, but the air was still cold. There was dew on the grass. A young robin was bouncing about near my feet. The first bees were flying into the garden to start their work. And there was a big dragonfly darting this way and that. As I sat there, enjoying the life of the garden, eating a wild raspberry I had just picked, my imagination stirred, and a series of visions came to me about a possible future that could happen on earth if we are willing to choose love and live our purpose. One of those visions turned into this poem:

I'm voting for a new kind of politics.
Based not on opposition, but on imagination.
A politics with an international heart.
A climate change from fear to love.
With a defense budget for trees,
and a Ministry for Bees.
A new flag for Planet Earth.
An end to debt economies.
No need for charities.
No third world. Just one world.
Where leaders who dare to love
the most always win the
majority vote.

ENDNOTES

Introduction

1. *Shift Happens! radio show.* This was an internet talk-radio show for Hay House Radio. I hosted most of my shows live every Thursday, between 6 and 7 P.M. UK time. You can listen to episodes on the Hay House Unlimited Audio App and also at my website, www.robertholden.com.

2. *"Yew-Trees" by William Wordsworth.* You can find this poem in most editions of his collected works. I recommend *The Book of Nature: Wordsworth's Poetry on Nature* (Bristol, UK: Ragged Hand, 2020).

PART I: THE CALL

A Bigger Me

1. Robert Holden, *Authentic Success*, formerly titled *Success Intelligence* (Carlsbad, CA: Hay House, 2011), 2–3.

2. *My grandpa's briefcase.* When Grandpa died (I was 21 years old by then), I asked Granny if I might have his briefcase. I keep it here in my office by my desk.

3. *Biography counseling.* Also called biography work, this is described as a practice to help you become the Self you truly are. The work helps you to understand your life story by observing significant stages, cycles, and dates. To learn more, read *Why on Earth? Biography and the Practice of Human Becoming* by Signe Eklund Schaefer (Hudson, NY: SteinerBooks, 2013).

4. William Wordsworth, "Ode: Intimations of Immortality from Rec-ollections of Early Childhood," in *Poems, in Two Volumes* (London: Longman, Hurst, Rees, and Orms, 1807).

5. Rudolf Steiner, *The Illustrated Calendar of the Soul: Meditations for the Yearly Cycle*, trans. John B. Thomson (East Sussex, UK: Temple Lodge Publishing, 2004).

6. Jean Houston, *Godseed: The Journey of Christ* (Wheaton, IL: Quest Books, 1987).

7. *Grain of wheat parable.* John 12:24–26 (New Revised Standard Version).

8. *Jesus's warning to us.* "Those who love their life lose it, and those who hate their life in this world will keep it for eternal life." John 12:25 (NRSV).

9. *Not glory for the self.* "Yet I do not seek my own glory, there is one who seeks it and he is the judge." John 8:50 (NSRV).

10. *Not self-made glory.* "If I glorify myself, my glory is nothing. It is my Father who glorifies me, he of whom you say, 'He is our God.'" John 8:54 (NSRV).

11. *The hero journey.* To learn more about the hero journey, I recommend Joseph Campbell's book *The Hero with a Thousand Faces* (New York: Pantheon Books, 1949). Also visit The Joseph Campbell Foundation at www.jcf.org.

Questions to Live By

1. *300 questions a day.* I recommend two articles from the British press, one from *The Daily Telegraph*, the other from *The Independent*:
    "Mothers Asked Nearly 300 Questions a Day, Study Finds," *The Telegraph*, March 28, 2013, https://www.telegraph.co.uk/news/uknews/9959026/Mothers-asked-nearly-300-questions-a-day-study-finds.html.
    Emma Elsworthy, "Curious Children Ask 73 Questions Each Day—Many of Which Parents Can't Answer, Says Study," *The Independent* December 3, 2017, https://www.independent.co.uk/news/uk/home-news/curious-children-questions-parenting-mum-dad-google-answers-inquisitive-argos-toddlers-chad-valley-tots-town-a8089821.html.

2. Rainer Maria Rilke, *The Book of Hours: Prayers to a Lowly God*, trans. Annabelle S. Kidder (Evanston, IL: Northwestern University Press, 2001), 15–17.

3. Robert Holden, *Stress Busters* (New York: HarperCollins, 1992).

4. *The Happiness Project.* For further information about the Happiness Project and references to happiness research, read my books *Happiness NOW!* (Carlsbad, CA: Hay House, 2007) and *Be Happy* (Carlsbad, CA: Hay House, 2009).

5. *True Vision.* To find out more about the work of True Vision, visit www.truevisiontv.com.

6. *How to Be Happy.* This BBC documentary is currently available to watch on YouTube. The book that accompanies the documentary is Brian Edwards and Wendy Sturgess, *QED How to be Happy* (BBC Education, 1996).

7. *Success Intelligence Ltd.* For further information about my S.I. keynotes, workshops, and Mastermind programs on Success Intelligence, visit www.robertholden.com.

8. Holden, *Authentic Success*, 120.

9. Rainer Maria Rilke, *Letters to a Young Poet* (New York: Penguin Classics, 2012).

10. Rilke, *Letters to a Young Poet*, 30.

11. Hollie Holden, "Holy Church of Noticing." To read more of Hollie's poetry, visit her website: www.hollieholden.me.

A Sense of Destiny

1. William Wordsworth, "Ode: Intimations of Immortality."

2. *The Selected Poetry of Rainer Maria Rilke*, trans. Stephen Mitchell (New York: Random House, 1982), 69. I also recommend Rainer Maria Rilke, *A Year with Rilke*, trans. Joanna Macy and Anita Barrows (New York: HarperCollins, 2009).

3. *My great-uncle, Derek Hill.* Read Grey Gowrie, *Derek Hill: An Appreciation* (London: Quartet Books, 1987). Visit Glebe House and Gallery in Donegal, Ireland, www.glebegallery.ie.

4. *Senselessness and aimlessness.* C. G. Jung, *The Practice of Psychotherapy*, vol. 16 of *Collected Works* (Princeton, NJ: Princeton University Press, 1985), 41. Also visit www.carljungdepthpsychologysite.blog.

5. *Addressed by a voice.* C. G. Jung, *The Development of Personality*, vol. 17 of *Collected Works* (Princeton, NJ: Princeton University Press, 1981), 176.

6. *A sense of destiny.* C. G. Jung, *Memories, Dreams and Reflections: An Autobiography* (New York: Pantheon Books, 1963).

7. *The inner voice.* Jung, *The Development of Personality*, 175.

8. *True personality.* Jung, *The Development of Personality.*

9. *The Stages of Life essay.* C. G. Jung, *Structure and Dynamics of the Psyche*, vol. 8 of *Collected Works* (Princeton, NJ: Princeton University Press, 1970), 387–403.

10. *What is the myth you are living?* Read Mr. Purrington, "Carl Jung on 'What Is the Myth You Are Living?,'" *Carl Jung Depth Psychology*, April 7, 2020, https://carljungdepthpsychologysite.blog/2020/05/05/carl-jung-on-what-is-the-myth-you-are-living/#.YoKnmYvMI2w.

11. *"You are the light of the world."* Matthew 5:14 (NSRV).

Answering the Call

1. *Glebe House and Gallery.* Website: www.glebegallery.ie.

2. Holden, *Stress Busters*, 35.

3. Viktor E. Frankl, *Man's Search for Meaning: Revised and Updated* (New York: Washington Square Press, 1997).

4. Frankl, *Man's Search for Meaning,* 111.

5. Frankl, *Man's Search for Meaning,* 138.

6. Frankl, *Man's Search for Meaning,* 121.

7. Viktor E. Frankl, *Yes to Life: In Spite of Everything* (London: Rider, 2019).

8. *Logotherapy in a nutshell.* Read a great introduction to Logotherapy in Part Two of Frankl, *Man's Search for Meaning.*

9. Frankl, *Man's Search for Meaning,* 121.

PART II: THE PATH

The Hero You Are

1. *Power of Myth.* There are three ways to watch and read about this documentary. The first is the *Power of Myth* DVD box set, 30th Anniversary Edition, released by Kino Lorber. The second is to visit Bill Moyers's website: https://billmoyers.com/series/joseph-campbell-and-the-power-of-myth-1988. The third is to read the illustrated paperback that accompanies the series, called *The Power of Myth.*
   Joseph Campbell and Bill Moyers. *The Power of Myth* (PBS: 1988).
   Joseph Campbell and the Power of Myth with Bill Moyers, 30th Anniversary Edition (New York: Kino Lorber, 2018).
   "Joseph Campbell and the Power of Myth," BillMoyers.com (PBS,

August 28, 2015), https://billmoyers.com/series/joseph-campbell-and-the-power-of-myth-1988.

Joseph Campbell and Bill Moyers, *The Power of Myth* (New York: Doubleday, 1988).

2. *Hero Journey courses.* For further information about my Hero Journey workshops, retreats, and Mastermind programs, visit the Events page on my website: www.robertholden.com.

3. Joseph Campbell, *Pathways to Bliss: Mythology and Personal Transformation* (Novato, CA: New World Library, 2004).

4. Joseph Campbell, *The Hero with a Thousand Faces* (New York: Pantheon Books, 1949).

5. Campbell and Moyers, *The Power of Myth*, 53.

6. *Sleepy Land.* Diane K. Osbon, ed., *Reflections on the Art of Living: A Joseph Campbell Companion* (New York: HarperCollins, 1991), 77.

7. *One hero journey after another.* Campbell, *Pathways to Bliss*, 133.

8. See Part I, "A Bigger Me," note 3.

9. Stephen Larsen and Robin Larsen, *Joseph Campbell: A Fire in the Mind: The Authorized Biography* (Rochester, VT: Inner Traditions, 1991), 3.

10. Campbell, *The Hero with a Thousand Faces*, 18.

11. Robert Thurman, *Wisdom Is Bliss: Four Friendly Fun Facts That Can Change Your Life* (Carlsbad, CA: Hay House, 2021).

Joy Is Your Compass

1. *"Blank Joy."* This poem appears in many collections of Rilke's poems. To enjoy more of Rilke's poetry, I recommend you visit https://rilkepoetry.com/poems/by-title/.

2. *Thinking one's own thoughts.* Read Rudolf Steiner, *Intuitive Thinking as a Spiritual Path* (Hudson, NY: SteinerBooks, 1995).

3. *George Bernard Shaw on joy.* From George Bernard Shaw, *Man and Superman* (New York: Penguin Classics, 2000), 34.

4. *Whales and dolphins.* A great source for research on the sentient and sapient nature of whales and dolphins is the Whale and Dolphin Conservation Project: https://uk.whales.org/.

5. *Life on earth is made possible for us all.* To learn more about swimming in the wild with dolphins and whales, visit Ocean of Love Pilgrimages: https://oceanoflove.nl.

A Meditation on Success

1. Martin Heidegger, *What Is Called Thinking?* (New York: HarperPerennial, 1963).

2. *Destination addiction.* Read Holden, *Authentic Success*, 235–248. Watch the TED Talk on destination addiction on YouTube and at my website: www.robertholden.com.

3. *Frankl on success.* Frankl, *Man's Search for Meaning*, 16–17.

4. See Part I, "Questions to Live By," note 7.

5. Danah Zohar and Ian Marshall, *Spiritual Intelligence* (London: Bloomsbury Publishing PLC, 2001).

6. *An experience of being alive.* Joseph Campbell and Bill Moyers, *The Power of Myth*, 5.

7. Carlos Castaneda, *The Teachings of Don Juan: A Yaqui Way of Knowledge* (Oakland: University of California Press, 1968).

8. Zohar and Marshall, *Spiritual Intelligence*, 296.

9. *Dove Real Beauty Campaign.* Read about Dove campaigns at https://www.dove.com/us/en/stories/campaigns.html.

10. "The 'Dove Real Beauty Pledge,'" Dove, https://www.dove.com/us/en/stories/about-dove/dove-real-beauty-pledge.html.

Doing What You Love

1. *The Loveability Project.* Read Robert Holden, *Loveability: How to Love and Be Loved* (Carlsbad, CA: Hay House, 2013). For more information on my talks, retreats, and Mastermind programs on love, visit my website: www.robertholden.com.

2. *A Course in Miracles.* Read *A Course in Miracles: Combined Volume*, 3rd ed. (Novato, CA: Foundation for Inner Peace, 1975).

3. *Tom Carpenter.* I wrote a foreword for Tom's books *Let Love Find You*, volumes 1 and 2. I also recommend Tom Carpenter and Linda Carpenter, *Dialogue on Awakening* (The Carpenter's Press, 2012).

4. *A Course in Miracles*, 15.

5. Sigmund Freud, *On Narcissism: An Introduction* (New Haven, CT: Yale University Press, 1991).

6. C. G. Jung, *The Red Book* (New York: W. W. Norton & Company, 2009).

7. Erich Fromm, *The Art of Loving* (New York: HarperPerennial, 2000).

8. Rilke, *Letters to a Young Poet*, 49.

9. Eileen Caddy, *Opening Doors Within: 365 Daily Meditations* (Rochester, VT: Findhorn Press, 2019).

10. Frankl, *Man's Search for Meaning*, 57.

11. Thomas Berry, *The Great Work: Our Way into the Future* (New York: Three Rivers Press, 1999).

12. "United Nations Millennium Development Goals," United Nations, www.un.org/millenniumgoals.

13. Caddy, *Opening Doors Within*, 172.

PART III: THE ORDEAL

Make Me an Instrument

1. Thomas of Celano, *Francis Trilogy: Life of Saint Francis, The Remembrance of the Desire of a Soul, The Treatise on the Miracles of Saint Francis* (Hyde Park, NY: New City Press, 2004).

2. Saint Francis of Assisi, *Little Flowers of St. Francis of Assisi*, trans. Brother Ugolino (New York: Cosimo Classics, 2007).

3. Thomas of Celano, *Francis Trilogy*.

4. Saint Francis of Assisi, "Canticle of the Creatures" (1224). Francesco loved all of God's creatures with equal love, and this inspired him to write "Canticle of the Creatures," which is a song of love to brother sun and sister moon.

5. Robert Holden, *Finding Love Everywhere: 67½ Wisdom Poems to Help You Be the Love You Are Looking For* (Carlsbad, CA: Hay House, 2020), 29.

The Death of Normal

1. *Mental health and COVID-19*. "Mental Health and Psychosocial Considerations during the COVID-19 Outbreak," World Health Organization, March 18, 2020, https://www.who.int/docs/default-source/coronaviruse/mental-health-considerations.pdf.

2. Arundhati Roy, "The Pandemic Is a Portal," *Financial Times*, April 3, 2020, https://www.ft.com/content/10d8f5e8-74eb-11ea-95fe-fcd274e920ca.

3. Ed Yong, "How the Pandemic Defeated America," *The Atlantic*, August 4, 2020, https://www.theatlantic.com/magazine/archive/2020/09/coronavirus-american-failure/614191/.

4. Roy, "The Pandemic Is a Portal."

5. Pema Chödrön, *When Things Fall Apart: Heart Advice for Difficult Times* (Boulder, CO: Shambhala, 1996), 71–72.

In a Dark Place

1. St. John of the Cross, "Dark Night of the Soul," trans. David Lewis (London: Thomas Baker, 1908). St. John of the Cross wrote a poem and two book-length commentaries about the poem, *Ascent of Mount Carmel* (*Subida del Monte Carmello*) and *The Dark Night* (*Noche Oscura*). Both commentaries can be found in *The Collected Work of St. John of the Cross*, trans. Kieran Kavanaugh and Otilio Rodriguez (Washington, D.C.: ICS Publications, 1991).

2. Thomas Moore, *Dark Nights of the Soul: A Guide to Finding Your Way Through Life's Ordeals* (New York: Gotham Books, 2004), xviii–xix.

3. Dante Alighieri, *The Divine Comedy*, illus. Paul Gustave Doré (San Diego, CA: Canterbury Classics, 2013).

4. *On Liz Trubridge.* Liz had heard that Julian Fellowes's favorite children's book was *The Chimneys of Green Knowe* by Lucy M. Boston (London: Faber & Faber, 1958), and she approached him through his agent with the idea of adapting it for screen. While Julian was working on *From Time to Time*, which he directed, he told Liz about a new series he was writing for Carnival Films and Gareth Neame, and before long, she was invited to join the team to produce *Downton Abbey*.

5. Sogyal Rinpoche, *The Tibetan Book of Living and Dying* (New York: HarperCollins, 1992), 11.

6. Richard Sylvester, *I Hope You Die Soon: Words on Non-Duality* (Oakland, CA: Non-Duality Press, 2006).

7. Eugène Ionesco, *Exit the King* (New York: Grove Press Inc., 1963).

8. Corinthians 15:51 (NRSV).

9. *In Praise of Mortality: Selections from Rainer Maria Rilke's Duino Elegies and Sonnets to Orpheus*, trans. and ed. Anita Barrows and Joanna Macy (Echo Point Books & Media: Brattleboro, VT, 2005).

10. *Fruitful darkness.* Read Joan Halifax, *The Fruitful Darkness: A Journey Through Buddhist Practice and Tribal Wisdom* (New York: Grove Press Inc., 2004).

11. *Sweet darkness.* Read the poem "Sweet Darkness" by David Whyte. David Whyte, *River Flow: New and Selected Poems, Revised Edition* (Langley, WA: Many Rivers Press, 2012).

12. *Holy darkness*. Listen to the hymn "Holy Darkness" by Dan Schutte, who was inspired by the poem "Dark Night of the Soul" by St. John of the Cross. Colleen Toole, "History of Hymns: 'Holy Darkness' by Dan Schutte," Discipleship Ministries, May 18, 2016, https://www.umcdiscipleship.org/resources/history-of-hymns-holy-darkness-by-dan-schutte.

13. Moore, *Dark Nights of the Soul*, 117.

14. *Nicodemus*. Watch Robert Holden and Reverend Peter Dewey in conversation about Nicodemus in the documentary *The Gospel of John–Decoded and Revealed* (Robert Holden Film, 2019). You can watch it at https://www.robertholden.com/shop/gospel-of-john-decoded-and-revealed/.

15. Hollie Holden, "What Wants to Be Born in You, Beloved?" To read more of Hollie's poetry, visit her website: www.hollieholden.me.

The Enneagram Chapter

1. *Marika Borg*. Marika is a much-loved teacher of the Enneagram. She is a student of *A Course in Miracles* and author of many books. You can find out more about her courses and books at www.marikaborg.fi.

2. *About the Enneagram*. To learn more about the Enneagram, visit the International Enneagram Association website: www.internationalenneagram.org.

3. *Don Riso and Russ Hudson*. Don and Russ are co-authors of several classic books on the Enneagram. A good place to start is Don Richard Riso and Russ Hudson, *The Wisdom of the Enneagram: The Complete Guide to Psychological and Spiritual Growth for the Nine Personality Types* (New York: Bantam, 1999). Also visit their website: www.enneagraminstitute.com.

4. P. D. Ouspensky, *In Search of the Miraculous* (San Diego: Harcourt, Inc., 2001), 294.

5. *About Nassim Haramein*. For more information about Nassim's work, visit the Resonance Science Foundation website www.resonancescience.org.

6. *Rudolf Steiner verses*. There are many translations of Steiner's verses. A good resource is this website: www.awaldorfjourney.com/verses.

7. *Wayne Dyer documentary*. Wayne W. Dyer, *The Shift*, dir. Michael A. Goorjian (Carlsbad, CA: Hay House, 2009). Also see the accompanying book by Wayne Dyer, *The Shift: Taking Your Life from Ambition to Meaning* (Carlsbad, CA: Hay House, 2010).

8. *"A troubled guest on the dark earth."* This is from the last line of the poem "The Holy Longing" by Wolfgang von Goethe.

9. *About Shawn Gallaway.* To find out more about Shawn Gallaway's music, concerts, workshops, and I Choose Love movement, visit his website: www.shawngallaway.com.

10. *Patanjali yoga sutras.* There are many translations of this classic work. Read Sri Swami Satchidananda, *Yoga Sutras of Patanjali* (Buckingham, VA: Integral Yoga Publications, 2012).

11. Louise Hay and Robert Holden, *Life Loves You* (Carlsbad, CA: Hay House, 2015).

12. Louise Hay, *Trust Life: Love Yourself Every Day with Wisdom from Louise Hay,* compiled and edited by Robert Holden (Carlsbad, CA: Hay House, 2018).

13. Hay, *Trust Life*, entry for November 24.

14. *About Martin Luther King Jr.* Visit the website www.thekingcenter.org. Read Martin Luther King Jr., *Where Do We Go from Here: Chaos or Community?* (New York: Harper & Row, 1967).

PART IV: THE VICTORY

A Commencement Speech

1. *About the University of Santa Monica.* Visit the USM website: www.universityofsantamonica.edu.

2. Ron Hulnick and Mary Hulnick, *Loyalty to Your Soul: The Heart of Spiritual Psychology* (Carlsbad, CA: Hay House, 2011).

3. *Why USM.* Visit www.universityofsantamonica.edu/why-usm.

4. Whyte, *River Flow.*

5. Abraham H. Maslow, *Motivation and Personality* (New York: Harper & Row, 1954), 162.

6. Maslow, *Motivation and Personality*, 46.

7. Fromm, *The Art of Loving*, 9.

8. *On Albert Einstein.* Read Albert Einstein, *The World as I See It* (New York: Citadel Press, 2006).

9. Berry, *The Great Work*, 170.

10. *OneSpirit Interfaith Foundation.* For information on courses, trainings and services offered by One Spirit, visit the website: www.interfaithfoundation.org.

11. *On Alternatives.* For information about talks, workshops, and retreats, visit www.alternatives.org.uk

12. William Blake, *The Complete Poems* (New York: Penguin Classics, 1978).

13. William Stafford, *The Way It Is: New & Selected Poems* (Minneapolis: Graywolf Press, 1999).

14. C. G. Jung, *Jung on Christianity* (Princeton, NJ: Princeton University Press, 1999), 195.

15. Rudolf Steiner, *From Jesus to Christ* (Hudson, NY: SteinerBooks, 2005).

Not Selling Yourself Short

1. "How Happy Are You?," *The Oprah Winfrey Show*, April 11, 2007, https://www.youtube.com/watch?v=r-7q7QbHMvg.

2. PBS, *Shift Happens!* This show is available for purchase at www.robertholden.com.

3. Natalie Goldberg, *Writing Down the Bones* (Boulder, CO: Shambhala, 2005), 129.

4. Holden, *Finding Love Everywhere*, 117

5. Ernest Hemingway, *A Moveable Feast* (Cedar Rapids, IA: Arrow Books, 2004), 7.

6. Denise Breton and Christopher Largent, *Love, Soul & Freedom* (Center City, MN: Hazelden, 1998), 12.

Presence of Love

1. *Rainbow in the clouds.* Genesis 9:13 (New International Version).

2. Maya Angelou, *The Complete Poetry* (London: Virago, 2015), 269.

3. Maya Angelou, *I Know Why the Caged Bird Sings* (New York: Random House, 1969).

4. Jung, *The Practice of Psychotherapy*, 229.

5. Paul Laurence Dunbar, *The Complete Poems of Paul Laurence Dunbar* (Charlottesville: University of Virginia Press, 1993).

6. Angelou, *The Complete Poetry*, 261.

7. Angelou, *The Complete Poetry*, 301.

8. John Howlett, *Invictus: Selected Poems and Prose of W. E. Henley* (Brighton, UK: Sussex Academic Press, 2017).

9. *Forgiveness is my function. A Course in Miracles*, Lesson 62.

10. Nelson Mandela, *Long Walk to Freedom: The Autobiography of Nelson Mandela* (London: Abacus, 1995).

11. Caroline Myss, *Intimate Conversations with the Divine: Prayer, Guidance, and Grace* (Carlsbad, CA: Hay House, 2020).

Sing the Whole Song

1. Rudolf Steiner, *Bees: Lectures by Rudolf Steiner* (Hudson, NY: Steiner-Books, 1998).

2. *On bees and biodiversity.* Laura Petersen, "Global Economy Must Tally Environmental Costs—Report," *New York Times*, October 20, 2010, https://archive.nytimes.com/www.nytimes.com/gwire/2010/10/20/20greenwire-global-economy-must-tally--environmental-costs--4664.html. Also visit TEEB: The Economics of Ecosystems & Biodiversity at the website: www.teebweb.org.

3. Dorothy G. Maclean, *Memoirs of an Ordinary Mystic* (Douglas, MI: Lorian Press, 2010).

4. Maclean, *Memoirs of an Ordinary Mystic*, 2.

5. Dorothy G. Maclean, *Messages from God* (Forres, Scotland, UK: Findhorn Press, 2012).

6. *Love Button Global Movement.* Visit www.lovebutton.org.

7. William Wordsworth, *Poems: The Collected Poems of Wordsworth* (Bristol, UK: Ragged Hand, 2020).

8. Steiner, *The Illustrated Calendar of the Soul*.

9. *Longest stride of soul.* From Christopher Fry, *A Sleep of Prisoners* (New York: Dramatists Play Service, Inc., 1998).

10. Holden, *Finding Love Everywhere*, 127.

HIGHER PURPOSE
LIBRARY

Here is a list of resources I recommend to students who attend my seminars, retreats, and Mastermind programs.

Books

Angelou, Maya. 1984. *I Know Why the Caged Bird Sings*. London: Virago.

Berry, Thomas. 2000. *The Great Work*. New York: Crown.

Caddy, Eileen. 2019. *Opening Doors Within*. Rochester, VT: Findhorn Press.

Campbell, Joseph. 2008. *The Hero with a Thousand Faces*. Novato, CA: New World Library.

Chödrön, Pema. 2020. *Welcoming the Unwelcome*. Boulder, CO: Shambhala Publications.

Dyer, Wayne W. 1998. *Manifest Your Destiny*. New York: HarperCollins.

Foundation for Inner Peace. 2007. *A Course in Miracles*, Third Edition. Novato, CA: Foundation for Inner Peace.

Fox, Matthew. 1995. *The Reinvention of Work*. New York: HarperOne.

Frankl, Viktor E. 2004. *Man's Search for Meaning*. London: Rider.

Frankl, Viktor E. 2020. *Yes to Life*. Boston, MA: Beacon Press.

Hemingway, Ernest. 1994. *The Old Man and the Sea*. Cedar Rapids, IA: Arrow Books.

Holder, Jackee. 1999. *Soul Purpose*. London: Piatkus Books.

Houston, Jean. 1992. *Godseed: The Journey of Christ*. Wheaton, IL: Quest Books.

Houston, Jean. 1997. *A Mythic Life: Learning to Live Our Greater Story*. New York: HarperOne.

Hulnick, H. Ronald, and Mary R. Hulnick. 2011. *Loyalty to Your Soul*. Carlsbad, CA: Hay House, Inc.

Johnson, W. J., tr. 2008. *The Bhagavad Gita*. Oxford: Oxford University Press.

Lorimer, David. 2021. *A Quest for Wisdom*. London: Aeon Books.

Maclean, Dorothy. 2007. *Come Closer*. Douglas, MI: Lorian Press.

Myss, Caroline. 2002. *Sacred Contracts*. New York: Three Rivers Press.

Rilke, Rainer Maria. 2011. *Letters to a Young Poet*. Translated by Charles Louth. London: Penguin Classics.

Seeley, Thomas D. 2010. *Honeybee Democracy*. Princeton, NJ: Princeton University Press.

Spangler, David. 1997. *The Call*. New York: Putnam Publishing Group.

Tolle, Eckhart. 2008. *A New Earth*. New York: Penguin Books.

Warren, Rick. 2002. *The Purpose Driven Life*. Grand Rapids, MI: Zondervan.

Williamson, Marianne. 2019. *A Politics of Love*. New York: HarperOne.

Winfrey, Oprah. 2019. *The Path Made Clear*. New York: Flatiron Books.

Zohar, Danah. 2001. *Spiritual Intelligence*. London: Bloomsbury Publishing.

Films

Campbell, Joseph, and Bill Moyers. 1988. *The Power of Myth*. Arlington, VA: Public Broadcasting Service.

Dyer, Wayne W. 2010. *The Shift*. Carlsbad, CA: Hay House.

ACKNOWLEDGMENTS

Thank you, Hollie Holden, for the many ways you support me and for creating a purpose-centered life together. Thank you, Bo Holden, for your creative soul, and for always wanting to sing the whole song. Thank you, Christopher Holden, for your big heart, and for wanting to be a bigger me. Thank you to my mother, Sally, my father, Alex, my brother, David, and my great-uncle, Derek Hill, whose life as an artist gave me inspiration, direction, and courage.

Higher Purpose features many of my mentors. Thank you, Avanti Kumar, for introducing me to the spiritual path. Thank you, Tom and Linda Carpenter, for being my spiritual godparents and most beloved friends here on earth. Thanks to Joseph Campbell and the Joseph Campbell Foundation for your inspiring work with the Hero Journey. Thanks to Thomas Berry for your writing *The Great Work* and for being such a wonderful example of your message. Thanks to Russ Hudson for your pioneering work with the Enneagram. Thanks to Peter Dewey for your mentoring on mysticism and the Christ consciousness.

Higher Purpose is full of stimulating, helpful, liberating, pivotal conversations with friends and teachers. Thank you to everyone whose story I have shared in this book. Thanks again to Maya Angelou, Caroline Myss, Jean Houston, Matthew Fox, Andrew Harvey, Bob Thurman, Jean Houston, Danah Zohar, Liz Wenner, Chuck and Lency Spezzano, Shawn Gallaway, Thomas Moore, and Daniel Ladinsky for your inspiration and generous support.

In addition, I'd like to thank Raina Nahar, Phil Cartwright, Ziggy Marley, Rachel John, Jasper Morris, Michael Furber, Marianne Adjei, and Jackee Holder.

Thank you to everyone I have collaborated with over the years on talks, retreats, and Masterminds to do with living your purpose. Thanks to Nina Hirlaender, for your deep love and respect for St. Francis and St. Clare. Thanks to Michael Neil, for our work together on Spiritual Resilience. Thanks to Caroline Myss for the programs we co-presented together while I was writing *Higher Purpose*. Teaching and learning with you is a joy. Thanks to Venetia David and the Alternatives team for your inspiring purpose-centered work in the world and for hosting my events for 30 years now!

Thank you to all our teachers at The Children's Garden and at The St Michael Steiner School. It is so inspiring to experience the many ways you love the children in your care. Thank you to Régine Charrière, Eleni Karakonstanti, Leigha Hipkin, Maria Da Costa, Amanda Bell, Michèle Hunter, Serene Fong Ho, Katie Sharrock, Grace, and Sarka Kubschova. Thanks to Margli Matthews and Julia Dvinskaya for teaching and mentoring me on Rudolph Steiner's work on biography counseling.

Thank you to my Findhorn family. Thank you, John Willoner and Sylvia Black, for making Findhorn home to the Holdens. Thanks to Adele Napier, Will Russell, Angie Alexandra, Joanne Van Zyl and Keanu (KK), Nicola Coombe, Elmer Postle, and Lucien Coombe-Postle, the Winn family, and the Prior family, for all our wonderful gatherings around the dinner table, at the Blue Palace, by the river, on the pier, and at the beach. And thank you to the Angel of Findhorn Who oversees everything.

Thanks to the co-founders of Findhorn, who include Peter and Eileen Caddy and Dorothy Maclean. Taking tea with Eileen Caddy one afternoon in Cornerstone, I knew I was in the presence of a true Christ mystic. Thank you, Janet Limb and the Findhorn team who host and focalize my events in the Universal Hall. Thanks to Jonathan Caddy, Jason Caddy, Christine Lines, Kathy Tyler, Joy Drake, Lori Forsyth, John Talbott, Geoff Dalglish, Yuko Sato, Ash

Balderson, Jewels Kinnair and the team at Cullerne, and everyone who is helping to grow Findhorn.

Thank you to the Hay House team. Thank you, Reid Tracy, for the idea to write *Higher Purpose*. "Have you ever thought about writing a book on purpose?" you asked me, at the end of a dinner at the Merrion Hotel, in Dublin. We hadn't talked about work all night until then! Thank you, Margarete Nielsen, for your generous love and constant support for my work. Thank you, Patty Gift, for being a wonderful friend and editor. Thank you, Anne Barthel—if this book were a baby, I'd ask you to be its godmother. Thanks to Sheridan McCarthy for your masterful editing. Thanks to Jemima Giffard-Taylor for your cover design and your illustrations.

Thank you to the Hay House community of writers and teachers who inspire me in so many ways. Thanks to Louise Hay for encouraging us to listen to our "inner ding" and for showing us that it is never too late to live our purpose. Thanks to Wayne Dyer for showing us how to manifest our destiny and live with intention. Thanks to Gabby Bernstein for being a spiritual shooting star who lights up the night sky and guides us so boldly and lovingly on our journey. And a big thank-you for writing the foreword to *Higher Purpose*.

Thank you to Kyle Gray, Rebecca Campbell, and David Hamilton for living your purpose-centered lives, for living close by, and for being just a phone call away. Thank you to my fellow Hay House authors in the U.S., who include Deborah Egerton, Cheryl Richardson, Brian Weiss, Meggan Watterson, Anita Moorjani, Colette Baron-Reid, Marianne Williamson, Alan Cohen, Denise Linn, Pam Grout, Kris Carr, Nancy Levin, Mike Robbins, and many more.

Thank you to "my team." Thank you, Laura Samuel, for the countless ways you have helped me these past nine years. There isn't a job title or description—manager, captain, boss, COO, commander-in-chief, Prime Minister—that covers what you do or conveys how much love you put into your work. Thank you to Brenton Hughes—"Brother Brenton"—for a million visible and invisible acts of kindness Thanks to Sohini Sinha for being part of our family and for injecting your love and expertise into all we do. Thanks to Moly Yim, Avi Levi, Wioletta Stangreciak ("Lola"), and Sergio Garcia, and a big thanks to Jemima Giffard-Taylor for your brilliant designs, artistry, and creative input to all my projects.

Thank you to everyone who has participated in my retreats, Masterminds, and mentoring programs while I've been writing *Higher Purpose*. Your presence in my life, along with our deep and meaningful conversation, is a blessing. Thanks to those on my current Living Your Purpose mentoring journey, who include Donna Bond, Mary Hill, Terry Adamson, Amber Krzys, Nana Askov, Nicola Albini, Debby Handrich, Karen Auld, Nadim Bitar, Camilla Egelund Naef, Kisser Paludan, and Alpa Patel. And thank you to Jean-Laurent Inglis for the journey of the past 15 years, and the many invitations to work together on purpose-inspired projects.

And, lastly, thank you to the WME Agency, to Sabrina Taiz, and to Jennifer Rudolph Walsh, for representing me.

CREDITS

ABOUT THE AUTHOR

Robert Holden's innovative work on psychology and spirituality has been featured on *The Oprah Winfrey Show*, *Good Morning America*, a PBS special *Shift Happens!* and two major BBC-TV documentaries on happiness – *The Happiness Formula* and *How to Be Happy*. He has presented two popular TEDx talks on *The Tea Meditation* and *Destination Addiction*.

Robert works as a consultant to leaders and organizations on the theme of purpose and leadership. He gives keynote talks on living a purpose-centred life worldwide. His clients include universities, schools, charities, businesses, publishing companies, theatre groups and global brands such as Dove and the Real Beauty Campaign, Unilever, the Body Shop, IBM, Virgin and Google.

Robert teaches a series of public programmes on living your purpose. He hosts Masterminds on the Hero Journey, the Golden Thread, Purpose Club and Success Intelligence. He teaches on the *Living Your Purpose* retreat in Assisi and a *Make Me An Instrument* online course. He teaches a *Purpose & the Enneagram* programme. He has led spiritual retreats to Jerusalem, Galilee, Montserrat, Glastonbury and Findhorn.

Robert is a *New York Times* bestselling author of 13 books, including *Happiness NOW!*, *Shift Happens!*, *Authentic Success*, *Loveability*, *Holy Shift: 365 Meditations from A Course in Miracles*, *Life Loves You*, co-written with Louise Hay, and a book of poetry, *Finding Love Everywhere*. **www.robertholden.com**

Hay House Titles of Related Interest

YOU CAN HEAL YOUR LIFE, the movie,
starring Louise Hay & Friends
(available as an online streaming video)
www.hayhouse.com/louise-movie

THE SHIFT, the movie,
starring Dr. Wayne W. Dyer
(available as an online streaming video)
www.hayhouse.com/the-shift-movie

***

*A COURSE IN MIRACLES MADE EASY: Mastering the Journey
from Fear to Love,* by Alan Cohen

*HAPPY DAYS: The Guided Path from Trauma to Profound Freedom
and Inner Peace,* by Gabrielle Bernstein

*INTIMATE CONVERSATIONS WITH THE DIVINE:
Prayer, Guidance, and Grace,* by Caroline Myss

*RAISE YOUR VIBRATION: 111 Practices to Increase
Your Spiritual Connection,* by Kyle Gray

TRUST LIFE: Love Yourself Every Day with Wisdom from Louise Hay,
by Louise Hay

All of the above are available at www.hayhouse.co.uk

***